I0643702

THE DISTRICT'S DEPARTED

THE DISTRICT'S DEPARTED

A Guidebook to DC Cemeteries

KIM ROBERTS MEIKLE

RIVANNA BOOKS
UNIVERSITY OF VIRGINIA PRESS
Charlottesville and London

The University of Virginia Press is situated on the traditional lands of the Monacan Nation, and the Commonwealth of Virginia was and is home to many other Indigenous people. We pay our respect to all of them, past and present. We also honor the enslaved African and African American people who built the University of Virginia, and we recognize their descendants. We commit to fostering voices from these communities through our publications and to deepening our collective understanding of their histories and contributions.

Rivanna Books
An imprint of the University of Virginia Press

Printed in the United States of America on acid-free paper

First published 2026

9 8 7 6 5 4 3 2 1

ISBN 978-0-8139-5523-0 (hardback)
ISBN 978-0-8139-5524-7 (paperback)
ISBN 978-0-8139-5525-4 (ebook)

Library of Congress Cataloging-in-Publication Data is available for this title.

Photographs by Kim Roberts Meikle
Maps by Nat Case, INCase, LLC

Frontispiece: Pierre Charles L'Enfant Monument at Arlington National Cemetery

Cover art: Details of graves in Rock Creek Cemetery (*top*); Civil War graves in Soldier's Home National Cemetery (*bottom*). (Photographs by Kim Roberts Meikle)
Cover design: Cecilia Sorochin

CONTENTS

THE DISTRICT'S DEPARTED

INTRODUCTION

I have always been drawn to old cemeteries. When I moved from North Carolina to New England as a child, I was amazed at the age of such places, struck by how a cemetery from the 1700s could exist among modern suburban neighborhoods, giving a tantalizing glimpse of an earlier era. They seemed to me places where time was suspended. Later, living in Boston, I sought out old cemeteries as a hobby. On weekend afternoons, I rode on the back of a friend's motorcycle to all the surrounding small towns, stopping at the town hall or a real estate office to ask for directions to the oldest burial ground. I loved the odd first names—Lemuel, Bezaleel, Ezekiel, Aphra, Theophilus, Phineas, Eliphaletta, Sophronia—and the engraved bits of verse.

> Remember me as you pass by
> As you are now so once was I
> As I am now, you soon shall be
> Prepare for God and follow me.

I remember one graveyard in particular, with two large headstones next to a line of twelve smaller ones—all for children who had died soon after birth. The first few stones said that the babies were sleeping in the arms of Jesus, making their fate sound almost fortunate. The next few began to speak more openly of grief, and each successive stone got more and more resigned, saying "our loss is heaven's gain" and "we cannot question God's will." The penultimate stone spoke of "paying a debt to God." But the final stone was the saddest: it said simply, "She is flown."

I learned to look for hints of a community's history. I noted the colonial cemeteries with sections for African American and Native American graves—separate in life, separate in death. I loved the handmade quality of some of the engravings, the mistakes where the local carver had to continue a word on the line below, the carved skulls, the hourglasses flanked by open wings. I looked for the prominent male citizens with larger stones, marked as doctors, ministers, deacons, captains, or esquires, and the smallest stones for infants, topped with sleeping lambs.

There were stories implied in all the old stones—half-glimpsed lives of the women who died in childbirth or from smallpox, the sailors lost at sea, and the farmers whose last names remained local landmarks, repeated as the names of the town's roads. I loved the claims of high morals, the firm hopes of future redemption. Women were always "loyal consorts" or widowed "relicts."

In Cambridge, Massachusetts, I also visited Mount Auburn Cemetery, the earliest of the garden cemeteries, and began thinking more deeply about how Americans' ideas of the best ways to commemorate their beloved dead have changed over time.

EARLY TRADITIONS: A LANDSCAPE OF MEMORY

Most cultures have some form of ancestor veneration that demands respect and prescribes rituals for the handling of human remains. The places we set apart for the bodies of the dead remind us of the transience of our own lives, mixing a sense of dread with some relieving beauty. They hold a sublime power and play a therapeutic role for mourners. Gravestones are often meant to evoke the shape of a door—they are portals to the next world.

Family burial grounds, on private land, make up some of the earliest American burial traditions. The Washington family plot at Mount Vernon is an excellent example of this type of burial—but there are remnants of family sites throughout the greater Washington, DC, region representing lesser-known individuals. Of course, this burial option was only available to landholders and thus to more upper-class individuals.

Municipal cemeteries were also important sites. Although no longer extant, several municipal cemeteries once existed in crossroads communities that have now been absorbed into the city of Washington, including Tenleytown, Hillsdale, and Brightwood. Community graveyards were more democratic than church burial grounds, as they were maintained by secular authorities. For those who were excluded from church burials as a result of their race, ethnicity, minority religion, sexual nonconformity, or questionable morals—or simply because they were strangers who had the misfortune of dying while traveling through the area—there were segregated sections to accommodate them in many municipal burial grounds.

Pierre Charles L'Enfant's plan for the city of Washington (1791) made no provisions for burial grounds within the city limits, although churchyard cemeteries, family cemeteries, and other small burial grounds were already in existence. In 1798, the city government rectified the lack of planned burial grounds by creating two municipal ones: Eastern and Western Cemeteries. Eastern Cemetery, in Northeast DC, was quickly abandoned as too marshy to be of practical use. Western Cemetery (also known as Holmead's Cemetery for an earlier landowner) was bounded by Florida Avenue, S Street, and Nineteenth and Twentieth Streets, north of today's Dupont Circle. Western remained in active use through the mid-1800s, open to residents of all denominations, but with a separate, segregated section for African Americans outside its protective fence.

In the 1880s, more than three thousand bodies were exhumed from Western when the cemetery was closed to make room for new land development; most white citizens' remains were reinterred at Rock Creek Cemetery, and most African American citizens' remains went to

Graceland Cemetery. Graceland, once located on thirty acres in Northeast DC (in today's Carver Langston neighborhood), closed in 1894, so all those bodies had to be moved yet again at a later date—along with additional burials—and they mostly went to Historic Woodlawn Cemetery. Other major disinterments in DC also took place at Foundry Methodist Church and Payne's Cemetery as burial grounds were moved farther outside the city limits.

CHURCH BURYING GROUNDS

One of the oldest models of church burying grounds in the region can be seen in the Old Presbyterian Meeting House Burial Ground in Alexandria, Virginia. Laid out on the plot of land surrounding the church, the colonial-era graves make a direct connection to a community in faith, a membership in life that was believed to continue after death.

The aesthetic of early grave carvings seen in these church burying grounds emphasized the severe consequences of death, with images of skulls and inscribed verses about repentance and redemption. The burying ground was intended as a lesson in religious submission. Later headstones softened the message, with representations of angels and more abstract images, such as hands pointing toward heaven, along with natural images of flowers and weeping willow trees. But the religious message was always clear: to die well, one must live within the church's teachings.

For all churchyard burial sites, the land was consecrated and usually fenced or walled in. Most were designed to allow bodies to be laid from east to west (an orientation that expressed a will for the dead to arise in the afterlife looking toward Jerusalem). Only church members were allowed, creating a whole class of excluded dead, which could include strangers, those who died from communicable diseases, unbaptized babies, purported witches, "whores," and suicides. (The term "whore" could be used to denote an actual sex worker but was also used to derogate women who did not meet the culture's strict gender and sex norms.)

In the earliest European churchyards, the dead were buried atop one another, with an intermingling of corpses and coffins in various states of decay. Bones might be moved to catacombs or stacked up in charnel houses, or the land might simply be leveled every few centuries and the human remains thrown away to make more room. Only the very rich were guaranteed a permanent resting place, often within a church.

Eventually, in both European and American urban areas, there were simply too many bodies filling too little space. Many churches opened off-site burying grounds to accommodate the increased need. There was also an increasing concern about public health. Burying grounds were thought to contain miasmas—bad smells that transmitted disease—and many jurisdictions began to legislate the placement of cemetery grounds outside city limits. Waves of cholera, yellow fever, and typhoid outbreaks throughout the mid-Atlantic in the 1820s increased this fear.

In 1852, a District ordinance required all existing cemeteries within the original city boundaries to move. Any cemeteries located south of Florida Avenue (what was then Washington City, as opposed to the more rural areas of upper Northwest and Northeast DC, then known as Washington County) had to exhume all bodies and relocate them to new cemeteries farther out. Exhumations took place throughout the nineteenth century and beyond. Thus we have National Harmony Memorial Park in Hyattsville, twice relocated from earlier locations in Washington City (in 1857 and 1958), and, as mentioned above, the entire exhumation of Graceland Cemetery.

In Alexandria, a "hygienic" law was enacted even earlier, after a yellow fever epidemic killed more than three hundred residents. Although some earlier churchyard cemeteries were allowed to remain, the city opened the Wilkes Street Cemetery Complex in 1803 for new burials in thirteen adjoining sections administered by thirteen separate church and civic entities. The Wilkes Street Complex was considered far enough away from town to prevent the contamination of well water (reflecting a misunderstanding of how yellow fever actually spreads, which is through mosquito bites). Today, though, the city of Alexandria has expanded to completely surround the complex, with modern housing overlooking the graves.

Health concerns were matched by rising land values in urban centers. As city populations increased in size, the economic concern about land use made the idea of exhumation more palatable to most Americans. But the process of moving graves was unevenly accomplished: cemeteries serving the beloved dead of people of color, poor people, and religious minorities were the first targeted for removal. And some remains were always left behind with every mass exhumation.

GARDEN CEMETERIES

Mount Auburn Cemetery in Cambridge, Massachusetts, opened in 1831 as the country's first garden cemetery, with winding carriage roads, lakes, trees, and scenic vistas. This new type of cemetery was sentimental, a soothing landscape that changed the view of death from something severe, morbid, and inevitable, as often expressed in early urban cemeteries and church graveyards, to a romanticized idea of eternal rest. Parklike landscapes and plantings made death seem part of a natural process, and artfully designed tombs added variation and elegance to the scenic views. This was a landscape intended to inspire visitors with lessons in morality and uplift, made up of equal parts botanical garden and outdoor museum. The style quickly caught on and spread to other cities: Woodlawn in New York, Laurel Hill in Philadelphia, Graceland in Chicago, and Oak Hill Cemetery in Washington, DC.

With the rise of the garden cemetery came the concurrent rise in the public profile of cemeteries as cultural amenities. Before there were museums or parks in most cities, there were cemeteries, which were often understood to be repositories for learning local history and places in which to gain an appreciation for horticulture and religious sculpture. Garden cemeteries became places of recreation, where visitors were encouraged to take inspiration from great men (and, less commonly, women) and to feel a sense of patriotism. Families often picnicked on cemetery grounds.

Garden cemeteries were privately owned and managed places, often endowed by a rich, civic-minded businessman (as Oak Hill was) or a group of businessmen forming a joint-stock corporation. These large cemeteries, intended for the public good, were profitable investments that were also widely appreciated as contributions to a community's welfare. Designed by professionals, they were scenic retreats from city life that also led to the professionalism of landscape architecture in the United States and gave rise to a golden age of funerary sculpture. Rock Creek Cemetery, which began as a churchyard burying ground, took on a new identity as a garden cemetery at this time, and it now boasts some of the finest funerary sculpture in the entire nation.

New iconography dates from this period. Obelisks—based on ancient Egyptian monolithic monuments that Americans thought were a reference to eternity and resembled rays of light descending from heaven—became prevalent. So did draped urns, broken columns signaling a life cut short (often used for early deaths), and anchors, which recall the shape of crosses. Egyptian- and Roman-style tombs, lambs (symbols of innocence favored for children's graves), doves, praying angels, graves in the form of beds: all created a symbolic language that emphasized sentimentality and was more secular than earlier funerary design. Engraved garlands of laurel and ivy and stone tree stumps mimicked the natural world. Elaborate family mausoleums, representing wealth and high social class, also became popular in the mid-1800s. Thus we have such gems as the Van Ness Mausoleum, modeled after the Temple of Vesta in Rome, at Oak Hill Cemetery.

The landscape was varied, with monuments of different heights and sizes adding charm and surprise to the experience of walking burying grounds. Garden cemeteries became a visual jumble of aesthetic borrowings from Egyptian, Roman, Mogul, and Gothic architecture. But, beautiful as they were, these landscapes also reinforced class differences and cultural norms. Many Americans who could afford to do so spent lavish sums on funeral arrangements and cemetery art, creating an aspirational funerary culture that favored traditional nuclear families, Christian zeal, and middle-class morality.

MILITARY GRAVEYARDS

The first graveyards specifically designed for members of the military opened during the Civil War. Americans had never experienced a war where such vast numbers of soldiers were killed. Hardly a family was immune from war's stark consequences. In some towns, all the men who qualified to enlist volunteered at the same time to serve in a single regiment—and if that regiment happened to be at the front line of a major battle, an entire town's male population could be decimated in a single day.

Death, once considered a private or family matter, was transformed by the Civil War into a national affair—a nationwide mourning that resounded in the culture for decades. The US Congress enacted a law in July 1862 to create a new type of cemetery, with orderly rows of uniform stones lined up in military formation. These new cemeteries were places of patriotism, with overtly nationalistic imagery, meant to soothe a wounded nation with a message of honor and shared sacrifice.

The design for military cemeteries was first developed in Washington, DC, by US Quartermaster General Montgomery C. Meigs and then used throughout the nation. Military cemeteries thus represent the District's major contribution to the history of the cemetery. Meigs's plan was based on rational ideas with a symbolic resonance that could easily be replicated. Fourteen military cemeteries were founded in 1862, and over the next few decades, designs first used in DC were replicated in 130 national cemeteries across the country. (There are now 155 military cemeteries on American soil.) The unified design called for a stone or iron fence enclosing the grounds, an entrance gate embellished with flags and American eagles, an administrative lodge house, and identical small white headstones at the graves. Alexandria National Cemetery and Battleground National Cemetery are excellent examples of this original design, and both preserve their Meigs-designed lodge houses.

Traditions still used in military burials, including the use of color guards, playing taps, and draping flags over coffins, were also first developed in DC in the aftermath of the Civil War. These rituals helped Americans make sense of the war's carnage, when over a half million soldiers died. And like the uniform design of the gravestones, the ceremonies emphasized a remarkably egalitarian spirit: all soldiers, regardless of rank or length of service, were to be honored equally.

The Civil War was also a time of new advances in mortuary science. Improved embalming techniques made it possible to transport dead soldiers home for burial closer to their families. More people were dying in hospitals than in their homes, and care for the dying passed to nurses and doctors rather than female family members. This professionalism and medicalization continued after death as well: the job of undertaker dates to this period.

Washington, DC, has one of the largest concentrations of military cemeteries in the country. Perhaps this was inevitable in the capital city, with the headquarters of various armed forces nearby. Only two military cemeteries remain under the administration of the US Army (rather than the National Park Service), and both are in the city. The first military cemetery, the US Soldiers' and Airmen's Home National Military Cemetery, opened in 1861 and holds the mausoleum of General John A. Logan, who established the first official Memorial Day services (then called Decoration Day). The country's largest military cemetery, Arlington National Cemetery, dates to 1864 and is the most important of such military sites. It contains several monuments that attempt to address national losses, such as the assassination of President John F. Kennedy and the space shuttle *Challenger* disaster.

SPECIAL GROUP CEMETERIES

Since religious and ethnic minorities were frequently excluded from church or private cemeteries (and even some municipal cemeteries), these groups established their own burial grounds. African Americans, Catholics, and Jews were most often subject to this exclusion, and thus such places as the Mount Zion Methodist and Female Union Band Society Historic Memorial Park, Mount Olivet Cemetery, and National Capital Hebrew Cemetery can be found in DC.

Other specialized groups also set up their own cemeteries. These include fraternal organizations such as the Freemasons, trade unions, hospitals (including St. Elizabeths Hospital), jails, and religious orders (such as Georgetown Visitation Convent). Schools, too, including the Industrial Home School and the National Training School for Boys, had their own burying grounds. Their cemeteries are long gone but were once part of the landscape of DC.

Pet cemeteries, such as Aspin Hill Memorial Park in Silver Spring, Maryland, began appearing more widely in the 1920s. The first pet cemetery in the United States was inaugurated much earlier, however: a veterinarian in New York founded the Hartsdale Canine Cemetery in 1896.

The ancient tradition of potter's fields, where communities placed the remains of indigent people who could not afford their own burial expenses—always set apart from more fortunate others—was brought from Europe with the founding of the nation. An inactive plot in Southeast DC called Blue Plains Cemetery has no visible grave markers, but records show that it was the burial site for individuals from the Home for the Aged and Infirm, the Washington Almshouse, and the Washington Asylum. It was also where many smallpox victims were interred. You can still visit one potter's field, dating from 1796, that remains part of the Wilkes Street Cemetery Complex in Alexandria. Penny Hill is at the rear of the complex, closest to the modern highway, with only eleven grave markers. (There is historic documentation for at least 906 burials, however, with the last in 1976.)

In 1968, the US Supreme Court outlawed racial discrimination against African American people in the sale and rental of property by private owners and public authorities—a ruling that also applied to cemeteries for the first time. Although it is now illegal to segregate in death, many people of color and other minorities still choose cemeteries with historic ties to their racial, ethnic, or religious groups.

MEMORIAL PARKS

By the 1950s most American cemeteries had abandoned picturesque garden cemetery designs and opted instead for a simpler, less cluttered layout. Memorial parks offered open space that could be more easily maintained. Lawn mowers (first patented in 1830) and leaf blowers were a sign of the new efficiency. Suburban-style lawn parks were more coherent in design than garden cemeteries, with less vegetation and smaller, more standardized grave markers. Some used only markers flush with the ground. The effect of these pastoral landscapes was more modern and more sunny, both literally (as there were few trees) and emotionally: the place was bereft of the shadows of sorrow. The overall aesthetic was more formal and cultivated, emphasizing a flat, carefully maintained expanse of green. Instead of a tangle of winding paths, the land was broken into easily navigated blocks like a suburban subdivision, a grid plan that better fit a scientific age and made death seem rational—almost cheerful. This became the dominant design of cemeteries by the end of World War II.

With the rise of memorial parks, a new cemetery professional emerged. Cemeteries began to offer new, service-oriented features, including "pre-need" sales packages. "Perpetual care" services transferred the care of graves from individual families to cemetery directors. Burial became a business. Managers developed a language that deliberately masked direct references to death, bodily decay, or finality. The selling of plots became a specialized form of the real estate business, with professional administrators equally skilled in sales, overseeing crews of workers, and managing budgets and payrolls.

The first modern memorial parks developed in the suburbs around Los Angeles in 1913 and quickly spread across the country. In the DC area, National Harmony Memorial Park, Washington Hebrew Memorial Park, and Cedar Hill Cemetery are good examples of the evolving form.

CREMATION AND NATURAL BURIALS

Cremation started in the United States in 1876, with Dr. F. Julius LeMoyne of Pennsylvania building the first crematory. The practice remained rare, however, until the 1980s. The year 2015 marked a turning point, when a larger percentage of Americans chose cremation over burial. That trend is expected to continue. Cremation is not only less expensive but is increasingly seen as more ethical: it eliminates the need for large lawns (usually maintained with pesticides) and embalming chemicals. Without coffins, there is no need for wood or metal trimmings of copper, bronze, and steel, all of which can potentially leach into the soil. (Of course, this view that cremation is eco-friendly may not take into account the amount of fuel needed to burn a body or the carcinogenic particles and carbon dioxide released into the atmosphere during that process. Cremation involves running a furnace at very high heat for up to two hours.)

Cremations also appeal to a modern sensibility: we no longer have the uncomfortable and messy experience of displaying a dead body at a funeral. Although families of the cremated dead have more often eschewed cemeteries and opted instead to scatter ashes, cemeteries have recognized that they must adapt to changing attitudes. Most have responded by adding columbaria, where cremated remains can be stored in smaller spaces that allow for personalized commemoration.

The Green Burial Council was established in 2005 to set standards for burials with an even smaller environmental impact. In specific, accredited sites, the deceased could be covered with a simple shroud and placed directly into the ground. This approach circumvents the need for embalming chemicals, a casket, or a concrete vault. (Such vaults, in common use, reduce the chance of subsidence of the soil over each grave, simplifying the maintenance of the grounds.) Green burial uses fewer resources than cremation but still allows for a graveside service. Individual graves are typically not marked; many cemeteries use a collective commemorative monument to identify the green burial area. Individual records are kept by the cemetery, however. A good example is Congressional

Cemetery, which established a green burial "Circle of Life" section on its grounds in 2019.

ENDANGERED LANDSCAPES

The continued and increasing adoption of cremation leaves cemeteries in a precarious situation. Without new burials, they are in danger of becoming less financially viable and less relevant as meaningful cultural spaces. As older cemeteries fill, new revenue streams dry up, and keeping up with basic maintenance costs gets harder.

Some cemeteries are combating the problem in innovative ways. Congressional Cemetery offers annual memberships to dog owners. Members pay dues in exchange for the privilege of walking their dogs on the property, and they are expected to fulfill a commitment of volunteer hours as well. Oak Hill Cemetery, once considered full, recently opened up thousands of additional burial sites as it upgraded its walkways, locating cremation urns under newly placed pavers that can be personalized with engraved inscriptions. Some cemeteries now offer tours, Halloween parties, movie nights, and book clubs. But cemeteries tend to be conservative places, slow to change—and their managers are not always willing to dilute their solemn commemorative spaces with popular public events. Those unwilling to adapt will only face greater hardship. Will the social connection that cemeteries represent soon be permanently severed? Should we continue to support expensive public amenities beyond their economic viability?

Economic and social changes inevitably affect our relationship to traditional death rituals. Americans are more mobile, and family ties have weakened. We have distanced ourselves from the dead and dying as we have medicalized end-of-life care. Increasingly, in the last few decades, Americans have turned to creative new types of public mourning via web pages and social media.

These digital spaces provide interactive ways to confront death for those people (particularly younger people) who feel alienated from conventional religious or cultural traditions.

Other notable public mourning rituals have also sprung up. Examples include the AIDS Memorial Quilt (begun in 1985 and displayed in such places as the National Mall), the masses of flowers and candles left at Ground Zero at the World Trade Center in New York after the terrorist attacks of 9/11, and grassroots memorials, such as roadside shrines commemorating those who have died in car accidents, ghost bicycles memorializing victims of bicycle accidents, and R.I.P. murals recognizing the victims of gun violence. As the cemetery decreases in public consciousness, new forms of memorial are taking its place, many of them performative and public.

An additional impediment to the viability of cemeteries, one specific to DC, was the adoption of an impermeable surface tax in 2009. Implemented in an effort to comply with the federal Clean Rivers Project, the tax penalized properties with hard surfaces that diverted stormwater into sewers and storm drains. This placed a high burden on nonprofits such as the National Arboretum and churches with large parking lots—but it was especially catastrophic for historic cemeteries, which saw their water bills skyrocket to thousands of dollars per month. In 2019, the DC City Council finally adopted a Clean Rivers Impervious Area Charge (CRIAC) Nonprofit Relief Program. But this monetary relief is only partial—and the program requires annual renewal by the City Council, so its future is not secure.

On the other hand, I take hope from several African American cemeteries that have recently been in the news as activists for racial justice fight to reclaim the sacred lands where ancestors were buried. A greater public awareness of the issue of endangered Black forebears began in 1992 with the New York African Burial Ground

Project, when the remains of hundreds of people of color were unearthed in lower Manhattan during construction of a federal office building. A bioarchaeologist, Dr. Michael Blakey (then teaching at Howard University), led a study of the remains and artifacts that construction had unearthed and created new standards for community engagement. The National Park Service now administers a memorial on Broadway above the ancestral chamber (where remains were reinterred) as well as an interpretive center and research library.

More locally, the Morningstar Tabernacle No. 88 Order of Moses Cemetery in Cabin John, Maryland, threatened by an expansion of the Beltway, was listed in 2021 on "America's 11 Most Endangered Historic Places," a list compiled by the National Trust for Historic Preservation. Attention in the media resulted in a highway diversion and a victory for preservation of the site.

In another preservation battle, the Sons and Daughters of Liberty Lodge Cemetery in Annandale, Virginia, won only a partial victory. The cemetery land, and all the surrounding houses in a historically African American neighborhood, was taken by eminent domain for construction of a new high school in the 1960s—a school that was never built. In 2000, the Fairfax County Park Authority purchased the land to create Pine Ridge Park. Although a playing field covers part of the cemetery, a quarter-acre parcel has been preserved and fenced in, containing forty-five graves (though only one has its original gravestone). New markers were placed over the remaining graves.

And of course there have been complete losses. Moses Macedonia African Cemetery was paved over in the 1960s for a parking lot in front of Westwood Tower Apartments in Bethesda, Maryland. When the complex was sold to new developers, the Bethesda Cemetery Coalition sued, trying to protect the land where up to four hundred known burials had taken place—but the Maryland Supreme Court allowed for the sale to proceed in 2020, further erasing the historic site. This unethical judicial ruling went forward despite written evidence of cemetery records and the pleas of living descendants.

In yet another sad case, human remains are unearthed every time construction occurs in the residential block of 3300 Q Street NW in the Georgetown neighborhood. At least twenty-eight remains have been found to date, which archeologists report is evidence of a lost African American burial ground. That former cemetery remains unmarked.

Mount Pleasant Plains Cemetery is another prominent example of a cemetery for people of color that has been completely lost; it is now the site of Walter Pierce Park in the Adams Morgan neighborhood. A few historical markers have been placed there, functioning as the only reminders of this lost history. The list goes on.

In 1990, Congress passed the Native American Graves Protection and Repatriation Act, which has helped Native American descendants reclaim human remains in the collections of museums and universities. In 2022, the Smithsonian Institution enacted its own Shared Stewardship and Ethical Returns policy, which should hopefully serve as a model for other institutions. Recognizing that it held one of the world's largest collections of human remains, the Smithsonian made a commitment to "promote respectful engagement with descendants and descendant communities . . . for the appropriate care, shared stewardship, or ethical return of human remains." Since 2019, the secretary of the Smithsonian has been Lonnie Bunch III, the first African American to lead the organization. In 2023, Congress passed the African American Burial Grounds Preservation Act, establishing a new program through the National Park Service to aid jurisdictions (through grants and technical assistance) in identifying, researching, surveying, and preserving cemeteries.

Clearly, cemeteries remain significant cultural institutions—even as our ideas of the best ways to commemorate our beloved dead evolve. In this book, I hope to reengage readers with the District's landscapes of the dead. These "libraries in stone" are repositories of our history. They are also compelling places to explore, combining elements of beauty with dread, and they give us a tangible and sublime connection to our ancestors.

I recently learned that there's a word for cemetery enthusiasts like myself. We are "taphophiles," from the Greek words *taphos* (funeral) and *-phile* (lover). (I also learned that there's a psychological condition called "coimetromania" that takes this love too far, when people have an abnormal attraction to anything to do with the dead. Let's leave it at that.)

Even if it doesn't make you into a taphophile, if this book convinces you to become a tombstone tourist, to connect more deeply with the architectural and spiritual traditions surrounding Americans' death rituals, and to learn more about our cultural history, I will feel my efforts have not been in vain. I hope you will take this guidebook with you on some trips to explore the rich taphonomy of Washington, DC.

I began this project because of my interest in funerary sculpture. The District is home to some of the best-known funerary sculpture, especially one masterpiece—the Adams Memorial by Augustus Saint-Gaudens in Rock Creek Cemetery—that many critics consider the finest funerary art in the United States. I had already conducted research on this work for an earlier book on DC's literary history, *A Literary Guide to Washington, DC,* and that became my starting point.

But I quickly realized that each new cemetery had its own specific story to tell, and I needed to adapt my interests to best highlight each site. The length of each tour in this book varies, matching the cemeteries' range in size, from the single-acre Battleground National Cemetery to the 639-acre—and growing!—extent of Arlington National Cemetery. I continue to develop my interest in funerary sculpture, so where there are notable designs, I include that information. Some cemeteries are the resting places of famous individuals or people whose life stories deserve to be better known. I was also influenced by the challenge of the walking tour format. The need to create a circular walk (beginning and ending at the cemetery entrance) with stops at regular intervals meant that some sites at the further reaches of graveyards were omitted.

Tours in the book are arranged chronologically, by the founding date of each cemetery. Practical information and links to cemetery websites are noted following the "Before You Go" headings at the start of each tour.

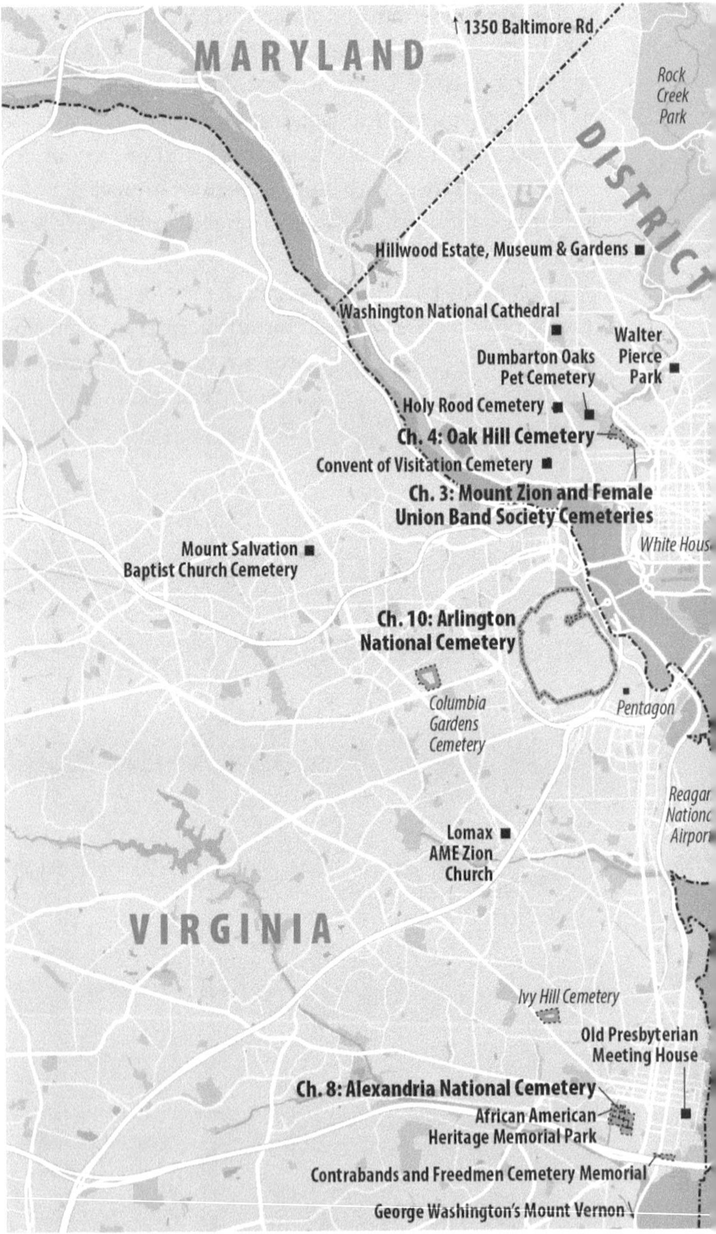

Cemeteries and tours included in this book

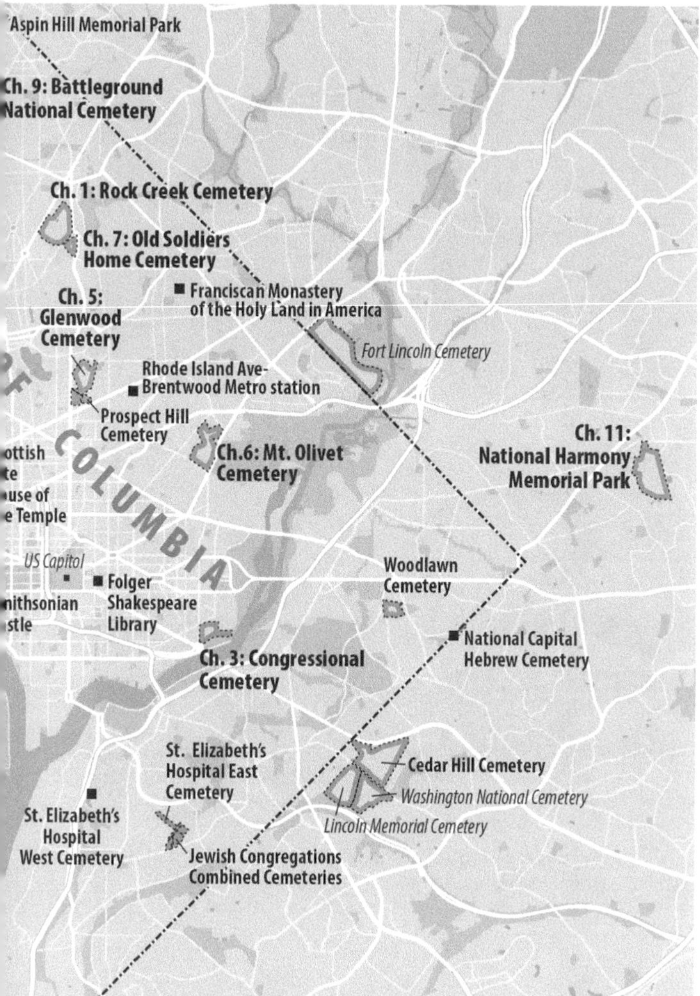

Aspin Hill Memorial Park
Ch. 9: Battleground National Cemetery
Ch. 1: Rock Creek Cemetery
Ch. 7: Old Soldiers Home Cemetery
Ch. 5: Glenwood Cemetery
Franciscan Monastery of the Holy Land in America
Fort Lincoln Cemetery
Rhode Island Ave-Brentwood Metro station
Prospect Hill Cemetery
Ch.6: Mt. Olivet Cemetery
Ch. 11: National Harmony Memorial Park
COLUMBIA
US Capitol
Folger Shakespeare Library
Woodlawn Cemetery
National Capital Hebrew Cemetery
Ch. 3: Congressional Cemetery
St. Elizabeth's Hospital East Cemetery
Cedar Hill Cemetery
Washington National Cemetery
Lincoln Memorial Cemetery
St. Elizabeth's Hospital West Cemetery
Jewish Congregations Combined Cemeteries
MARYLAND

Clockwise from upper left: Adams Memorial (5); Kauffmann Memorial (10); Houser Memorial; Frederic A. Keep Monument (20)

ROCK CREEK CEMETERY (1719)

One Old Rock Creek Church Road, Petworth neighborhood, DC

Founded in 1719 and encompassing eighty-six acres, Rock Creek Cemetery is the oldest in Washington, DC, and actually predates the city's founding by over eighty years. Although the burial grounds are nondenominational, they are under the stewardship of St. Paul's Episcopal Church.

A note on the street address: in 1998, the US Postal Service switched to automated sorting and required all addresses in the city to have a nine-digit zip code. The cemetery couldn't get one, because up to that time it had no actual street number (and 1 Rock Creek Church Road had already been taken). To avoid the confusion of taking on a "dummy address" on one of the cemetery's side streets, the Ward 4 councilmember introduced legislation to rename the small stretch of road in front of the cemetery gate. That tiny block is now Old Rock Creek Church Road, a change that enabled the cemetery to, as the *Washington City Paper* reported, "make a leap into the numerical age."

Before You Go

https://rockcreekcemetery.org
Open daily 9:00 am to 7:00 pm
Nearest public transportation: Georgia Avenue–Petworth Station to bus
Limited parking available; restrooms available during office hours

→ **Enter through the gate and walk downhill toward the church. You will see an unpaved path on your right**

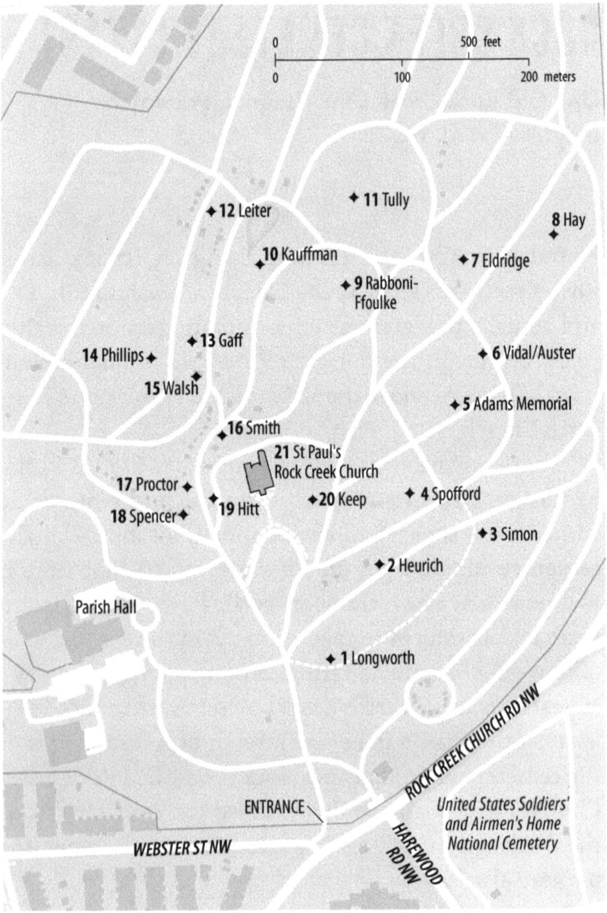

Rock Creek Cemetery

marked by a large boulder. Turn right onto the path and look for a large gravestone on your left.

1 ALICE ROOSEVELT LONGWORTH GRAVE

Section F, Lot 351

Alice Roosevelt Longworth (1884–1980) is the author of an autobiography, *Crowded Hours* (1933). The oldest daughter of President Theodore Roosevelt, she married Congressman Nicholas Longworth and was a famous Washington socialite.

Known for her wild and unconventional ways, she gambled, smoked in public, and had extramarital affairs. Gossip columns of the times reported her antics: plunging into a swimming pool fully clothed, placing bets at the Benning Race Track, wearing a boa constrictor around her neck. She became a formidable and opinionated Washington presence for many decades. An embroidered sofa pillow in her home read, “If you haven’t got anything good to say about anybody, come sit next to me.”

Her husband, who died in office, is buried in Cincinnati. Longworth is buried with her daughter, Paulina Sturm (1925–1957), who died from an overdose of sleeping pills. Paulina was the result of an affair Longworth had with Senator William E. Borah. Longworth took custody of her granddaughter, Joanna, after her daughter’s death and doted on her; the two became extremely close. Joanna, a philanthropist and historian, is still living.

→ **Cut diagonally downhill to the paved road and turn to your right. You will see a large mausoleum on your left.**

2 HEURICH TOMB

Section 30, Lot 13

The Heurich family is buried here, including Christian Heurich (1842–1945), who founded the Heurich Brewing Company in 1872. The brewery was located first near Dupont Circle and later in Foggy Bottom (on the site of the Kennedy Center) and was the largest brewery in the city’s history, producing five hundred thousand barrels of beer annually at its height. The company closed in 1956. Heurich was one of DC’s largest landowners and became a noted philanthropist. He died at age 102. Also interred in the tomb are his two wives and two of his four children.

Created by Louis Amateis (1855–1913), the large mausoleum is decorated with four caryatids with wings and clasped hands. Amateis was born in Turin, Italy, but settled in Washington, DC, in 1889 to found the School of Architecture and Fine Arts, which later became part of George Washington University. He worked on the US Capitol sculptures as well as busts of such famous men as President Chester A. Arthur, General Winfield Scott Hancock, General John Logan, and the industrialist Andrew Carnegie. The mausoleum was moved in 1951 from the family's dairy farm in Hyattsville, now the site of the Mall at Prince George's. The stained glass on the back wall of the mausoleum was designed by Louis Comfort Tiffany (1848–1933). Underneath, an inscription in German says, "In deep pain, there is no worldly wisdom for the heart."

→ **Continue down this road; just past another spur road on your left, look to the right for a large statue with two arms raised.**

3 SIMON MEMORIAL (1917)

Section O, Lot 45

This depiction of a winged figure with wide-flung arms was created for the poet, musician, and artist Anne C. McConnor Simon (1870–1916). The inscription reads, "A Soul Whose Eyes Were Keener Than the Sun / A Soul Whose Wings Were Wider Than the World / There Is No Death."

As if to prove the inscription, today Simon is best known for three books published by her husband, Otto Torney Simon (1860–1944), purported to be posthumous "spiritualistic messages" sent from beyond the grave: *The Message of Anne Simon* (1920), *The Second Message of*

Anne Simon (1920), and *The Later Message of Anne Simon* (1924). For the first book, Otto (whom she called "Dick") reported that he received "inspirational influences" for twenty-five days, usually in the evening hours, and was able to transcribe them as "a passive instrument" of her will. This happened two more times; her husband was able to report her reassurances that the "darkness will disappear and the rosy dawn will reach to the morning-star."

The memorial's sculptor, Brenda Putnam (1890–1975), was the daughter of Librarian of Congress Herbert Putnam and a close friend of the Simons. She studied at the National Cathedral School, the School of the Museum of Fine Arts Boston, the Art Students League of New York, and the Corcoran School of Art. Putnam was the cofounder of Brookgreen Gardens, a major sculpture garden in Murrells Inlet, South Carolina. She was a member of the National Academy of Design, the National Association of Women Artists, and the National Sculpture Society. Her works are in the collections of the Metropolitan Museum of Art, the National Gallery of Art, and the Smithsonian Institution. She created the iconic statue of Puck in front of the Folger Shakespeare Library, a bust of her father at the Library of Congress, a portrait of William Dean Howells at the American Academy of Arts and Sciences (Cambridge, Massachusetts), and a group sculpture of the Beecher sisters at the Stowe-Day Foundation (Hartford, Connecticut).

→ **Take the small spur road past the Lemon Memorial and turn left. By a large oak tree, you will see an obelisk on the upward slope to your right.**

4 AINSWORTH RAND SPOFFORD GRAVE

Section E, Lot 32

Ainsworth Spofford (1825–1908) was the sixth librarian of Congress and one of the longest serving. He was appointed by Abraham Lincoln and served under eight presidents from 1864 to 1897. During his tenure, the Library of Congress was transformed from a resource for senators and congressmen into a national institution. He wrote that the library should be "a comprehensive collection of the literature of the nation" and advocated for a revised copyright law that would include a mandate stipulating that two copies of every published book, pamphlet, map, print, photograph, or piece of music be deposited into the Library's expanding collections. Spofford also shepherded the appropriation of funds for a new, separate building for the collections, now known as the Thomas Jefferson Building, one of the most glorious architectural treasures in the city.

Spofford is the author of a significant abolitionist text, *The Higher Law, Tried by Reason and Authority* (1851), and a nonfiction work on the training of librarians, *A Book for All Readers* (1900). While serving as librarian of Congress he simultaneously held the post of professor and department head of library science at Columbian College (forerunner to today's George Washington University). After stepping down as head librarian, Spofford served under his successor, John Russell Young, until his death in 1908.

Although his ashes were interred in the family plot in Rock Creek Cemetery in 1908, his name was left off the obelisk for ninety-six years. A researcher, John Y. Cole, eventually brought the omission to the attention of Spofford's descendants, and his great-grandson, John Spofford Morgan, had the inscription added in 2004.

→ **Go back to the road and continue past the spur you took earlier. Go a few hundred feet and look to your left. Up a slight rise, you will see a series of boxwood hedges planted closely. Walk up the slope and look for a short set of marble steps leading through the hedges.**

5 ADAMS MEMORIAL (1890)

Section E, Lot 202

Although their names do not appear, this is the grave of Henry Brooks Adams (1838–1918) and his wife, Marian Hooper Adams (1843–1885), known to friends as Clover. Henry Adams is best remembered as the author of two novels, *Democracy* (1880) and *Esther* (1884), and his autobiography, *The Education of Henry Adams* (1918). He also wrote biographies of Albert Gallatin and George Cabot Lodge, a critical study of Mont Saint-Michel and Chartres, and the multivolume *History of the United States During the Administrations of Thomas Jefferson and James Madison* (1889–1891). His homes in Lafayette Square became celebrated salons for a small, elite group of intellectuals called the Five of Hearts.

Clover Adams was a skilled amateur photographer, known for her portraits of great men such as historian George Bancroft and secretary of state John Hay. Her photographs are now in the collections of the Massachusetts Historical Society. After her father's death, Clover went into a deep clinical depression, and in December 1885, she committed suicide in her home by poisoning herself with potassium cyanide, one of her photographic chemicals. She was forty-two years old.

Newspapers covered the suicide widely, and there was much public speculation about her mental health and her marriage.

Henry Adams wanted to memorialize his wife, but he knew that a conventional grave marker would not do: because she had died by suicide, no angel or wreath or cross, no conventional signs of grief, would be appropriate for her cemetery plot. Adams commissioned a friend, the sculptor Augustus Saint-Gaudens (1848–1907), to create a memorial for Clover's grave. Saint-Gaudens was the foremost American sculptor of the second half of the nineteenth century. Henry Adams asked Saint-Gaudens to create a figure that symbolized, like the Buddhist figure of Kwannon (also known as Guanyin), "the acceptance, intellectually of the inevitable."

In *Beyond Grief: Sculpture and Wonder in the Gilded Age Cemetery* (2014), Cynthia Mills writes that Augustus Saint-Gaudens

> understood Adams's desire to use the monument and the evocative questions it would pose to counter any sense of shame or guilt that arose from Clover's suicide and the ensuing scandal. Beauty could serve a palliative function, perhaps easing pain, but it could also be equated to something that was good and true, with a moral life and outlook. It could cloak or assist in denying ugly truths. Ideally, it could be a means to transform, address, or mask the unspeakable, the trauma subject beyond the scope of normal language. The goal was to turn a tragedy into poetry, to counterbalance the horrific and convert a sense of grief to one of awe or wonder, something positive that awaited in a realm beyond grief.

Although Henry Adams steadfastly refused to discuss his wife's death publicly, the memorial became a favorite retreat of his, and he visited often. In an undated letter to his friend Elizabeth Cameron, he wrote that he was starting to "look with yearning eyes to my happy home at Rock Creek where I can take off my flesh and sit in the sun on my stone bench to eternity, and see my friends at quiet intervals of thousand-year naps." He died in 1918 and was interred next to his wife. His will stipulated that "no inscription, dates, letters, or other attempt at memorial" should be placed at the grave. Noted architect Stanford White (1853–1906), another friend of Adams's, created the bench, with its stylized owl's wings at each end, and the setting for the memorial: a raised hexagonal outdoor room surrounded by boxwoods.

The sculpture's mysterious form seems to seek continual reinterpretations of its meaning. The figure tries to balance several tensions at once: to be both male and female and both Eastern and Western in influence. Perhaps because of this, the memorial has inspired an outpouring of written responses. Poems began to appear in print almost immediately after Clover's interment, and they continue to be written. I've been collecting these poems: I've found ones by Anne Kelledy Gilbert, Cecil Arthur Spring-Rice, Julia Caroline Ripley Dorr, Pepita Crounse, Max Eastman, Louis Zukofsky, Eleanor Wilner, Adrienne Rich, Paul Kane, Linda Bierds, W. D. Fenza, and Joyce S. Brown. I've even written one of my own. These lines from Harriet Monroe's "Quatrains" stand out: "I was a woman who now sleeps so still. / I laughed and wept. I loved and had my will." Leonora Speyer's sonnet "The Saint-Gaudens Statue in Rock Creek Cemetery, Washington" warrants quoting in full:

> Are there no tears for other hearts to shed?
> Those heavy eyes have drained the world of grief,
> And yet no solace found, no drear relief,
> Such as my heart would seek, and find, I know,
> Had I been given the weight of that vast woe,
> And wept through pain to peace! But you, instead,
> Have drowned all healing in a shoreless sea
> Of unforgiven wrong, whose every breath
> Lifts windy clamor through the soul's hushed space,
> Fanning to greater grief, to swifter glow,
> The flame that smolders still in that bronze face,
> Sadder than life, and sadder far than death,
> Because of love renounced and joy to be,
> And faith and hope and immortality.

The Adams memorial is arguably the most important piece of figurative art in Washington, DC, and is certainly one of the most significant pieces of funerary art in the nation. It was a favorite retreat for Eleanor Roosevelt. She brought a reporter to the site in 1933 and told her,

"In the old days, when we lived here, I was much younger and not so very wise. Sometimes I'd be very unhappy and sorry for myself. When I was feeling that way, if I could manage it, I'd come out here, alone, and sit and look at that woman. And I'd always come away somehow feeling better. And stronger. I've been here many, many times."

John Galsworthy included the sculpture in his novel *Two Forsyte Interludes,* writing that "this statue awakened the connoisseur within him" and "seemed to carry him down to the bottom of his own soul." Mark Twain said it embodied all human grief and kept a print of the sculpture on display on a mantel in his home. The writer and critic Alexander Woollcott, a member of the Algonquin Round Table, wrote about it in his collection of essays *When Rome Burns* (1934), and Anthony Hecht wrote about it in his book *On the Laws of the Poetic Art* (1995).

Although sometimes referred to by the name *Grief,* Burke Wilkinson, Saint-Gaudens's biographer, asserts that this is "a misconception, for the figure transcends grief and has an element of the supernatural. She seems to sit at some far meridian of the known and unknown, some outer boundary where the finite touches the infinite."

The monument was completed in 1891 at a total cost of $20,000. In 1972, the Adams Memorial was added to the National Register of Historic Places.

→ **Exit out the other side of the memorial and make an immediate right to cut across the grass to the next paved road. Turn left and look for the horizontal dark gray marble grave marker on your left.**

6 GORE VIDAL / HOWARD AUSTER GRAVE

Section E, Lot 293

Eugene Luther Gore Vidal (1925–2012) is the author of twenty-five novels and twenty-eight works of nonfiction. He also wrote plays, short stories, memoirs, and screenplays. His books include *Washington, DC* (1967), *Myra Breckinridge* (1968), *Burr* (1973), *Lincoln* (1984), *The Decline and Fall of the American Empire* (1992), *United States* (1993, winner of the National Book Award for Nonfiction), *Palimpsest* (1995), and *Point to Point Navigation* (2006). He made an unsuccessful bid for a congressional seat in 1960 and was a political commentator for such journals as the *Nation*, the *New Statesman*, the *New York Review of Books*, and *Esquire*. He also appeared in a number of movies.

In his obituary, the *Los Angeles Times* called his writing "among the most elegant in the English language," and the *New York Times* wrote, "Few American writers have been more versatile, or gotten more mileage from their talent."

Vidal was raised in the District but spent his entire adult life in other locations, particularly the Amalfi Coast in Ravello, Italy, where he owned a villa called La Rondinaia ("The Swallow's Nest"). Vidal is buried here with Howard Auster, his partner of fifty-three years. But he chose this plot because it is in close proximity to that of his first lover, Jimmy Trimble (1925–1945), a friend from St. Albans School who was a star high school athlete and died at the Battle of Iwo Jima. According to an article in the *New Yorker*, Trimble "lived for the rest of Vidal's life in fevered fantasies." Vidal also prized this location for its proximity to the Adams Memorial, which is of course "the most visited site" in the cemetery and gives Vidal what he imagined would be a connection to a descendant of two presidents. The careful placement of his grave at this site would put him "midway between heart and mind, to put it grandly."

→ **Continue on this road until you reach the intersection. You'll see the large Vogt Mausoleum in front of you. Go behind the mausoleum and look for a modest-sized grave marker on the right side of the tomb.**

7 CHARLES W. ELDRIDGE GRAVE

Section K, Lot 12

Charles W. Eldridge (1837–1903) was one half of the Boston-based abolitionist publishing firm Thayer and Eldridge, which issued the third edition of Walt Whitman's *Leaves of Grass* in 1860. In December 1862, Whitman stopped in Washington while on his way to find his brother George, a Union soldier who had been injured in battle in Fredericksburg, Virginia. Whitman encountered Eldridge, who had become a clerk in the office of the army paymaster, Major Lyman Hapgood. Eldridge eventually obtained a position for Whitman in Hapgood's office, and Whitman remained in the District for the next ten years, working as a federal clerk and volunteering in area Civil War hospitals.

In addition to publishing, Eldridge also worked as a newspaper editor. He remained an activist for the rest of his life, embracing social justice and Republican causes. The Washington Friends of Walt Whitman had the metal plaque installed when the engraving on the stone became too weather-damaged to read. At the dedication of the plaque, members read Whitman's "Recorders Ages Hence":

Recorders ages hence,
Come, I will take you down underneath this impassive
exterior, I will tell you what to say of me,
Publish my name and hang up my picture as that of the
tenderest lover,
The friend the lover's portrait, of whom his friend his
lover was fondest,
Who was not proud of his songs, but of the measureless
ocean of love within him, and freely pour'd it forth,
Who often walk'd lonesome walks thinking of his dear
friends, his lovers,
Who pensive away from one he lov'd often lay sleepless
and dissatisfied at night,

Who knew too well the sick, sick dread lest the one he
lov'd might secretly be indifferent to him,
Whose happiest days were far away through fields, in
woods, on hills, he and another wandering hand in
hand, they twain apart from other men,
Who oft as he saunter'd the streets curv'd with his arm
the shoulder of his friend, while the arm of his friend
rested upon him also.

→ **Go back out to the paved road (to the right of the Vogt Mausoleum) and continue downhill. Look for a bronze bust of a man atop a gravestone on your right.**

8 EDWIN B. HAY MONUMENT (1906)

Section I, Lot 74

This bronze bust with a beatific expression portrays Edwin Barrett Hay (1849–1906), the author of the novel *The Vivians* (1907), a lawyer, and an avid club member whose grave proclaims him to be "A Friend of All Mankind." Although the grave gives his birth year as 1850, he was actually born a year earlier.

Hay attended DC public schools and Columbian College. He worked as an attorney in the District from 1874 until his death, and he was also a chirographer, an expert in the study of handwriting (for which he provided testimony at numerous trials). He was a member of the American Arabic Order of the Nobles of the Mystic Sciences, the Gridiron Club, and the Shakespeare Club (serving as its president for sixteen years) as well as a vestryman of St. Paul's Church. Note the Masonic symbols included on his grave marker.

The bust was created in 1906 by Vinnie Ream, and you can see the signature "Hoxie" (the sculptor's married name) on Hay's neck. Lavinia Ellen Ream Hoxie (1847–1914) is best known for her sculpture of Abraham Lincoln in the rotunda of the US Capitol, which made her the first woman artist commissioned to create a work of art for the US government. Ream was born in Madison, Wisconsin, and moved to Washington, DC, in 1861. After her father's health began to fail, she became one of the first women to be employed by the federal government, working as a clerk for the US Post Office during the Civil War. Beginning in 1863, she apprenticed to sculptor Clark Mills (who created the iconic statue called *Freedom* atop the US Capitol and the equestrian statue of Andrew Jackson in Lafayette Square). After creating a bust of Lincoln from life at age eighteen, Ream continued her studies in Paris and Rome, opened a studio in New York in 1871, and then returned to the District to open a studio on Pennsylvania Avenue.

Ream was renowned for her beauty and conversational skills, and she developed friendships with influential men, becoming effective in self-marketing. Her works include the statue of Admiral David G. Farragut in Farragut Square and portraits of Sequoyah and Samuel Jordan Kirkwood in Statuary Hall at the US Capitol. She also exhibited at the American Institute Fair in New York City, the Centennial Exhibition in Philadelphia, and the Columbia Exposition in Chicago. The town of Vinita, Oklahoma, was named in her honor.

→ **Retrace your steps and continue back uphill. Look to your right for a section of older graves arranged in a loose semicircle. When the city of Washington was founded, provisions were made for two government cemeteries. This group of stones (and their respective interments) were moved in the 1870s or 1880s from Western Cemetery, formerly located on the north side of Dupont Circle. Only the bodies of white citizens were moved to this location; disinterments of African American bodies were sent from Western to Graceland Cemetery (and were then moved to Woodlawn Cemetery when Graceland was closed). A total of 1,665 bodies were moved from Western Cemetery to a mass grave here, and the land where they formerly reposed**

was developed by John McLean, publisher of the *Washington Post*. This section and the area around St. Paul's Church are now the parts of the cemetery with the oldest remains. The gravestones do not relate to what lies beneath them but are arranged in the general area of the mass grave.

Continue to the intersection (with the Vogt Mausoleum on your right) and turn right, heading toward a modern columbarium in the middle of an intersection. Cross past the columbarium and continue on the grass on the opposite side to a large standing stone, which is the back side of the Rabboni-Ffoulke Memorial.

9 RABBONI-FFOULKE MEMORIAL (1909)

Section B, Lot 164

This is the grave of investment banker Charles Mather Ffoulke (1841–1909), a collector of rare tapestries. He is buried with his wife, three children, and father-in-law. The Ffoulkes were prominent in Washington social circles; they built a mansion on Massachusetts Avenue near Dupont Circle with a ballroom and a gallery for displaying their antique tapestries, including the famous seventeenth-century Barberini tapestries now in the collections of the Philadelphia Museum of Art and at New York's Cathedral of St. John the Divine. Their house no longer stands. Ffoulke was also one of the early presidents of the National Society of the Fine Arts. Three of his five children died in their twenties of tuberculosis and are also buried here. Two daughters survived, married, and raised families of their own.

The funerary sculpture was created in 1909 by Gutzon Borglum (1867–1941), best known as the sculptor of Mount Rushmore. The life-size bronze sculpture depicts Mary Magdalene, dressed in robes and a cape, stepping forward to recognize the risen Jesus Christ on Easter morning. The name of the sculpture refers to John 20:16: "Jesus saith unto her, Mary. She turned herself and saith unto him, Rabboni; which is to say, Master."

Borglum, the son of Danish immigrants, was raised in the Idaho Territory in a Mormon family that practiced polygamy. He married his former art teacher, the sculptor Elizabeth Putnam Janes (1848–1922), who was nineteen years his senior, and they lived in California until their divorce. He later settled in New York, married a second time, and became active in the Masons and the Ku Klux Klan.

Borglum's other works in the DC area include the statue of General Philip Sheridan in Sheridan Circle and a bust of Abraham Lincoln in the US Capitol Crypt.

→ **Facing the sculpture, look to your left. You will see a large, curved granite wall across the grass.**

10 KAUFFMANN MEMORIAL (1897)

Section B, Lot 88

Samuel H. Kauffmann (1829–1906) was publisher of the *Washington Evening Star,* DC's newspaper of record from 1852 to 1981. Kauffmann moved to the District in 1861, became the newspaper's third publisher in 1867, served on the board of trustees of the Corcoran Gallery of Art, and became the patron of select local painters. At the time of his death, his home on Massachusetts Avenue held one of the finest private art collections in the city, and he was considered one of the top authorities on equestrian statues in America.

The *Evening Star* Building still stands at 1101 Pennsylvania Avenue NW, now home to the Securities and Exchange Commission. Built in 1898 in the Beaux Arts style, it has a thirteen-story marble façade and was designed by Marsh and Peter.

The grave memorial, also known as *Seven Ages,* was created in 1897. It features a curved granite wall exedra with seven relief panels. On the curved bench sits a bronze figure of a woman holding a wreath of asphodel, a symbol of the underworld that was connected to the myth of Persephone. The panels depict the scenes from William Shakespeare's Seven Ages of Man from *As You Like It.* Shakespeare wrote:

All the world's a stage,
And all the men and women merely players;
They have their exits and their entrances,
And one man in his time plays many parts,
His acts being seven ages. At first the infant,
Mewling and puking in the nurse's arms;
And then the whining schoolboy, with his satchel
And shining morning face, creeping like snail
Unwillingly to school. And then the lover,
Sighing like furnace, with a woeful ballad
Made to his mistress' eyebrow. Then a soldier,
Full of strange oaths, and bearded like the pard,
Jealous in honor, sudden and quick in quarrel,
Seeking the bubble reputation
Even in the cannon's mouth. And then the justice,
In fair round belly with good capon lin'd,
With eyes severe and beard of formal cut,
Full of wise saws and modern instances;
And so he plays his part. The sixth age shifts
Into the lean and slipper'd pantaloon,
With spectacles on nose and pouch on side;
His youthful hose, well sav'd, a world too wide
For his shrunk shank; and his big manly voice,
Turning again toward childish treble, pipes
And whistles in his sound. Last scene of all,
That ends this strange eventful history,
Is second childishness and mere oblivion,
Sans teeth, sans eyes, sans taste, sans everything.

The artist, William Ordway Partridge (1861–1930), was a New York–based sculptor whose other works include the Pocahontas sculpture for Jamestown, Virginia, as well as the Thomas Jefferson statue at the New-York Historical Society, the equestrian statue of General Ulysses S. Grant in Grant Square in Brooklyn, and the James Smithson statue at the Smithsonian Institution Castle.

→ **Walk downhill to the paved path and cross over to the section on your right. Look for an unusual horizontal grave marker topped with a bronze chair.**

11 MEMORIAL FOR A DEMOCRAT (2014)

Section C, Lot 120

The memorial for Paul Raymond Tully (1944–1992) is a bronze cast of Tully's favorite wooden office chair, topped with a copy of the *New York Times* proclaiming the election of President Bill Clinton, and two of Tully's ubiquitous take-out coffee cups: an opened one for him, and a closed one to give to a visitor such as yourself. The memorial was made by Tully's daughter, Jessica Tully (1970–), and installed twenty-two years after his death.

Tully was the political director of the Democratic National Committee and one of the Democratic Party's main strategists at the time of his unexpected death at age forty-eight. He was an advisor to President Clinton, to Senators Edward Kennedy, Walter Mondale, and Gary Hart, and to Governor Michael Dukakis, working behind the scenes on every presidential election from 1968 through 1992.

→ **Retrace your steps to the paved road. Walk around the pond. If you visit in the summer months of July and August, the pond will be filled with water lotuses. Note**

the large raised grave to the right of the pond, encased in glass.

12 LEVI Z. LEITER GRAVESITE (1904)

Section L, Lot 19N

Levi Ziegler Leiter (1834–1904) was a Maryland dry goods merchant who moved to Chicago to open a department store with Marshall Field. When he sold his share to his partner, Leiter became a wealthy man—and he built on that fortune with investments in commercial real estate, coal mines, and stock market speculation.

High society in most East Coast cities was insular, but the District's oldest families were decimated by the Civil War, and official society had always fluctuated as new elections and foreign postings brought continual change to the governmental cast of characters. From the 1880s on, Washington's elite classes seemed to value money over pedigree. As Kathryn Allamong Jacob writes in her book *Capital Elites: High Society in Washington, D.C. After the Civil War* (1995),

> Rebuffed by Chicago's high society, the Leiters decided in 1883 to try their luck in Washington. Mrs. Leiter hoped to make matches for her three beautiful daughters. . . . To their delight, the unaffected Leiters were indeed a hit in Washington. Their entertainments were spectacular but usually tasteful. . . . Mrs. Leiter threw herself into committee work to preserve Mt. Vernon. . . . The elderly, extremely respectable historian George Bancroft and Levi Leiter shared a love of history and books and spent many evenings together. Mrs. Leiter was the recipient of vast bouquets of Bancroft's famed roses. Even the discriminating Henry Adams and Mr. and Mrs. John Hay soon became the Leiters' friends. . . . Their enormous fifty-five-room white brick mansion . . . dominated Dupont Circle for half a century.

One of Leiter's daughters, Mary Victoria, married George, Lord Curzon of Kedleston, the former British viceroy of India. According to an article in the *Washington Post* from 2013, "Supposedly, the fictitious Cora Crawley, countess of Grantham on 'Downton Abbey,' is modeled after this Leiter daughter."

When the Leiters built their mansion at 1500 New Hampshire Avenue NW on the circle, it was the largest private house in Washington. After Levi Leiter's death, his wife continued to host elaborate parties there until World War II. The house was demolished in 1947 and is now the site of the Dupont Circle Hotel.

Levi Leiter is buried with his wife beneath a raised sarcophagus of white Carrara marble covered with handsome bas-relief carvings, including one of the Last Supper. Carrara marble comes from Tuscany and is valued for its pure white color; it has been favored by sculptors as a medium since the time of ancient Rome. But because this marble is so porous, a glass structure was placed over the sarcophagus at a later date to better preserve the site. In 2018, the glass was replaced, the stone walls and staircase rebuilt, and the entire sarcophagus cleaned. Other members of his family are under more modest stones nearby.

Leiter was extremely nervous about his mortal remains. His grave is so overbuilt that, as the *New York Times* reported after his interment, "Only an earthquake or heavy charges of explosives could move the mass." Leiter requested extra precautions to ensure that grave robbers would not steal his body and hold it for ransom. His coffin, which was buried twelve feet underground (double the normal depth), was surrounded by steel beams bolted to the casket, and the grave was filled with concrete.

→ **Exit at the top of the gravesite and take the paved road to your left. Look to your right for a bronze male figure with a raised arm on the slope of the hill.**

13 GAFF MEMORIAL (1922)

Section L, Lot 139

Thomas Trueman Gaff (1854–1923) was an industrialist who made his fortune in the distillery and heavy machinery industries. He moved to the District in 1904, and President Taft appointed him as a commissioner on the Panama Canal. Gaff was a committed clubman: he belonged to the Chevy Chase Riding Club, the Cosmos Club, the University Club, and the Harvard Club of New York. His mansion, at 1520 Twentieth Street NW in the Dupont Circle neighborhood, is now the ambassador of Colombia's diplomatic residence. Built in the French Château style, the house was a center for DC society events. It was added to the National Register of Historic Places in 1978.

The memorial was created by Jules Déchin (1869–1947), a French sculptor best known for his World War I memorials in France. This is his only work in the United States. Sited on a steep slope, a bronze sitting male figure in a loose hooded robe raises his left hand above a plaque with the Latin motto "Excepit illum magna et aeterna pax," a quote from the playwright and Roman Stoic philosopher Seneca the Younger. It translates as "Great and eternal peace to the people who gladly received him."

→ **Continue just a little further on this paved road. Look to your right for a large rectangular grave with the name "PHILLIPS" in capital letters, flanked by two decorative swags.**

14 DUNCAN PHILLIPS GRAVE

Section R11, Lot 52

Duncan Phillips (1886–1966) was a major art collector and critic based in Washington, DC, from 1895 until his death. He established the Phillips Memorial Gallery (now the Phillips Collection) in memory of his father and brother as a "joy-giving, life enhancing influence, assisting people to see beautifully as true artists see." His gallery had a major role in introducing modern art to the United States, and as a collector, Phillips had the foresight to recognize excellence among such artists as Georgia O'Keeffe, Arthur Dove, John Marin, and Milton Avery before they were well known. His museum in Dupont Circle now houses nearly three thousand major works by American and European impressionist and modern artists. Phillips is the author of *The Enchantment of Art* (1914).

Also buried at this site is Marjorie Acker Phillips (1894–1985), a painter who studied at the Art Students League in New York. She married Duncan Phillips in 1921 and served as associate director of the Phillips Collection from 1925 to 1966, taking on the role of director from 1966 to 1972.

The couple are buried with Duncan's brother, James Laughlin Phillips (1894–1918), also an art collector and associate director of bureau personnel for the American Red Cross. He died in the influenza pandemic of 1918.

→ **Continue on this road a little further and then cross the swath of grass to your left by a large rectangular grave marked "Oliphant." Take care, as the slope is steep here, and look for the short flight of marble steps leading from the Oliphant grave to the road below. When you reach the road, look to your left and walk to the first mausoleum built into the hillside on your left.**

15 WALSH TOMB

Section L, Lot 1, Grave 6

This handsome mausoleum is built into the hill; its front pediment is supported by four Ionic columns. Although the door to the tomb is solid bronze, you can peek through the windows on either side to see the remains of Evalyn Walsh McLean (1886–1947), famous as the last private owner of the Hope Diamond.

Walsh was the daughter of an Irish immigrant who rose up from poverty, making a vast fortune operating one of the richest gold mines in the world—the Camp Bird Mine, located in Colorado. Her parents took her on trips to Europe as a young girl and sent her to the best private schools, but Walsh was always aware of her nouveau riche status. In her memoir, *Father Struck It Rich* (1936), cowritten with Boyden Sparkes, she wrote, "An agreement was reached in our family for me to go to Paris to study—music, French and other parlor tricks of ladies. By some school magic, I was to become a lady!"

When her father built a mansion in 1903 in Dupont Circle, it was the most expensive house in the city. This neobaroque palace still stands at 2020 Massachusetts Avenue NW, now the Indonesian embassy chancery. The mansion still retains its original Y-shaped grand staircase, the stained glass ceiling in the huge entry hall, and the large slab of unrefined gold ore (shipped here from the Camp Bird Mine) built into the front porch.

In 1908, against her family's advice, Walsh eloped with Edward Beale McLean (1889–1941), the publisher of the *Washington Post.* A notorious alcoholic and playboy, McLean was famous for his galas. The couple built two mansions, since destroyed: a family estate called Friendship (now the site of the McLean Gardens apartments off Wisconsin Avenue NW) and a house for formal entertaining off Lafayette Square (now the site of the Import-Export Bank at 811 Vermont Avenue NW). During their marriage, the McLeans had four children, Evalyn became addicted to morphine, and they managed to quickly decimate two family fortunes worth millions. The couple separated in 1927. Her final house, located at 3308 R Street NW in the Georgetown neighborhood, still stands.

McLean was renowned for her jewels. On her honeymoon, she purchased a diamond called the Star of the

East. But she is best known for the Hope Diamond, tinted a deep and rare blue, which she conspicuously wore to parties (and which was said to carry a horrible curse). The Hope Diamond is now one of the most visited items in the collections of the Smithsonian Institution's National Museum of Natural History.

→ **Walk back toward the stairs you came down; before you get there, you will come to a complex intersection, where you'll see the back of the church. Bear left to walk toward the church and look to your left for the mausoleum built into the slope of the church's hill, with a sheet of corrugated metal covering the door.**

16 SAMUEL HARRISON SMITH TOMB

Section A, Lot 56

Samuel Harrison Smith (1772–1845) was the founder of the District's first newspaper, the *National Intelligencer,* which began publishing in 1800. He also served as commissioner of the revenue for the US Treasury, secretary of the Treasury, and president of the Bank of Washington. He was a close friend of Thomas Jefferson's. In addition, he volunteered as treasurer of the Washington National Monument Society.

Smith married his second cousin, Margaret Bayard (1778–1884); they moved to Washington in the fall of 1800 and lived in the capital for the rest of their lives. Margaret Bayard Smith was one of the first novelists to use the District as a setting for her fiction. Her novels include *A Winter in Washington* (1824) and *What Is Gentility?* (1825). She also wrote children's literature and a biography of First Lady Dolley Madison, and she is best remembered for her posthumous collection of letters and journal entries, *The First Forty Years of Washington Society* (1906). The Smiths were one of the earliest "power couples" in Washington. In addition to a home on New Jersey Avenue on Capitol Hill, now razed, they owned a country estate, called Sidney, on a tract of land known as Turkey Thicket (now the grounds of the Catholic University of America).

→ **Continue on the paved road to your right, walking around the back of the church. You will see a large old evergreen on your right shading a mausoleum.**

17 JOHN CLAGETT PROCTOR TOMB

Section 14, Lot 5

John Clagett Proctor (1867–1956) lived his entire life in Washington, DC. He began working at age fifteen as a printer, then earned a law degree from the National University Law School and was admitted to the bar in 1894. Proctor was active in several DC organizations, including the Masons, the Society of Natives, the Association of the Oldest Inhabitants, Sons of Union Veterans of the Civil War, the Columbia Historical Society, and the DC Federation of Citizens Associations.

He wrote articles for the *Sunday Star* newspaper from 1928 until the early 1950s; several were collected in the 1949 volume *Proctor's Washington and Environs*. In 1950, he self-published *Proctor's Poems*, a volume of collected verse. He is buried with his wife, Annie Maud Proctor, and son Francis. Note the stained glass seen through the mausoleum door, which depicts a sun setting over a river, symbolizing the end of a journey.

John Clagett Proctor's poem "Georgia Avenue" was first published in a periodical called the *Come-Back* on June 18, 1919. Walter Reed General Hospital had opened in 1909 with eighty beds and expanded in World War I to twenty-five hundred beds. (The Georgia Avenue facility closed in August 2011.) The lower section of Georgia

Avenue was first paved in 1916, just three years before this poem was written, but upper Georgia Avenue remained unpaved until after the war.

Oh, what a road to Walter Reed!
A rocky road is it indeed!
The ditches in the thoroughfare
Make angels weep and preachers swear.

The wounded in the ambulance
Imagine they are still in France
As over hump and bump they go
To where they hardly ever know.

A ride upon a camel's back
Is pleasant to the reel and rack
Endured as your auto hits
The gulleys and the open pits.

And should you take a trolley car
You'll find it worse, indeed, by far,
For crooked track and flattened wheel
May make you lose your latest meal.

Of all the streets of Washington
This one will surely take the bun;
It is the most unusual street
That you, perhaps, in life will meet.

They call it Georgia Avenue—
But what on earth did Georgia do
To merit such a big disgrace?
(A slap, it seems, right in the face.)

For Georgia is a good old State
Where everything is up to date,
And if I represented it
I'd start right in and do my bit.

I'd tack right to the District bill
An item which they could not kill:

I'd make the delegation aid
And soon I'd have asphaltum laid.

→ **Continue on this road to the intersection, then turn right and look to your right. Directly behind the Proctor Mausoleum, you'll see a large bronze figure of a woman.**

18 JOHN SPENCER MEMORIAL (1919)

Section 14, Lot 48

John Spencer (1811–1854) is buried with his wife, Catherine, and daughter Mary Ann. I could find little information about the Spencers; they were born in Ireland and immigrated first to Canada, where their daughter was born, and then to the United States.

This site is important for its neoclassical sculpture that hints strongly at the Art Deco style that was to come. A memorial figure leans on a funeral urn. She has downcast eyes and holds a bouquet of flowers to symbolize the transience of life.

The sculptor was Adolph Alexander Weinman (1870–1952), a German-born American artist who was a member of the National Sculpture Society, the US Commission of Fine Arts, the American Academy of Arts and Letters, and the National Academy of Design. All of Weinman's most famous works are in the District; they include pediments for the Jefferson Memorial and the Library of Congress as well as sculptures in the interior of the US Supreme Court.

→ **Cross the grass back past the Proctor Mausoleum to the road. You will see the Hitt Memorial just on the other side, marked with a short set of stairs.**

19 HITT MEMORIAL (1931)

Section A, Lot 37

This is the gravesite of Robert Stockwell Reynolds Hitt (1876–1938), who worked for the State Department as ambassador to Panama and Guatemala. He earned an undergraduate degree from Yale and a law degree from Harvard, after which he followed his father into foreign service, including postings in Paris, Berlin, and Rome. He died of pneumonia at age sixty-one and is buried with family members: Catherine E. Hitt, Edith Gray Hitt, Sally Reynolds Hitt, William Hitt, and Elizabeth Hitt de Hertelendy. His Georgian Revival mansion in Dupont Circle was designed by noted local architect Jules Henri de Sibour and is now the Hong Kong Economic and Trade Office, located at 1520 Eighteenth Street NW.

The Hitt Memorial consists of three bronze relief plaques on a pink granite base. The quote under the plaques, "Out with the ebb tide on some farther quest," is the final line of "With the Tide" by the writer Edith Wharton.

> Somewhere I read, in an old book whose name
> Is gone from me, I read that when the days
> Of a man are counted, and his business done,
> There comes up the shore at evening, with the tide,
> To the place where he sits, a boat—
> And in the boat, from the place where he sits, he sees,
> Dim in the dusk, dim and yet so familiar,
> The faces of his friends long dead; and knows
> They come for him, brought in upon the tide,
> To take him where men go at set of day.
> Then rising, with his hands in theirs, he goes
> Between them his last steps, that are the first
> Of the new life—and with the ebb they pass,
> Their shaken sail grown small upon the moon.

Often I thought of this, and pictured me
How many a man who lives with throngs about him,
Yet straining through the twilight for that boat
Shall scarce make out one figure in the stern,
And that so faint its features shall perplex him
With doubtful memories—and his heart hang back.
But others, rising as they see the sail
Increase upon the sunset, hasten down,
Hands out and eyes elated; for they see
Head over head, crowding from bow to stern,
Repeopling their long loneliness with smiles,
The faces of their friends; and such go forth
Content upon the ebb tide, with safe hearts.

But never
To worker summoned when his day was done
Did mounting tide bring in such freight of friends
As stole to you up the white wintry shingle
That night while they that watched you thought you slept.
Softly they came, and beached the boat, and gathered
In the still cove under the icy stars,
Your last-born, and the dear loves of your heart,
And all men that have loved right more than ease,
And honor above honors; all who gave
Free-handed of their best for other men,
And thought their giving taking: they who knew
Man's natural state is effort, up and up—
All these were there, so great a company
Perchance you marveled, wondering what great ship
Had brought that throng unnumbered to the cove
Where the boys used to beach their light canoe
After old happy picnics—

But these, your friends and children, to whose hands
Committed, in the silent night you rose
And took your last faint steps—
These led you down, O great American,
Down to the winter night and the white beach,

And there you saw that the huge hull that waited
Was not as are the boats of the other dead,
Frail craft for a brief passage; no, for this
Was first of a long line of towering transports,
Storm-worn and ocean-weary every one,
The ships you launched, the ships you manned, the ships
That now, returning from their sacred quest
With the thrice-sacred burden of their dead,
Lay waiting there to take you forth with them,
Out with the ebb tide, on some farther quest.

The bronzes were created by Laura Gardin Fraser (1889–1966), a prominent sculptor who studied under James Earle Fraser before becoming his wife. She is less well known than her husband, largely owing to sexism and also, perhaps, to the fact that her best works are in smaller formats: medallions and coins, including the Charles A. Lindberg Congressional Medal, the George Washington Bicentennial Medal, the Benjamin Franklin Congressional Medal, the Oregon Trail Memorial half dollar, and the George Washington commemorative five-dollar gold coin. Her large-scale work includes a Flying Pegasus for Brookgreen Gardens in South Carolina, the Elks National Memorial in Chicago, and four ten-foot panels installed on the Roosevelt Bridge in Washington, DC. Her more famous husband also has sculptural work in this cemetery, which we'll look at next.

→ **Continue around the church, passing the main entrance. Look to your left for two bronze figures against a granite base.**

20 FREDERIC A. KEEP MONUMENT (1920)

Section A, Lot 210

Frederic A. Keep (1854–1911) is buried here with his wife, Florence (1867–1954), and an infant child who died immediately after birth. Keep was a prominent Washington businessman; Florence was a socialite, and some of her personal belongings are now in the collections of the National Museum of American History.

The monument, called *Journey of Life,* features two half-nude figures in bronze on a granite base. James Earle Fraser (1876–1953) created some of the District's most iconic sculpture, including *The Authority of Law* and *The Contemplation of Justice* outside the US Supreme Court, the south pediment and the *Guardianship* and *Heritage* sculptures at the National Archives, statues of Alexander Hamilton and Albert Gallatin outside the US Treasury, and two heroic bronze equestrian statues, called *The Arts of Peace,* at the entrance to the Rock Creek and Potomac Parkway on the DC side of the Arlington Memorial Bridge. He also created the Second Division Memorial on the Ellipse and the William Howard Taft Monument at Arlington National Cemetery (see site 4 in that tour on page 225).

Fraser was a member of the National Academy of Design, the National Sculpture Society, and the Architectural League of New York. He was inducted into the National Institute of Arts and Letters and served on the US Commission of Fine Arts in Washington from 1920 to 1925. He was apprenticed to Augustus Saint-Gaudens beginning at age twenty-two, and he credited the older man's influence on his own aesthetic—so it is entirely fitting that works by both not only share these grounds but are the highlights of its sculptural offerings.

→ **Backtrack to the church entrance.**

21 ST. PAUL'S ROCK CREEK CHURCH

The oldest religious institution in DC and the one in longest continual use, St. Paul's Rock Creek Church was built in 1775, incorporating parts of an older wooden church that dates to 1719. It was remodeled in 1853, restored after a fire in 1922, and restored again in 2004. The church's stained glass windows depict the history of the Episcopal Church in America, and the church is also famed for its acoustics and its handsome Dobson pipe organ. In 1972, St. Paul's was added to the National Register of Historic Places.

Although the cemetery has long been associated with the burial of the city's wealthy white residents, the church itself has had a majority African American congregation since the mid-1970s. According to the rector of St. Paul's, the Reverend Allan Johnson-Taylor, the congregation was white for the first 130 years or so of the church's existence, with the first Black church member joining around 1940. As the demographic makeup of the congregation has changed, so has the diversity of more recent burials in the cemetery.

CONGRESSIONAL CEMETERY (1807)

1801 E Street SE, Capitol Hill neighborhood, DC

Founded in 1807, Congressional is the only remaining cemetery from L'Enfant's city plan still in use. Why was this single cemetery exempt from the District's 1852 ordinance requiring that all cemeteries in the center of the city disinter remains and move farther out? Congressional Cemetery was spared because of its unique relationship to the US Congress, which is reflected in its name. Originally the site was just 1.5 acres, but the cemetery expanded in size six times between 1849 and 1869, and it now encompasses 32.75 acres. It was added to the National Register of Historic Places in 1969 and to the National Historic Landmarks list in 2011.

Congressional holds approximately sixty-five thousand graves and twenty-five thousand headstones; it also has a section where pets can be buried. Underground scanning has revealed numerous unmarked graves. In addition to traditional graves and columbaria, the cemetery is certified by the Green Burial Council and, in 2019, opened a "Circle of Life" section for natural burials.

Although the cemetery went through a notable period of disrepair, today it is a model of modern funerary upkeep and has found numerous creative ways to involve the public. The K9 Corps (established in 1997) is a membership group that supports ongoing conservation in exchange for the privilege of dog walking on the private grounds. Members must also pledge volunteer hours. (Unless you come on a Saturday, when they are prohibited, be prepared to see some dogs on your visit!)

Before You Go
https://congressionalcemetery.org
Open daily 9:00 am to 5:00 pm
Nearest public transportation: Potomac Avenue Station
No parking; restrooms available

1 GATEHOUSE

Built in 1923, this is the second gatehouse on this site, which combines a residence and office for the cemetery keeper. The original gatehouse (constructed in 1832) had a bell tower, which tolled each time there was a graveside funeral, with the tradition of one toll for each year the deceased person had lived. You can see the second of the cemetery's old bells, from 1894, on the left, hanging on a specially built wooden structure. That bell was restored in 2015 by the McShane Bell Foundry in Baltimore, the original company that cast it—still in business over the decades. The restored bell is back in use today.

Congressional Cemetery's first owner was Christ Church, Washington Parish, which managed the burial ground from 1807 through 1976. A renovation to the gatehouse was the last major project undertaken by Christ Church before the cemetery went into years of steep decline. After that time, the cemetery was given to a nonprofit organization, the Association for the Preservation of Historic Congressional Cemetery.

→ **Proceed down the main walkway (Congress Street). About midway from the entrance to the chapel, look for two large modern headstones side by side on your right, just before the brick path. The first includes a bas-relief portrait in bronze on the front of the gravestone.**

Cenotaphs (5)

2 WARREN M. ROBBINS GRAVE

Range 62, Site 89

Warren Robbins (1923–2008) was a collector of African art. He opened a private museum in his Capitol Hill home that operated from 1964 to 1979 and was the first museum in the United States dedicated solely to African art. Robbins's museum was located at 316–18 A Street NE in a former residence of Frederick Douglass. As his collection expanded, he ultimately owned nine adjoining properties, as well as sixteen garages and two carriage

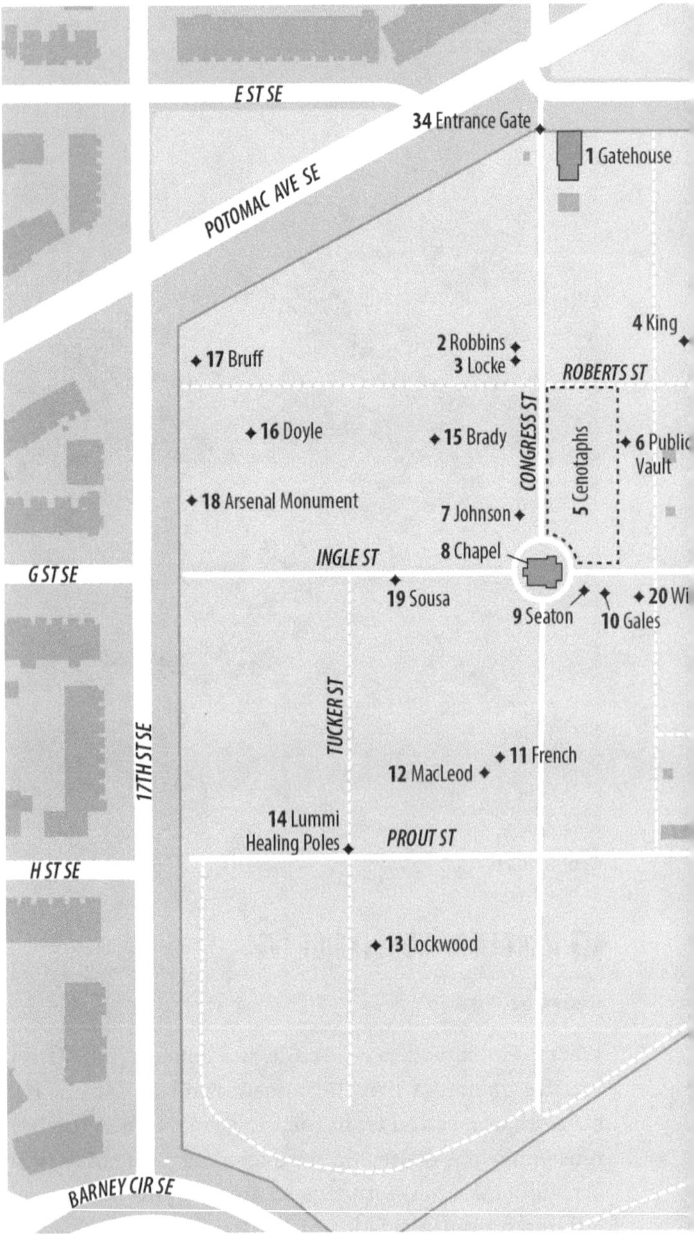

Congressional Cemetery

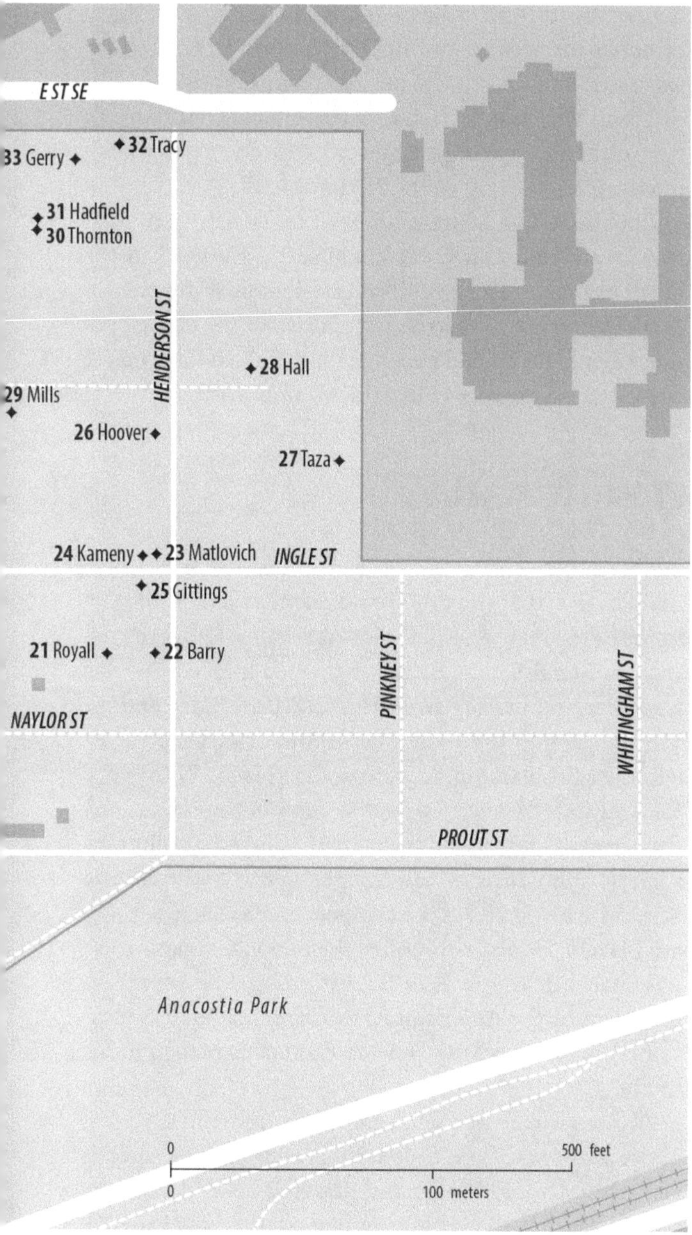
E ST SE
33 Gerry
32 Tracy
31 Hadfield
30 Thornton
HENDERSON ST
28 Hall
29 Mills
26 Hoover
27 Taza
24 Kameny
23 Matlovich
INGLE ST
25 Gittings
21 Royall
22 Barry
PINKNEY ST
WHITINGHAM ST
NAYLOR ST
PROUT ST
Anacostia Park
0
500 feet
0
100 meters

houses, to store all his artwork and his extensive library of books on African culture and history. His collection was later donated to the Smithsonian Institution, and Robbins was the National Museum of African Art's first director, serving from 1979 to 1983, prior to the museum's relocation to the National Mall.

Robbins was a white man born to Jewish Ukrainian immigrant parents in Massachusetts. He worked for much of his career as a cultural affairs officer for the US State Department. A strong supporter of the civil rights movement, he considered his collecting to be a major contribution to cross-cultural communication.

3 ALAIN LOCKE GRAVE

Range 62, Site 90

Alain Locke (1885–1954) is best known as one of the critics who created the artistic movement now known as the Harlem Renaissance. He distinguished himself early as a scholar, graduating from Harvard University and, in 1907, becoming the first African American recipient of a Rhodes Scholarship. A professor at Howard University for over four decades, Locke was chair of the philosophy department, faculty advisor for the university literary society, and editor of the campus literary journal, the *Stylus*. He helped form the campus drama club, the Howard Players. He also cofounded the national organization Associates in Negro Folk Education, and he served as president of the American Association for Adult Education. A building on the Howard campus is named in his honor.

Although it is not what he is best remembered for, Locke was one of the first serious collectors of African art in the United States and donated his collection to the Howard Gallery of Art. Perhaps that is why Robbins bought a gravesite adjoining his.

Locke edited the landmark anthology *The New Negro*

(1925), which helped define the Harlem Renaissance. His other books include *Diversity Within National Unity* (1945), *World View on Race and Democracy* (1943), *When Peoples Meet: A Study of Race and Culture Contacts* (1942), *Plays of Negro Life* (1927), and *Race Contacts and Interracial Relations* (1916).

Locke's tombstone was erected sixty years after his death, when it was discovered that his cremated remains had been languishing in storage at the Moorland-Spingarn Research Center at Howard University. He joined a large number of other LGBTQ+ individuals interred at Congressional.

→ **Cut across Congress Street. Not far in, look for a large rectangular monument shaped like a raised stone coffin. The grave uses a combination of rough "natural"-looking stone and carved, smooth surfaces.**

4 HORATIO KING GRAVE

Range 53, Site 78

Horatio King (1811–1897) was a journalist and the co-owner of a Maine newspaper, the *Jeffersonian.* In 1839 he moved to Washington, DC, for an appointment as clerk in the Post Office Department, rising into progressively more responsible jobs over the next two decades. By the time of his retirement, during the Civil War, he was postmaster general. Although a Democrat, King supported abolitionist causes. Abraham Lincoln appointed him to the committee that determined compensation rates for all enslaved people emancipated in the District in 1862. Under this law, all owners of enslaved people could apply for payment by the government of up to three hundred dollars per person whom they had freed. Lincoln hoped that this might serve as a model for a nationwide end to slavery. Instead, DC became the only place in the United States where owners were paid to release their slaves, and enslaved people in DC became the first in the nation to be freed by law.

After his retirement from government service, King opened a private law practice in Washington. He was a founding member of the Union Literary Society in the 1840s and hosted a popular salon in his house in the 1860s and '70s called King's Reunions. His salon evenings included readings by local and visiting authors of original poetry, essays, and memoirs, which led to the founding of the Washington Literary Society in 1874. King published *An Oration Before the Union Literary Society of Washington* (1841), *Sketches of Travel, or Twelve Months in Europe* (1878), and *Turning on the Light: A Dispassionate Survey of President Buchanan's Administration* (1895).

→ **Continue toward the chapel until you reach a small brick path. You will see rows of cenotaphs in front of you. Although "cenotaph" means a grave marker honoring a person who is not buried at that site, only some of these are true cenotaphs. Others actually mark burials.**

5 CENOTAPHS

As Abby Arthur Johnson and Robert Maberry Johnson write in *In the Shadow of the United States Capitol: Congressional Cemetery and the Memory of the Nation* (2012), the cenotaphs, 168 tombs that honor members of Congress who died in office between 1776 and 1876, are an example of "how the boundaries between public and private, sacred and secular, were blurred in the early republic." Although owned and operated at that time by Christ Church, and therefore on private land, the US government invested in the cemetery, not only by buying plots for the cenotaphs but also by making appropriations for the cemetery's upkeep. Because of this, the Johnsons argue, Congressional is "singular in its status as a U.S. national cemetery, it is in a category of its own. It is not a national military cemetery, like Arlington across the Potomac River, but a one-of-a-kind national public cemetery."

The House of Representatives endorsed a law in March 1839 to place a monument for each member who died in office, no matter where they were ultimately buried. The Senate adopted a similar law soon after. Cenotaphs were financed through the contingency funds of the US Congress. There are a total of nineteen senators, and seventy-one representatives, whose remains are actually buried in Congressional. In addition, this land holds six Cabinet members.

Designed by architect Benjamin Henry Latrobe (1764–1820) of local Aquia Creek sandstone, the distinctive shape of large square blocks with recessed panels topped by conical points was influenced by classical designs. (This sandstone was also used in the construction of the US Capitol and provides a further visual connection between the cemetery and Congress.) Although the sandstone is easily carved and has a depth of warmth in color and texture, it is also soft enough to be easily damaged by time and weather. The cenotaphs are part of 806 burial plots purchased by the US government within the cemetery, and they continue to be administered by the Department of Veterans Affairs.

There are a few exceptions to the rule that cenotaphs must honor senators and congressmen who died in office before 1876. William Thornton, architect of the Capitol, is the only person honored with a cenotaph who did not serve as a congressman (his grave is site 30 on this tour). And although Congress stopped paying for cenotaphs in 1875, one shared cenotaph is designated for two later deaths: Representatives T. Hale Boggs and Nicholas Begich died in a small airplane crash in 1972. A few modern cenotaphs, such as the one for Thomas Phillip "Tip" O'Neill Jr., continue the tradition, although they do not use the original sandstone block design.

→ **Take the small brick path to your left. Then turn right at the intersecting path to reach the next stop.**

6 PUBLIC VAULT

This partially subterranean receiving vault with wrought iron doors was built in 1835; it was substantially repaired in 2005. It temporarily held the remains of over six thousand individuals until arrangements could be made for burials elsewhere. Among the bodies temporarily in the vault were such notables as Presidents John Quincy Adams, William Henry Harrison, and Zachary Taylor as well as First Ladies Abigail Adams and Dolley Madison. Legend states that Lewis Powell, one of the men involved in the assassination of President Abraham Lincoln, hid in the public vault for one night while avoiding pursuit.

The vault was built with federal funds, and in the early periods of the cemetery's history, members of Congress could use the vault for "temporary disposition" at no cost. But the vault was always envisioned as a public amenity, as it clearly states on the iron doors, and it was open to all others at a fee (originally five dollars per month) for its use.

As advances in transportation and mortuary science made it possible for congressional members who died in Washington to be buried in their home districts, the vault became increasingly important. Many of the grandest federal funeral parades went through the city to the public vault so that public figures such as senators and congressional representatives could get federal recognition for their service to their country before getting a second, more private funeral back in their home jurisdictions.

→ **Continue on the path and then turn right at Ingle Street, heading toward the chapel. Bear right to walk around the chapel's circular drive and look for a small**

stone nearly level to the ground on the far side of Congress Street.

7 ADELAIDE JOHNSON GRAVE

Range 61, Site 152

Adelaide Johnson (1859–1955) was a feminist and suffragette, a vegetarian, and one of the first women whose husband took her name rather than the other way around. She studied art at the St. Louis School of Design and abroad in Dresden and Rome. Although she had trouble getting commissions, she exhibited work at the Woman's Building of the 1893 World's Columbian Exposition in Chicago as well as in the Capitol rotunda. Her most famous sculpture, *Portrait Monument to Suffrage Pioneers* (1920), is in the collection of the US Capitol. It depicts the busts of Lucretia Mott, Elizabeth Cady Stanton, and Susan B. Anthony rising out of a rough square of marble.

8 CHAPEL

Constructed in 1903, this small Gothic chapel of pebble dash with a slate roof was designed by Arthur M. Poyton and J. H. Gibbins. It stands on a circular plot of land at the center of the cemetery grounds, replacing an earlier fountain at this location. The rest of the cemetery is arranged in a grid pattern, an older style favored by church cemeteries that also has the advantage of echoing the L'Enfant design of the surrounding city. Even after this grid design fell out of fashion (and garden-style designs became popular), Congressional continued to use this rational, simple pattern. The chapel is the only section of the cemetery that gives some relief from the rigidity of the grid.

→ **Go to the left and look for the next two graves on the back side of the chapel. Both are the final resting places of former mayors of the city. The first can be found behind the chapel's rear rose window, in the shade of a tree. Although nearly illegible, you can make out a stars-and-stripes shield at the bottom of the gravestone.**

9 WILLIAM WINSTON SEATON GRAVE

Range 57, Site 165

William Winston Seaton (1785–1866) was one of two congressional reporters for the *National Intelligencer* newspaper from 1812 to 1820, and he was an expert in the debates and proceedings of both houses of Congress. He was active in the Columbian Institute for the Promotion of Arts and Sciences (a forerunner of the Smithsonian Institution) and a cofounder of St. John's Episcopal Church on Lafayette Square. He became a leader in District politics, first on the board of aldermen and then as the city's thirteenth mayor. During his decade as mayor, from 1840 to 1850, he oversaw the installation of telegraph lines, gas lines, and public water systems. He also put into place the beginnings of the city's free public education system, which initially only served white students (although residents of all races paid city taxes).

In addition to his house on E Street downtown, Seaton owned a farm in Prince George County, Virginia. He served on the executive committee of the American Colonization Society, and his experience with this organization convinced him to free all the enslaved people he owned. Seaton was a veteran of the War of 1812, a Unitarian, a Freemason, and a member of the Whig party. His wife, Sarah Weston Gales Seaton (ca. 1790–1863), buried next to him, was a translator from French and Spanish into English who also did occasional work for the *National Intelligencer.* The couple had eleven children together.

→ **Directly behind Seaton's grave is our next site. Look for a grave topped by an obelisk.**

10 JOSEPH GALES JR. GRAVE

Range 55, Site 168

Seaton's brother-in-law was Joseph Gales (1786–1860). Gales was born in England; he emigrated to the United States in 1795 and was educated at the University of North Carolina at Chapel Hill. In 1807 he moved to Washington, DC. Initially he worked as the junior partner for the *National Intelligencer* with Samuel Harrison Smith, but he became the newspaper's sole proprietor in 1810. The paper's printed records of congressional debates are considered the most accurate and complete historical accounts for Congress's early years.

Like his brother-in-law, Gales was an active member of the Columbian Institute for the Promotion of Arts and Sciences and a cofounder of St. John's Episcopal Church. His entry into local politics preceded that of his brother-in-law. Gales was elected the ninth mayor of Washington, DC, and served from 1827 to 1830. His major accomplishments as mayor were establishing relief committees for poor residents and breaking ground on the C&O Canal.

→ **Go back to the chapel and bear left to continue heading south on Congress Street. Look for a prominent brown obelisk on your right.**

11 BENJAMIN B. FRENCH GRAVE

Range 63, Site 228

Benjamin B. French (1800–1870) was clerk of the US House of Representatives and commissioner of public buildings under Presidents Franklin Pierce, Abraham Lincoln, and Andrew Johnson. He oversaw the expansion of the US Capitol and the Washington Monument. The Masonic Lodge in the Georgetown neighborhood is named for him. French is the author of historical sketches and poems; his books include *Fitz Clarence: A Poem* (1844), *Changes of Earth: A Poem* (1845), and *A Letter and Short Poem on the Death of Abraham Lincoln* (1870). His diaries were later collected and published as *Witness to the Young Republic: A Yankee's Journal, 1828–1870.*

French is best known for his associations with President Abraham Lincoln. He was present at the Gettysburg Address and in the room of the Petersen House in which Lincoln lay dying, and he was placed in charge of Lincoln's funeral arrangements.

→ **Further to your left, and two rows back, look for the next grave, marked by a flat, simple stone.**

12 WILLIAM MACLEOD GRAVE

Range 65, Site 238

William MacLeod (1811–1892) was the Corcoran Gallery's first curator—and one of the first museum professionals in the United States. He was a landscape painter who created regional scenes influenced by the Hudson River School painters, and he brought creativity and sensitivity to his role as curator, helping shape the museum field.

Born in Alexandria, Virginia, MacLeod studied medicine at the University of Glasgow in Scotland before turning to art. He showed work at the National Academy of Design's annual exhibitions in New York in 1852 and 1853, opening an art school and studio in Washington, DC, at Twelfth and F Streets NW in 1854. MacLeod directed the Corcoran from 1873 until 1889.

→ **Continue cutting over to the left and south. You will cross over the walkway; look for some tall cedar trees surrounding the next gravesite on all sides. A new**

monument was installed on the ground in front of the gravestone in 2023.

13 BELVA LOCKWOOD GRAVE

Range 78, Site 296

Belva Lockwood (1830–1917) worked as a teacher and temperance advocate before moving to Washington, DC, where she was a leader in the women's suffrage movement. She trained to be a lawyer but was denied admission to the bar in DC until 1873. When finally admitted, she became the first woman lawyer licensed in the city. She frequently argued against sex discrimination before congressional committees and ran her own legal practice. (Many of her clients were women suing for divorce.) In 1878, she made history when she became the first woman to argue a case before the Supreme Court. But she became more widely known in 1884, when she declared her third-party candidacy for US president as the Equal Rights Party's nominee. She ran for president again in 1888.

Lockwood's most famous legal victory, *U.S. v. Cherokee Nation,* came in 1906, when she won five million dollars as payment for tribal lands ceded to the government. It was a landmark case for Native American rights. Lockwood was posthumously inducted into the National Women's Hall of Fame in 1983.

Lura Ormes (1849–1894) shares a tombstone with her mother; see the back side of this grave. Like her mother, Ormes attended law school. She helped run her mother's law practice and served as campaign director for Lockwood's two presidential runs. She is buried alongside her husband and two children.

→ **A walkway, constructed as a 9/11 memorial, can be found just behind Lockwood's grave. Turn right and walk along this path.**

14 LUMMI NATION SEPTEMBER 11 HEALING POLE

After the terrorist attacks of 2001, the Lummi Nation of Washington State donated a totem pole gateway, created by the House of Tears master carvers, as a remembrance of those whose lives were lost in New York, Pennsylvania, and Washington, DC. The Healing Pole was originally displayed at the Pentagon before its rededication at this cemetery. On the two sides, large bears are carved; one has a sun on its torso, and the other a moon. A crossbar connects the two, carved with two eagles representing the faces of war and peace.

→ **Continue on this path all the way to Ingle Street. Cross Ingle and continue on the path. On your right and several rows in, cut across the grass to reach a large memorial topped by a skull and raven.**

15 MATHEW BRADY GRAVE

Range 72, Site 120

Mathew Brady (1822–1896) is best known for his Civil War photojournalism, including the first battlefield photos to gain a wide viewership, and his photographic portraits of Abraham Lincoln. In 1849, he opened his photography studio at 625 Pennsylvania Avenue NW, and in 1850 he published *The Gallery of Illustrious Americans* to much acclaim. Brady photographed every president from John Quincy Adams to William McKinley, with the exception of William Henry Harrison, who died young. He also made a series of portraits of all the senior officers of the Union Army.

Photography was relatively new when the Civil War began, and Brady's use of a mobile studio and darkroom enabled the creation of vivid imagery that captured the gruesome and graphic reality of the battlefield. He came under direct fire while documenting battles at Bull

Run, Petersburg, and Fredericksburg. As his eyesight began to worsen, Brady hired twenty-four employees who increasingly did most of the fieldwork; he concentrated on studio portraits. Some of the men he trained became accomplished artists who later worked under their own names: among them were Alexander Gardner, George Barnard, and Timothy H. O'Sullivan. Today, his photos are considered to be some of the greatest treasures of the US National Archives and the Library of Congress. Although immensely popular during the Civil War years, his photographs quickly fell out of fashion with a war-weary public, and Brady died in debt.

Brady's original gravestone, which still stands, incorrectly listed the year of his death. This modest marker was later replaced, and overshadowed, by a factually correct and visually confusing memorial installed in 2022. The new memorial, adjacent to his headstone, is a complex arrangement that includes small reproductions of some of Brady's famous photos; some photographs of people he knew (whose pictures he did not take); engraved quotations; two standing, life-sized bronzes of Abraham Lincoln and Frederick Douglass; and a bronze box camera atop a tripod. There are also elements that seem more evocative of the time period in which Brady lived than his actual life. These include a large plaque with a representation of Anna Murray Douglass (the first wife of Frederick Douglass), a raven sitting atop a white skull at the highest point of the monument (above the motto "The camera is the eye of history"), and a columbarium (along the sides of the large standing stone with the photos) for modern burials, mostly people who were collectors of historic photos. The modern memorial is a visual jumble that intends to honor Brady—but barely holds together all its ambitions.

→ **Retrace your steps to the brick path. Cross over the path and head due west across the grass toward**

Seventeenth Street. Look for a gravestone between two larger monuments topped by urns.

16 PETER DOYLE GRAVE

Range 91, Site 118b

Peter Doyle (1843–1907) was born in Ireland and moved to Virginia in 1852. He enlisted in the Confederate Army in 1861 and was wounded in the Battle of Antietam. He is best known for his associations with Walt Whitman (1819–1892) and is widely believed to have been the poet's greatest love. After he was released from service, Doyle worked at the Washington Navy Yard and as a streetcar conductor. In 1865, when Doyle was twenty-one and Whitman was forty-five, they met on a streetcar. Doyle stated, "The night was very stormy. . . . He was the only passenger, it was a lonely night, so I thought I would go in and talk with him. Something in me made me do it and something in him drew me that way. He used to say there was something in me had the same effect on him. Anyway, I went into the car. We were familiar at once—I put my hand on his knee—we understood. He did not get out at the end of the trip—in fact went all the way back with me. . . . From that time on we were the biggest sort of friends."

Doyle was present at Ford's Theater when Lincoln was assassinated. Whitman later made use of Doyle's eyewitness account of the events in his lectures and published writing. In 1897, the poet published *Calamus: A Series of Letters Written During the Years 1868–1880 by Walt Whitman to a Young Friend (Peter Doyle).* Doyle is buried with one brother, Edward, and near another, Francis, the first DC police officer killed in the line of duty.

→ **Continue toward the brick wall along Seventeenth Street. Look to your right for a section for Masons from**

the DC Chapter of the FAAM Grand Lodge, marked by a raised cube and a flagpole. In the row closest to Seventeenth Street, under a modest stone, you will find our next site. Joseph Bruff is buried with his wife, Eliza (whose name is easier to read than his), in the tenth grave in the last row.

17 JOSEPH GOLDSBOROUGH BRUFF GRAVE

Range 97, Site 103

Joseph Goldsborough Bruff (1804–1889) was an accomplished visual artist who worked for the US Bureau of Topographical Engineers as a cartographer. In 1849, he joined the California gold rush, forming the Washington City and California Mining Associates Expedition with sixty-three other men from the greater DC region. Bruff is best remembered for the extensive journals and sketchbooks he kept in the 1840s and 1850s as he traveled by stagecoach, wagon train, and steamboat to reach the mining camps. That work was published posthumously in two volumes titled *Gold Rush* (1944), considered by many historians to be one of the best sources of information on the subject. Bruff returned to Washington, DC, in 1853 without having struck gold. He worked for the next thirteen years in the Department of the Treasury as a supervising architect.

Congressional Cemetery has long been a favored burial site for explorers. Others in this cemetery include Joseph Nicollet, who charted the Mississippi River system; Thomas Fitzpatrick, who discovered the South Pass through the Rocky Mountains with Jedediah Smith; Henry Rowe Schoolcraft, who discovered the source of the Mississippi River; Charles Preuss, who mapped western trails from Missouri to Oregon; William Emory, who surveyed the trail from Santa Fe to California; and Middleton Smith, who explored Alaska and the Arctic on US government expeditions.

→ **Go back to cross the brick path and continue heading south along the brick wall. Look for a towering column topped with an angel.**

18 WASHINGTON ARSENAL MONUMENT

Range 98, Site 145

This monument marks the remains of sixteen of the twenty-two young women killed in an explosion in 1864 while they were working to fill cartridges by hand at the Washington Arsenal (now on the grounds of the Navy Yard). These young women were part of the largest civilian disaster of the Civil War. Most of the victims were Irish or of Irish descent. All were working inside a single room in a wooden building. Trays of explosives had been set outside the building to cure, but the intense heat of the sun ignited them, and a piece of burning fuse shot through an open window into the room, causing a huge explosion. The building went up in flames within seconds, and only eight of the twenty-nine women workers (and one male clerk) survived. Some of the women who died were caught by their large hoopskirts. These skirts—fashionable at the time—were so voluminous that one woman could only leave the bench pushed under her work table if all the other women beside her moved first. Thus, women were trapped as the flames quickly spread.

President Lincoln led the funeral procession, more than a mile in length, through the city to the cemetery and attended the graveside ceremonies. The memorial's twenty-foot-high pedestal, erected on the first anniversary of the disaster, was paid for by donations from District residents. The monument is topped by an allegorical figure of a grieving woman; it was sculpted in marble by Lot Flannery (1836–1922), an Irish-born artist who owned one of the largest stone-carving businesses in Washington. In addition to numerous tombstones,

Flannery sculpted the Abraham Lincoln statue located outside DC's City Hall as well as the statue of Chester Arthur in the collections of the Smithsonian American Art Museum. The Arsenal Monument is notable for depicting the gruesome cause of death on the front side of the granite plinth. Also depicted are winged hourglasses (symbolic of lives cut short) and a decoration of grapevines (symbolic of sacrifice). The names of the victims are carved into a separate marble plaque at the base of the monument.

→ **Continue on the path to Ingle Street and turn left. Pass the 9/11 Memorial Path on your right. Behind some bushes, you will see a bench and a large, flat grave marker.**

19 JOHN PHILIP SOUSA GRAVE

Range 77, Site 163 South

Director of the US Marine Corps Band for fifteen years, John Philip Sousa (1854–1932) is famous as the composer of popular and military marches, including "Semper Fidelis" (1888), "The Washington Post March" (1889), and "The Stars and Stripes Forever" (1896). Sousa also wrote an incredible 133 additional marches, as well as 70 songs and 15 operettas. He founded the Sousa Band in 1892, which he directed for the next forty years; he died while on a concert tour. The inventor of the sousaphone, he also wrote three novels and an autobiography. His books include *The Fifth String* (1902), *Pipetown Sandy* (1905), *The Transit of Venus* (1920), and *Marching Along* (1928), which was adapted into the Hollywood movie *Stars and Stripes Forever* (1952).

Sousa is the best known of the seven leaders of the US Marine Corps Band interred at Congressional. In addition, twenty-one musicians who once performed with the band are interred nearby. Every November 6, the date of his birth, a delegation from the Marine Corps Band comes to his grave to perform a selection of Sousa's marches.

→ **Continue on Ingle Street, passing the chapel. Turn right at the first path, paved in bluestone slabs, and look for a large square column monument, carved from marble, on the right.**

20 WILLIAM WIRT GRAVE

Range 50, Site 169

William Wirt (1772–1834) was the longest-serving attorney general in US history, serving a total of twelve years under Presidents James Monroe and John Quincy Adams. Wirt was admitted to the bar in Virginia in 1792, and in 1807 he was the prosecutor in Aaron Burr's trial for treason. He was elected to the Virginia House of Delegates in 1808 and served as attorney general from 1817 to 1829. In one of his most notable legal battles, he successfully defended Cherokee rights before the US Supreme Court—connecting him to another lawyer interred in this cemetery, Belva Lockwood (see site 13).

Wirt was an active member of the Columbian Institute for the Promotion of Arts and Sciences. Like Lockwood, he was also a third-party candidate for US president in 1832, nominated by the Anti-Masonic Party; unlike her, Wirt refused to campaign. Despite that, he was elected by Vermont, becoming the first third-party candidate to carry a state.

Wirt is the author of three collections of essays—*Letters of the British Spy* (1803), *The Rainbow* (1804), and *The Old Bachelor* (1814)—as well as the nonfiction books *The Two Principal Arguments in the Trial of Aaron Burr* (1808), *Sketches of the Life and Character of Patrick Henry* (1817), *Address to the Triumph of Liberty in France* (1830), and *Letters by John Q. Adams and William Wirt to the Anti-Masonic Committee for York County* (1831).

Sometime during the 1970s, a grave robber broke into Wirt's coffin and stole his skull, which was later sold to a memorabilia collector. It was then given to DC Ward One councilmember Jim Graham, who passed it along to experts from the Smithsonian Institution for authentication. The skull was finally reunited with the rest of Wirt's remains when it was returned to this gravesite in 2005.

→ **Continue along Ingle Street. Just before the intersection with Henderson Street, on your right, look for two marble benches. Walk on the grass between them to a thick black grave marker with the name "Royall" etched on the top.**

21 ANNE ROYALL GRAVE

Range 26, Site 194

Anne Royall (1769–1854) was one of the first professional female journalists in the United States. Born in a log cabin in Baltimore, as a youth she was living on the frontier of western Pennsylvania when she witnessed an Indian raid upon her family. That attack resulted in her stepfather's death. She married Major William Royall, a veteran of the American Revolution who was over twenty years her senior in age. After her husband's death, his relatives successfully contested his will, leaving her in poverty. She turned to writing to support herself.

Royall produced ten volumes of travel books. She moved to Washington, DC, and founded and edited *Paul Pry* (later renamed the *Huntress*) from 1831 until her death. The newspaper was famous for exposing political corruption and fraud. Her coverage included charges of nepotism against the US government, the laziness of government clerks, disclosures of wasteful spending, land fraud against Native Americans, and government interference in the private lives of citizens. Royall lived in a rented property that is now part of the grounds of the

Library of Congress, and she set up her printing press on the ground floor of her home. Royall is also the author of *Sketches of History: Life and Manners in the United States* (1826), the novel *The Tennessean* (1827), and *Letters from Alabama* (1830).

→ **Turn around and look for a large, modern black marble monument marked "Barry," which incorporates a bench, a column-flanked tombstone, plaques, and quotations.**

22 MARION BARRY JR. GRAVE

Range 20, Site 191

Marion Barry (1936–2014) was the longest-serving mayor of Washington, DC, in office from 1979 to 1991 and from 1995 to 1999. Barry was a leader in the civil rights movement in the 1960s: he was president of the National Association for the Advancement of Colored People (NAACP) chapter at his college, the first chairman of the Student Nonviolent Coordinating Committee (SNCC), and a cofounder of the Southern Student Organizing Committee. He was arrested several times at demonstrations to desegregate restaurants and eliminate segregation on public buses. He moved to Washington in 1965, where he led the Free DC Movement (advocating for home rule) and organized Pride Inc., a program to distribute free food in African American neighborhoods. In the 1970s, Barry served on the DC Board of Education and the DC Council.

As mayor, his notable successes included enhancing city sanitation services, instituting a popular summer jobs program for school-aged residents, requiring that at least 35 percent of city contracts go to minority-owned businesses, and expanding city support for the arts and culture. But his tenure was also marked by financial malfeasance, lack of governmental oversight, and long-standing addictions to cocaine and alcohol. Barry served a six-month sentence in federal prison for cocaine possession in 1990. In 2005, he pleaded guilty to misdemeanor charges stemming from his failure to file tax returns. None of these scandals appeared to diminish Barry's considerable influence in the city.

→ **Go north to the intersection of the two major paths, Ingle Street and Henderson Street. On the far left corner, under a tree, you will find a black marble tombstone.**

23 LEONARD MATLOVICH GRAVE

Range 20, Site 161N

Leonard Matlovich (1943–1988) followed his father into the military, enlisting at age nineteen. He served three tours of duty during the Vietnam War and received the Purple Heart and the Bronze Star. In 1974, he met with Frank Kameny (see site 24, below), and they formulated a plan to challenge the military's longtime ban on gay service members. Matlovich came out to his commanding officer, was ruled unfit for service, and subsequently sued for reinstatement. His challenge was widely covered in the press, and he appeared on the front page of the *New York Times,* on the cover of *Time* magazine, and on *CBS Evening News with Walter Cronkite.* After a long legal process, Matlovich accepted a financial settlement from the Air Force in 1980. He used his notoriety to advocate against LGBT discrimination and to fight for funding for HIV/AIDS treatment and education.

Matlovich died of complications from AIDS in Los Angeles one month before his forty-fifth birthday. Although he was eligible for burial at Arlington National Cemetery, he wanted to create the kind of memorial that Arlington would not allow, so he chose Congressional instead. Matlovich intended his grave to be a memorial to all gay veterans, so he did not include his name, hoping that other LGBTQ+ people would choose sites near his. Matlovich said in an interview that he "realized that there was no place in America for gay people to gather and remember their forebears."

His vision for Congressional has indeed come true. As James Kirchick writes in *The Secret City: The Hidden History of Gay Washington,* "Today, Congressional Cemetery boasts of having a 'gay corner,' believed to be the only such designated burial ground in the world, a fitting distinction considering how Congressional welcomed the remains of AIDS victims when even the corpses of those stricken with the disease were rejected."

→ **Just behind the Matlovich memorial is a small tombstone.**

24 FRANKLIN E. KAMENY GRAVE

Fired for homosexuality in 1957 from a federal job as an astronomer with the US Map Service, Frank Kameny (1925–2011) was the first known gay person to fight gay discrimination in the courts. He was a cofounder of the Mattachine Society of Washington, the Gay and Lesbian Activists Alliance, and the Gertrude Stein Democratic Club. Kameny also led gay rights protests at the White House, Pentagon, State Department, Civil Service Commission, and Independence Hall, among other well-publicized events.

His gravestone, a simple Army-issued memorial, notes his service during World War II. At a security clearance hearing in 1969, Kameny told the Defense Department, "I, personally, placed my life in jeopardy, in frontline combat, under enemy fire, for this country. . . . [I] did not do so in order that our government—or any agent or officer of it—might disparage our people, by which we mean our fellow American homosexuals, or our way of life—to our faces, or behind our backs. We are fully as entitled to our dignity, and to the respect of our government as the homosexual citizens that we are, as are all other American citizens."

Kameny is remembered locally with a section of Seventeenth Street NW given the honorary name of Frank Kameny Way. He was added to the National LGBTQ Task Force's Legacy Walk in 2013 for his "resolve to transform the way gay people were treated by society." In 2011, his former home at 5020 Cathedral Avenue NW was added to the National Register of Historic Places. Most significantly, in 2009 he was issued a formal apology from the US government for his original job dismissal.

A small plaque in front of the gravestone reprints Kameny's famous motto: "Gay Is Good."

→ **Look directly across Ingle Street and to the right for a marble bench.**

25 BARBARA GITTINGS GRAVE

In 1958, Barbara Gittings (1932–2007) founded the New York chapter of the Daughters of Bilitis, the first lesbian rights organization in the United States, and edited its magazine, the *Ladder.* She developed a widely distributed bibliography of books with positive LGBTQ themes, led the gay caucus of the American Library Association, and worked on the campaign to remove homosexuality from the American Psychiatric Association's list of mental illnesses.

Gittings, the daughter of a US diplomat, was born in Vienna, Austria. In 2003 she was awarded an honorary lifetime membership in the American Library Association. She is remembered by the Gay and Lesbian Alliance Against Defamation with an annual award in her name. She died of breast cancer at age seventy-four and was survived by her partner of forty-six years, fellow activist

Kay Tobin Lahusen. Their stone, in the shape of a bench, also proudly proclaims, "Gay Is Good."

→ **Go back to the corner and turn left. Look for a memorial on your left enclosed inside an iron fence.**

26 J. EDGAR HOOVER GRAVE

Range 20, Site 117

J. Edgar Hoover (1895–1972) was born in Washington, DC, and lived his entire life in the city. He attended DC public schools and earned his law degree from George Washington University. Hoover began his federal career at the Justice Department and was hired in 1919, at age twenty-four, by the Bureau of Investigation. When he was promoted to bureau director in 1924, he fired all female agents (and banned their future hiring).

Hoover built his reputation, and his considerable power, by targeting criminal gangs of bank robbers, mafia groups, suspected communists, spies, and radicals. He expanded and modernized the FBI, introducing forensic science—but he also regularly and systematically abused his authority, establishing a national blacklist, harassing political dissidents, blackmailing public figures, and violating some of the same laws he was charged with enforcing. Some of his most egregious campaigns targeted civil rights leaders.

Hoover was buried, as he requested, next to the graves of his parents. The location is also near the gravesite of Clyde Tolson (1900–1975), the associate director of the FBI, who was his presumed lover.

By the time Hoover was interred, the cemetery was at a low point, with untended grass and overturned headstones. Ironically, Hoover's fame—his funeral was televised—brought public attention to the cemetery's deterioration and helped make its reclamation as a historic site possible.

Christ Church had experienced a steep decline in membership beginning in the mid-1950s. By 1979, the church realized that it could no longer manage the burial ground. The nonprofit Association for the Preservation of Historic Congressional Cemetery was formed, and the vestry of the church transferred its responsibilities to the organization. The cemetery's long-term future was ensured by two congressional matching grants of one million dollars in 1997 and 2002, managed by the National Trust for Historic Preservation, as well as a grant from the Save America's Treasures program in 1998.

→ **Cross Henderson Street and take the brick path to the right. Walk to the end of the bricks and continue on the dirt path. Where it intersects with another dirt path (which follows the line of the cemetery's exterior brick wall), turn right. Look for a sculpted bust near the ground to your right.**

27 TAZA, SON OF COCHISE GRAVE

Range 2, Site 125

Taza (1843?–1876) came to Washington, DC, as part of a Chiricahua Apache delegation in order to conduct peace talks with representatives of the US government in the summer of 1876. When he died of pneumonia, he was buried in a grave at Congressional that remained unmarked for nearly one hundred years. In 1971, his dramatic sculpted bust, created by Native American sculptor Doug Hyde (1946–) based on a photograph, was erected in his memory. Taza was also the subject of the movie *Taza, Son of Cochise,* released in 1954. It was filmed in Utah, in part at Arches National Monument, and starred Rock Hudson as Taza and Barbara Rush as his betrothed, Oona.

Congressional contains the remains of thirty-five

Native Americans who died while representing their tribes in the capital, making this an important site of remembrance for Native rights. Of the thirteen tribes represented, there is one Apache individual (Taza), fourteen Cherokees, three Chippewas, six Choctaws, two Creeks, one Dakota, one Lakota, two Kiowa, one Nez Perce, two Pawnee, one Sac and Fox, and one Winnebago.

→ **Go back to the brick path and look for a column topped by the figure of a seated woman, her hand raised thoughtfully to her chin.**

28 MARY ANN HALL GRAVE

Range 11, Site 92

For over forty years, Mary Ann Hall (1814?–1886) owned one of the most renowned of DC's legal brothels. Located on the current site of the National Museum of the American Indian, her three-story brick "fancy house," known for its elegance and wealthy clientele, had a central location convenient for government workers. She employed eighteen women by the height of the Civil War, making hers the largest brothel in the city (at a time when the Federal Provost Marshal's Office catalogued 450 of them). Hall, who was born and raised in the Georgetown neighborhood, never married or had children; she left her considerable estate to her niece and sisters, who are buried nearby. Brothels were not banned in the city until 1914, and an obituary in the *Washington Evening Star* praised her civic integrity and charitable works, concluding, "Her memory will be kept green by many who knew her sterling worth."

→ **Take the brick path back to Henderson Street and cross Henderson, continuing down the brick path further west. The next few graves honor prominent architects. The first can be found on the left. Look for a large white**

marble standing rectangle with attached Ionic columns flanking either side.

29 ROBERT MILLS GRAVE

Range 35, Site 111

Robert Mills (1781–1855) was an architect who designed some of the most prominent sites in the capital: the Washington Monument, US Patent Office, Old Post Office, and the US Treasury. Born in South Carolina, he studied with James Hoban and later worked with him on the White House. His buildings enhanced the popularity of neoclassical architecture along the East Coast, with notable commissions in Philadelphia, Baltimore, and Augusta, Georgia. In South Carolina, he was superintendent of public buildings and designed at least eighteen courthouses.

Mills's neoclassical monument in Congressional Cemetery, measuring nine feet in height and four feet in width, is made of two kinds of marble. It is the sole memorial in Washington, DC, for this extraordinary and influential architect. Surprisingly, his grave was unmarked for approximately eighty years. In 1936, a group of architects, along with members of the Mills family, finally addressed this omission.

→ **Cross back over the path and continue north across the grass, toward a second group of cenotaphs. The next grave, a cenotaph set apart, will be found due north, under a holly tree.**

30 WILLIAM THORNTON GRAVE

Range 33, Site 40

William Thornton (1759–1828), the first architect of the US Capitol, was born in the British Virgin Islands and educated in England. He emigrated to the United States in 1786, settling first in Philadelphia. His design for the US Capitol was selected in 1793 (although the building was greatly modified from his original plans). He submitted his proposal after the deadline, but George Washington praised it for its "grandeur, simplicity, and convenience" and appointed Thornton as one of three federal commissioners of the District of Columbia, responsible for overseeing all the original government buildings. Thornton also designed notable houses in the region: Octagon House, Tudor Place, Brentwood Mansion (now razed, but once standing just north of Gallaudet University), and Woodlawn Plantation. Trained as a physician, he never practiced medicine. Thornton was a member of the American Philosophical Society and the Columbian Institute for the Promotion of Arts and Sciences. He was an avid horse racer, developed a method for teaching deaf pupils to speak, and was also an amateur painter and writer.

→ **Look for the next headstone just slightly further north, a small stone just past a grave made to look like a broken column.**

31 GEORGE HADFIELD GRAVE

Range 33, Site 30

Born in Italy to English parents, George Hadfield (1763–1826) emigrated to Washington, DC, and worked as an architect on the US Capitol from 1795 to 1798, resigning only after an argument with William Thornton. He is credited with altering (and strengthening) Thornton's plans for the US Capitol, and he remained in the city after his resignation, opening his own private architectural practice. Hadfield designed Arlington House, now on the grounds of Arlington National Cemetery (see site 11 in that tour on page 223), as well as the Old City Hall,

Marine Corps Commandant's House, District of Columbia City Hall, and the Van Ness Mausoleum now at Oak Hill Cemetery (see site 20 in that tour on page 129). He also patented the first brick- and tile-making machine in the United States.

A later architect of the Capitol, George Malcolm White (1920–2011), is buried just to the right of Hadfield.

→ **Continue toward the fence line that runs along E Street SE and look for the third grave on a brick plinth on your right.**

32 URIAH TRACY GRAVE

Range 24, Site 1

Uriah Tracy (1755–1807) served in battles in Lexington and Concord, Massachusetts, rising to the rank of major general. Tracy attended Yale University, graduating in 1778, and was admitted to the bar in 1781. He practiced law in Connecticut for many years prior to entering politics at age thirty-two. Noting his skills as a sharp debater, the *National Intelligencer* described him as "ever an able, popular, and pleasing advocate" who was "in argument acute and lucid . . . [whose] ardor of debate, the rapidity of his ideas, and the impetuosity of his eloquence" made him influential. Tracy was elected to the US House of Representatives (1793–1796) and to the US Senate (1796–1807). In 1800, he served as president pro tempore of the Senate during the Sixth Congress. When he died in office at age fifty-two (from an unspecified illness), he became the first member of Congress to be buried at Congressional Cemetery, and his funeral became a model for subsequent state funerals. The *National Intelligencer* reported that "he was interred with the honors due to his station and character, as a statesman, and to his rank as a major general; his pall being supported by the heads of departments and officers of government."

Tracy is one of 33 Revolutionary War soldiers interred at Congressional Cemetery. Prior to the Civil War and the establishment of the federal military system, Congressional served as a de facto military cemetery. In addition to Revolutionary War soldiers, there are 6 veterans of the Tripolitan and Algerian Wars, 124 veterans of the War of 1812, and 44 veterans of the Mexican-American War. Even after the rise of specific military cemeteries, Congressional was still a favored burying ground, especially for those veterans who wanted to be buried alongside their families. There are 545 Civil War Union veterans interred here, 12 of whom were senior officers—and 50 Confederate soldiers, 12 of whom were senior officers. Veterans of every war since have also been interred at Congressional.

→ **Retrace your steps along the fence line. Look to your left for a monument on a tapered base topped by a footed urn and flame.**

33 ELBRIDGE GERRY GRAVE

Range 29, Site 11

The fifth vice president of the United States, Elbridge Gerry (1744–1814), served under President James Madison from 1813 to 1814. The only original signatory to the Declaration of Independence buried in Washington, DC, Gerry was also a member of the Continental Congress and governor of the state of Massachusetts. During the Revolutionary War, he helped keep the Continental Army supplied, using his international business contacts. Gerry is perhaps best remembered today for an unpopular bill that he supported while governor, one that proposed to redistrict Massachusetts in a way that would favor the Republican Party in elections. The term "gerrymander" comes from his name.

Gerry's monument at Congressional Cemetery bears

a quote from his writings. It states, "It is the duty of every citizen, though he may have but one day to live, to devote that day to the good of his country." In 2023, the DC chapter of the Daughters of the American Revolution added a plaque to the graveside honoring the 250th anniversary of the founding of the United States and commemorating Gerry's status as one of fifty-six signers of the Declaration of Independence.

→ **Continue along the fence line past the gatehouse. The path continues behind the house and then reconnects with Congress Street. Turn right to return to the cemetery entrance.**

34 BACK TO THE ENTRANCE GATE

Congressional Cemetery is notable as the region's burial ground that does the best public outreach. The fact that it was almost lost to neglect makes this status all the more poignant.

Influenced by the cemetery's hybrid nature—privately owned grounds that maintain a significant symbolic governmental function—the new managers have committed to perpetuating this space as a public amenity. An array of specialized tour brochures by the entrance emphasize aspects of women's history, LGBTQ history, federal history, pre–Civil War Washington, and more, making this one of the best-interpreted cemeteries in the region (second, perhaps, only to Arlington National Cemetery). The cemetery complements its brochures with an attractive website, a blog, and active social media posts highlighting cemetery history.

The managers coordinate a large, dedicated group of volunteers through the innovative K-9 Corps. While most cemeteries ban dog walking (believing that dogs romping and urinating on the graves will be seen as a desecration), Congressional invites dog owners with open arms, and the members of the Corps not only gain the privilege of bringing their dogs to this scenic spot but also pledge annual volunteer hours. This program should be a model for other cemeteries.

In crowded urban areas, cemeteries become badly needed open space. Congressional has done more than any other cemetery to return to the idea of combining memorial space for the dead with parkland. The cemetery hosts temporary art installations, and in 2024 it began working with an inaugural curator-in-residence to make site-specific sculpture a regular part of its offerings. A robust schedule of public programs, such as tours, movie nights, a book club, and the popular Dead Man's Run 5K race, is part of the annual calendar. All of these events are designed to bring in people who are not already members and generate renewed interest and investment in the property.

MOUNT ZION METHODIST / FEMALE UNION BAND SOCIETY HISTORIC MEMORIAL PARK (1808–1950)

2501 Mill Road NW, Georgetown neighborhood, DC, located near the intersection of Twenty-Seventh and Q Streets NW

Two cemeteries share a 3.5-acre plot in the Georgetown neighborhood. The cemeteries, actively in use from 1808 to 1950, represent significant ties to the region's African American ancestors, and the nonprofit group Black Georgetown, formed in 2005, is dedicated to the site's preservation. In 1975, it was added to the National Register of Historic Places. The nomination for that honor reads, in part, "Mount Zion Cemetery's history and that of the generations of Blacks both free and slave interred therein uniquely convey the quality and thrust of Black life and evolving free Black culture in the District of Columbia from the earliest days of the city to the present. It is one of the few remaining physical reminders of the significant contributions of Black people to the development of Georgetown."

Mount Zion United Methodist Church is the oldest African American church in Washington, DC. The Female Union Band Society was a sororal benevolent society formed in the 1840s. Although the two hundred or so headstones in their combined cemeteries, as arranged today, bear little relation to what lies below, as many as 6,313 people may have been interred at this site, according to records from 1930 at the DC Office of Health. In the 1970s, after years of neglect, the cemetery once again began to receive regular care. In 2018, Black Georgetown began surveying, using ground-penetrating radar, to learn more about the cemetery's rich history.

The cemetery was founded as the Old Methodist Burying Ground, established by the Montgomery Street Methodist Church, formerly located on Twenty-Eighth Street NW between M and Olive Streets. It was unusual at that time to locate a cemetery away from a church, but not unheard of, and in the end it was a lucky occurrence. The cemetery's location—tucked away in a less populated part of the city, about half a mile distant from the church—helped save it from destruction. Montgomery Street Methodist's congregation was then half white and half African American (the latter group composed of both enslaved and free people of color), with the African American parishioners seated separately in the upstairs galleries. In 1814, a group of nearly 125 African American church members, disdaining the church's practice of segregation, organized a separate church. That splinter group raised enough money by 1816 to purchase land and build a brick church called The Little Ark at the corner of Twenty-Seventh and P Streets NW. It was renamed Mount Zion United Methodist Church in 1844. For the first two decades, governed by their mother church, Mount Zion was led by white ministers; beginning in 1864, congregants were allowed to select a minister on their own, and beginning with Rev. John H. Brice, the church leader was always a person of color.

In addition to being the first African American church in the District, Mount Zion was notable for its Sabbath School. Established in 1823 under the leadership of William Lang, it offered literacy classes for children and adults—a highly unusual and valued service for a Southern city. The church was an important social and recreational center as well, and in 1920, Mount Zion purchased a building next to the parsonage, called the Community House, for additional meeting space. Located at

Grave of Nannie (4)

2906 O Street NW, the building was renovated in 1984 and still stands.

Before You Go

Administered by Black Georgetown Foundation
https://www.mtzion-fubs.org/
Open daily dawn to dusk
Nearest public transportation: Dupont Circle Station to bus
Parking and restrooms not available

1 ENTRANCE

The original burying ground, with its high elevation above a ravine, would have allowed for peaceful views down to Rock Creek. Today, the view is obscured by a larger cemetery. When Oak Hill Cemetery was opened for burials (restricted to white people only) in 1849, most, but not all, of the remains of white people at the Old Methodist Burying Ground were disinterred and moved to Oak Hill, making today's Mount Zion Cemetery, by default, an African American cemetery. Mount Zion and the Female Union Band Society cemeteries are also notable as the only burial places within DC boundaries containing a significant number of remains of enslaved and formerly enslaved people.

The original plot of ground, like the church it was attached to, was segregated. The site was partially surrounded by a wooden fence, dividing the white part of the cemetery from the African American part. The original plot was also larger: some of the land has been lost over the years to erosion, and some land was transferred to the US government by eminent domain in 1931 for the creation of Rock Creek Parkway. Today, a steep path runs downhill along the fence line of Oak Hill Cemetery and meets up with the paved trail along Rock Creek Parkway, connecting the two. A few additional gravestones can still be seen along this trail, suggesting the original cemetery site's complexity and size beyond the markers atop the ridge.

In 1842, the western side of the plot was sold in trust to the Female Union Band Society. As the practice of burying the dead in an east-to-west orientation, common in Judeo-Christian cemeteries, evolved to include African traditions, this division of the land into east and west burying grounds may have been related to the placement of earlier burials. As Lynn Rainville writes in *Hidden History: African American Cemeteries in Central Virginia,* bodies were placed so their heads lay west and their feet to the east, a practice that "can be interpreted in two ways. The Christian interpretation is that the deceased will rise on Judgement Day to face his or her maker. A more poignant meaning within enslaved communities was that the deceased rested facing Africa." Today the two sides have merged, but the combination of the two cemeteries could have helped facilitate and respect this established tradition.

The Female Union Band Society was a benevolent society designed to provide community and financial support in the event of death or sickness. Members paid dues (initially two dollars per week), which were invested in real estate, businesses, and banks to build equity. In addition, members were expected to participate in the mourning process, from washing and dressing the bodies of the dead to commissioning headstones, planning funeral services, and providing succor to the bereaved. In addition to paying dues, Female Union Band members pledged to remain of "good moral character" and could be expelled if "convicted of immoral or disgraceful practices" or if they proved "disagreeable to a majority of the Society, either by words or actions." These societies were common in free African American communities, beginning in the antebellum period through the mid-1900s, before the rise of a more established funeral home industry.

Some burial societies also provided a wider range of services, including stipends for widows, education funds for orphans, and credit unions. (It is unclear whether that was the case for the Female Union Band Society, but it did provide a small amount of money per week when members fell ill.) All such burial societies provided the basics of a plot, gravedigger, hearse, pallbearers, and a horse for the burial procession. Most burial societies, unlike the Female Union Band, were connected to African American churches.

The fact that the Female Union Band Society was organized by and for women is notable: African American women (and in this case, some Native American women as well) were taking the lead to provide a valuable service for themselves and their families and to use a major life-cycle event to cement the bonds of community. In the early days of the cemetery, women could not legally own property—so a man named Joseph Mason was engaged to purchase the cemetery and hold the land in trust for use by members of the Society. In 1842, Mason purchased the land for $250. Membership in the Female Union Band Society was a tangible way these women worked for their own autonomy at a time when, historically, the laws denied them basic rights.

In the 1840s, African American communities in the mid-Atlantic felt especially imperiled, as a backlash among the general white population brought new restrictions to daily life in the wake of Nat Turner's Rebellion in 1831. The rebellion, which took place in neighboring Virginia, was the most significant act of resistance to enslavement and the deadliest revolt by enslaved people in the United States. In the period after the rebellion was quelled, harsh new laws proliferated throughout the United States. They prohibited the education of African Americans (whether free or enslaved) and codified laws restricting types of labor, enforcing curfews, and denying rights of assembly. African American groups were under greater scrutiny. To fully understand the achievement of the women who formed the Female Union Band Society, it's important to see it in the context of this charged political atmosphere.

2 THE LARGER MONUMENTS

When you walk around the grounds of this small cemetery, you will find several significant landmarks. The entrance to the cemetery, facing Mill Street, is marked with a modern sign. Just beyond the sign and to the right of the central path, you will see the Mary Burrill monument, one of the three larger memorials. Burrill is buried with her husband and son in a plot delineated by iron poles. The older Beck/Doughty monument, toward the center of the cemetery, marks the remains of two white families whose graves were never moved. Richard Beck and William Doughty and their families were active members of Mount Zion's precursor, Montgomery Street Church. William Doughty (1772–1859) was a master shipbuilder. The Logan Monument on the western side of the grounds (on the left side of the central path and enclosed in an old iron fence) is the third large monument in the graveyard. The families who purchased these monuments invested considerable money in hiring a professional stone carver and obtaining a larger plot, and some of the details of the monuments are beautifully rendered, such as the flowers on the Logan monument, which symbolize the transient nature of life.

3 CENTRAL SECTION

The majority of the grave markers are found in two concentrated groups, where they have been gathered by modern caretakers in an attempt to provide better maintenance. Stones range from sturdy, thick marble gravestones made by professional carvers to more modest stones in slate, soapstone, or fieldstone, with homemade carvings. Several stones say "At Rest" at the top, and some give a relationship to the bereaved at the bottom, such as "Mother." Some stones have eroded too badly to read with ease anymore, and many are broken, partial, or toppled. The combination of hand-carved and professionally carved stones (such as the kind that could be ordered from a stonemason or from a catalogue, such as Sears and Roebuck) was not unusual in rural cemeteries but is more rare in urban settings such as this.

Some of the well-known people buried in the cemetery include the Reverend Joseph Cartwright (1783–1851), who was born enslaved and purchased his own freedom in 1819. He was one of the first Black preachers at Mount Zion Church, and he purchased his wife and three children out of slavery in 1839. Cartwright was a member of the Grand United Order of Odd Fellows, a grocer in Georgetown, and an abolitionist. He was known to have worked with a white abolitionist, Charles Torrey, to facilitate the escape of multiple enslaved people in the District.

Also included is Henry Smallwood (?–1887), one of the participants in the largest attempted escape of enslaved people in the history of the nation. In April 1848, seventy-seven enslaved people sailed from the port of Washington on a schooner called the *Pearl.* Although ultimately unsuccessful, the incident, and the subsequent debate it caused, led directly to the Compromise of 1850, a law that (among other things) ended the importation and sale of enslaved people in the District. It is thought that the plans for the *Pearl* escape were made, in part, on the Mount Zion Church grounds.

The son of one of the planners of the *Pearl* escape is also interred here: Franklin Jennings. His prominent father, Paul Jennings, is famous as the first enslaved person who worked in the White House to publish a memoir, *A Colored Man's Reminiscences of James Madison* (1865). The *Pearl* planners were a multiracial group, and Paul Jennings was active in the capital's abolitionist community. Franklin Jennings (1836–1926) was born enslaved, escaped his enslavers in Virginia, and fought for the Union Army in the Civil War (in the 5th Regiment, Company B of the Colored Cavalry). After the war, he lived in DC with his wife and two children. You can find his headstone near the larger Logan family monument; note that he shares his gray marble tombstone with Mary Logan Jennings (1850–1950), the last person to be buried in the Female Union Band Society cemetery.

Also buried here are several Lees, members of a prominent African American family who owned multiple houses in Georgetown as well as the Lee Feed and

Grain Store, which operated into the 1940s at the corner of Nineteenth and M Streets NW. The *Washington Star* newspaper called it the "oldest business among Negroes in America."

Dr. Collins B. Crusor (1856–1904), one of two early, distinguished African American doctors in Georgetown, is also buried at Mount Zion along with members of his family; he operated an independent medical practice from 1883 through the early 1900s. Two prominent educators who worked for the Negro Division of the DC Public Schools are buried here as well: Joseph Logan (1928–1949), a principal of Shaw Junior High School, and Daniel B. Thompson (dates unknown), a business and accounting teacher at Dunbar High School. Thompson's wife, Elizabeth, also interred at this site, served as executive secretary of the Phyllis Wheatley YWCA. Sandy Cohen (1896–1918) is one of the sixty-two African American soldiers and sailors from the District who died during World War I. In addition to his burial here, Cohen's name is also listed in the District of Columbia War Memorial.

In 1984, Pauline Gaskins Mitchell, a church member whose forebears are buried at Mount Zion, wrote a history of the cemetery for the *Records of the Columbia Historical Society of Washington, D.C.* She provides some additional names of those buried: "Among them are . . . Clement Morgan, an honor graduate of Harvard University and a noted lawyer; George Beason, a fraternal leader and financial secretary of Mt. Zion Church . . . Charles Turner, sometimes referred to as the black mayor of Georgetown in those early days; Caleb Hawkins, a restaurant proprietor, officer of Mt. Zion, and real estate investor; businessmen including Simon Burnett, Robert Holmes, and John Ransom; Harriet Beason, a teacher and historian of Mt. Zion . . . musicians Charles Lee and Ralph Parrott; and Edgar Murphy, one of the builders of Mt. Zion." She concludes, "These few are typical of the many outstanding blacks interred there."

There are a few headstones to seek out in particular.

The more modest, hand-carved headstones, with their personal touches, reflect a tradition of amateur artisanal carving in the community. The Eliza Ogleton (d. 1911) grave, for example, has a beautiful number 8 in her death date, with the two circles of the number detached. The grave of Georgie Ferguson (dates unknown) originally gave his first name as George, and a small letter *i* was later inserted to correct that mistake. The stone for James A. Taylor (d. 1924) has evocative and unusual letter *M*'s and a period between the words "At.Rest." And the stone for Fredick Jenkins (1899–1917) may have misspelled his first name.

Several markers make use of common symbols of death and mourning from the nineteenth century. You will find a couple of headstones that show open curtains in bas-relief, symbolizing the new phase in a person's journey. A few picture a hand with a single finger pointing upward toward heaven. The John T. Lewis stone (1855–1913) pictures a dove in flight.

One of the larger stones, laid horizontally in the center of the graveyard, is broken in two. After some difficulty, I was able to decipher it. It reads:

Sacred
To the Memory of
MARY ELLISON
Born Jan. [unreadable]
Who departed this life
August 14, 1817
aged 46 years
She was a mother, [unreadable] and beloved
wife, the extent of whose endearing excellen-
ce could alone be appreciated by her husband;
friend, warm sincere and constant; and whose
memory will be long cherished in the circle in
which her influence was shed; and a christian
the uprightness of whose walk, practically illus-
trated the precepts of the Gospel.

I like to think that all of these graves represent leaders and community builders in DC's African American community who were long cherished in the circle in which their influence was shed.

4 GRAVE OF NANNIE

At the foot of a large tree, just north of the central group of headstones, is the grave of a young girl who died at age eight, in 1856, and was buried in a Female Union Band Society plot. This bluestone grave topped with a stylized crown shape is always covered with small toys and other offerings, and new toys are laid out annually on May 26, the date of her birthday. Grave offerings such as these are tied to ancient practices that allow the deceased to move from an earthly plane into the status of ancestor, and they are significant transitional objects that help the living transform their loss from one of personal mourning into a community asset. Little of Nannie's life is known beyond her birth and death dates—not even her last name—but she has been adopted by cemetery visitors as she continues to serve this important community function.

In 2023, in an abhorrent act of vandalism, a nighttime visitor burned all the grave offerings in front of Nannie's stone; scorch marks are still visible. The culprit was never found. Since that time, new toys and offerings have been brought to this site to begin the ritual anew.

5 THE BRICK VAULT

Down a few steps at the rear of the cemetery is one of the most notable features of the site: the brick vault. Built into the side of the hill, this eight-by-eight-foot structure would have been used to store bodies during the winter months, when the ground was too frozen to easily dig. Note the handmade iron door hinges and the other historic details of this structure, which dates from the early 1800s. The door is never locked, and visitors are allowed to open it (although the door is quite heavy and difficult to move, so this requires some physical effort). Strong anecdotal evidence suggests that this vault was used as a stop on the Underground Railroad and as a temporary shelter for fugitives eluding capture or punishment. The proximity of Rock Creek and the Potomac River would have made this a crucial stop on the route an enslaved person might have taken from the south toward freedom in Pennsylvania or Ohio.

The National Park Service has recognized the site as significant to the Underground Railroad. In 2018, the cemetery was added to the United Nations Education, Scientific and Cultural Organization (UNESCO) Slave Route Project. This designation is important for two reasons: the cemetery is the only UNESCO Slave Route Site of Memory in the city, and it represents the first time the United Nations gave this recognition to a cemetery.

6 PATH TO ROCK CREEK

If you take the steep path down the western side of the cemetery that divides Mount Zion from Oak Hill Cemetery, you will reach Rock Creek. The path has suffered from continued problems of erosion, especially along the sharp slope of the lower parts of the cemetery. This path is all that remains of Lyons Mill Road, which connected a flour mill on the opposite side of Rock Creek to Georgetown. Likely the largest of the mills located along the banks of Rock Creek, Lyon's Mill was a two-story brick structure built atop a bluestone basement, and it had two water wheels, one on either end of the building. The mill was constructed in 1780, prior to the cemetery's founding. It was part of a sixty-five-acre estate that also included other industries: a smokehouse, icehouse, and stables. Lyon's Mill remained in operation through 1875 and then had a brief afterlife as the location for barn dances. The mill finally collapsed in 1913. Lyons Mill Road, always steeply graded, was washed away by storms and erosion over the ensuing years, but the footpath has always remained in use.

One can only imagine the tension, while the mill was operating, between those memorializing their beloved dead to the east of the road and the constant commercial traffic bringing flour from Lyon's Mill to the Georgetown docks. Despite the fact that the cemetery today is not in active use, that tension remains a part of its modern history. The lowest section, where a bike path now runs along the river, was originally part of the cemetery but in 1931 was claimed by the city under eminent domain. A horse path was installed in the early 1930s right over buried human remains. The abutments to the bridge that carried Lyons Mill Road across Rock Creek were reused by the city for a new bridge, one used by horse carriages and pedestrians.

In 2021, the National Park Service decided to replace the pedestrian bridge and widen what is now a well-used bike path. Unfortunately, they started the work without notifying the foundation that now administers this historic property. In fact, according to *Washingtonian Magazine,* "the burial grounds had been left off the maps used by city and federal agencies." Lisa Fager, the executive director of the Mount Zion Methodist / Female Union Band Society Historic Memorial Park, discovered a construction crew from the Department of Transportation at work in September 2021, and, fearful that they might dig up human remains, intervened to stop the work. According to an article in *DCist,* the National Park Service has since been responsive, despite that earlier failure of communication. A study in 2022 "using ground-penetrating radar, magnetometry, and electromagnetic conductivity" assessed the construction area, and the NPS has retained an archeologist to "be present on site to monitor all further construction work." Fager has declared herself "pleasantly surprised by the rigor with which NPS has addressed her concerns, [but] she still feels the weight of disregard for Black cemeteries." This has been manifested by joggers and hikers "regularly traversing the marked-off area throughout the archeological assessment" despite clear signs barring the path's use during that temporary closure. Because of this, in June 2022, the DC Preservation League added Mount Zion to their list of Most Endangered Places.

7 BACK TO THE ENTRANCE

By the mid-twentieth century, maintenance of the cemetery grounds showed a marked decline. The interment in 1950 of Mary Logan Jennings, a past president of the Female Union Band Society, was the last recorded burial. In 1953, the DC Department of Health officially prohibited any further burials.

By 1957, the church that succeeded Mount Zion, named Dumbarton United Methodist Church, decided to sell the property to developers. But a title search revealed that direct descendants of Mary Logan Jennings—Mary and Ellen Sinclair—still lived in the area. They contested the sale by declaring themselves the reconstituted Female Union Band Society and won their case in the US District Court for the District of Columbia in 1964. Initially they planned to disinter bodies and move them to other locations and sell the property themselves. But other descendants of one of the deceased, Neville Waters (the son of Female Union Band Society member Gertrude Waters) and Vincent DeForest, worked with the Afro-American Bicentennial Corporation to save the site in perpetuity, winning a subsequent court case in 1975. They helped form and administer a nonprofit foundation, eventually called Black Georgetown, in 2005.

Among other accomplishments, Black Georgetown has maintained the grounds, restored the historic vault, installed park benches, worked with student groups to research the people who were interred, and hosted annual ceremonies of remembrance. Their stewardship of this historic property has been exemplary. Struggles to properly maintain the property continue, but the cemetery has benefited from greater public recognition; in 2023, the DC Council approved substantial funding for stormwater management to address what they called "perpetual, systemic neglect" from earlier eras. In honor of the cemetery's 215th anniversary in 2023, the DC Council released a ceremonial resolution honoring the site as one of the "priceless parts of our city's heritage and powerful illustrations of resilience, sacrifice and community during a time of profound segregation."

OAK HILL CEMETERY (1849)

3001 R Street NW, Georgetown neighborhood, DC

The District's most beautiful cemetery is Oak Hill, a twenty-two-acre graveyard in operation since 1849. Located on a wedge of land that stretches from the heights of Georgetown into the steep river valley of Rock Creek, this cemetery has gorgeous views, majestic trees, and winding paths that cover dramatic changes in elevation. Consequently, this tour is not recommended for people with limited mobility or problems with balance. Many of the walkways have tilting stones, and even very fit visitors must watch their feet on these paths.

The main gate opens onto R Street NW in the Georgetown neighborhood, but anyone who drives on Rock Creek Parkway can see tempting glimpses of the cemetery from that major road as well. The grounds are divided into fourteen named sections, with each gravesite clearly numbered with a system of small metal markers. The cemetery includes grand mausoleums, obelisks, a large round columbarium, an amphitheater, and a rugged stone bridge.

Visitors often notice deer and foxes on the grounds. The cemetery was spared from much of the clear-cutting of trees that happened during the Civil War as soldiers improved sight lines for their forts and batteries. Consequently, some of the city's oldest trees can be found here. Walking the pathways from North Hill through the amphitheater valley can provide an explorer with scenic vistas—and quite a workout.

Before You Go

https://oakhillcemeterydc.org/

Open weekdays 9:00 am to 4:30 pm, weekends and holidays 11:00 am to 4:00 pm

Corcoran Mausoleum (12)

Nearest public transportation: Dupont Circle Station to bus

No parking; restrooms available

1 THE GATEHOUSE

The red brick gatehouse was probably built in the 1850s. A handsome Italianate building with neo-Gothic features, it was designed by George F. de la Roche (1791–1861) and includes a bell tower, the residence of an

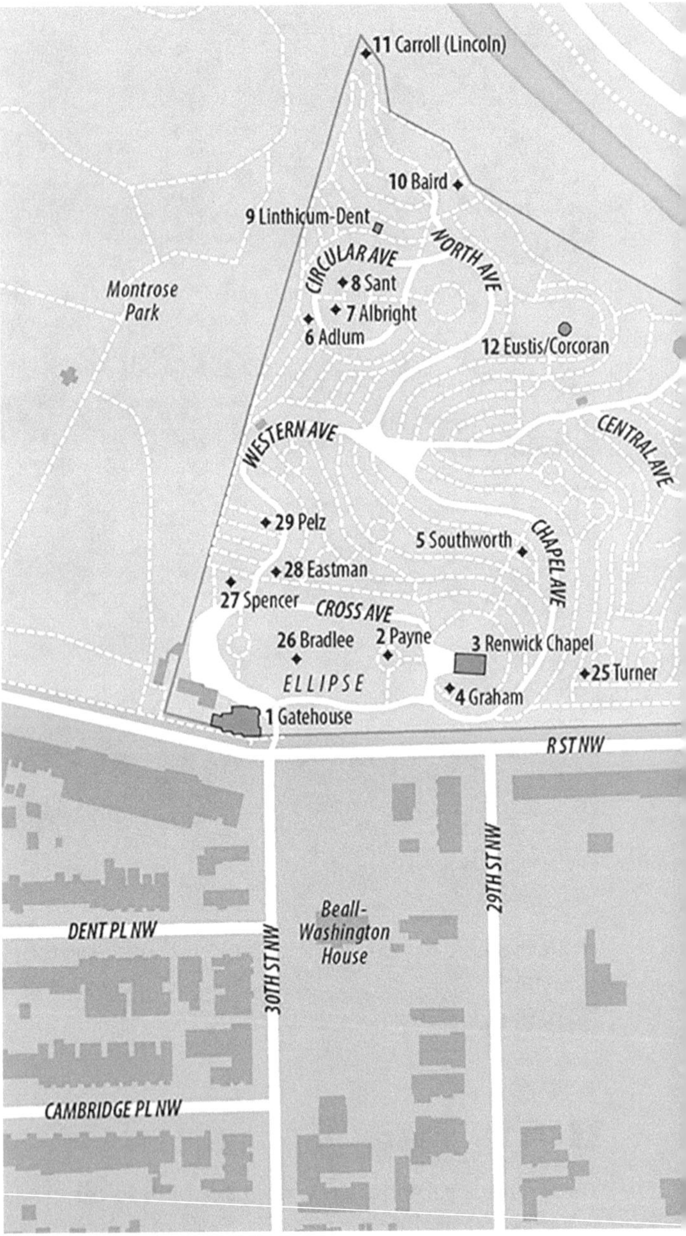

Oak Hill Cemetery

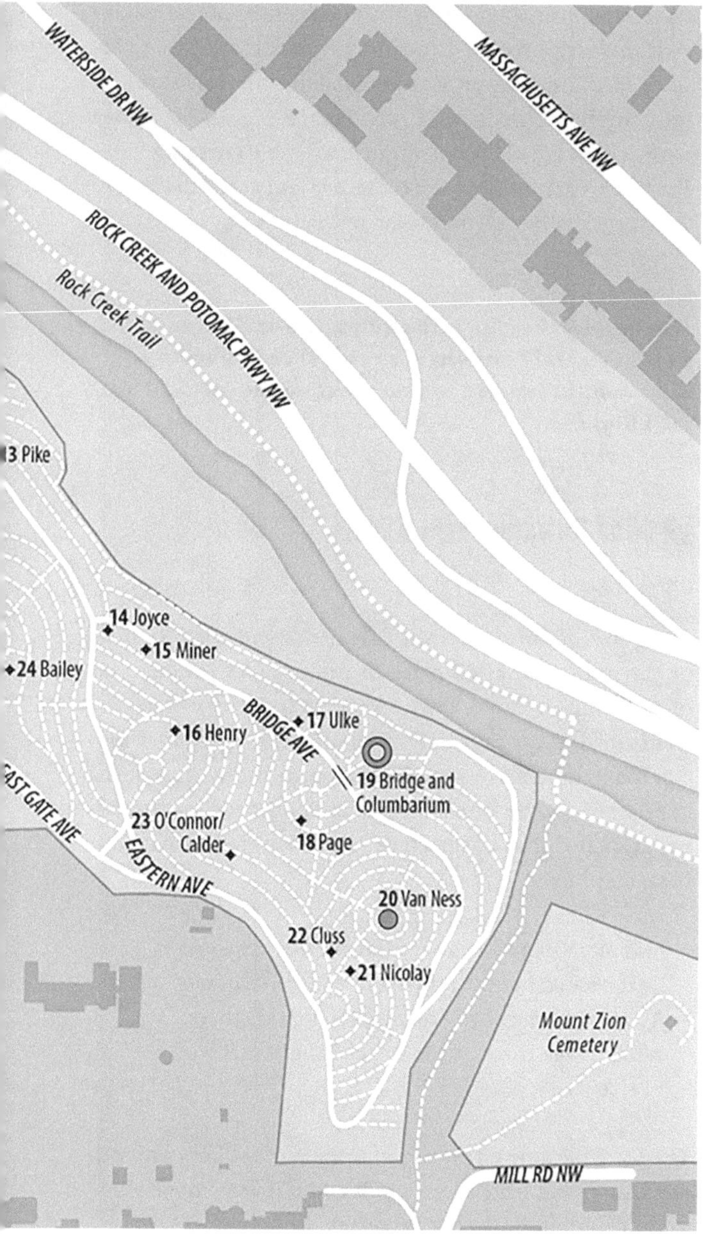
WATERSIDE DR NW
MASSACHUSETTS AVE NW
ROCK CREEK AND POTOMAC PKWY NW
Rock Creek Trail
13 Pike
14 Joyce
15 Miner
24 Bailey
BRIDGE AVE
17 Ulke
16 Henry
19 Bridge and Columbarium
EAST GATE AVE
23 O'Connor/ Calder
18 Page
EASTERN AVE
20 Van Ness
22 Cluss
21 Nicolay
Mount Zion Cemetery
MILL RD NW

on-site superintendent, and the cemetery office, where visitors can purchase brochures with a map. (Free versions of the site maps are also available for download on the cemetery's website.) Brick piers, designed by James Renwick Jr. (1818–1895), ground a double entrance gate. The fence surrounding the cemetery and at the main gate is impressively tall, made of wrought iron with triple flower finials.

→ **Just beyond the gate is the Ellipse, an oval of grass with an ornamental fountain of a crane shooting water out of its mouth. Proceed to your right, to the east end of the Ellipse.**

2 JOHN HOWARD PAYNE GRAVE

Ellipse, Lot 1

The grave of John Howard Payne, marked with its bust of the author, takes a place of prominence on one end of the Ellipse. Payne (1791–1852) is best known as the writer of the lyrics to "Home Sweet Home." That song, originally written in 1822 for the opera *Clari, the Maid of Milan,* became an international phenomenon, an enduring standard that has been recorded innumerable times. It starts:

> Mid pleasures and palaces though we may roam,
> Be it ever so humble, there's no place like home;
> A charm from the sky seems to hallow us there,
> Which, seek through the world, is ne'er met with
> elsewhere.

The song became a favorite of Civil War soldiers on both the Union and Confederate sides, and it was one of President Abraham Lincoln's favorites.

Payne also wrote adaptations of English and French plays and cowrote the comedy *Charles the Second* (1824) in collaboration with Washington Irving. He published his memoirs as well as several volumes advocating for Cherokee rights and culture. Payne believed that the Cherokee and Hebrew languages shared the same roots and advanced a specious theory that the tribe was one of the Ten Lost Tribes of Israel. He became an outspoken critic of President Andrew Jackson's Indian Removal Act and the depredations of the Trail of Tears, and he lobbied Congress on the tribe's behalf.

Payne pursued an acting career in the United States and England to much acclaim. He acted on stage with Edgar Allan Poe's mother, Elizabeth Poe, in *Romeo and Juliet* and was the first American actor to play the role of Hamlet. He courted Mary Shelley, but she did not return his affections, and Payne never married. He was constantly short of money and never received royalties for his famous song.

In 1842, President John Tyler appointed Payne the American consul in Tunis. When he died in present-day Tunisia, he was buried in a Protestant cemetery. Thirty-one years later, his body was disinterred, cremated, and brought back to the United States, where he was received with honors at New York's City Hall. Although he had never lived in Washington, DC, or been associated with the city, he was reinterred in a ceremony at Oak Hill in 1883 on the eighty-second anniversary of his birth. The memorial ceremony was attended by President Chester A. Arthur and prominent leaders from the Cabinet, State Department, and Supreme Court. The US Marine Corps Band (led by John Philip Sousa) played, and newspapers reported estimates of as many as three thousand attendees.

You can see the original gravestone from his grave in Tunisia to the left of the monument. In the original monument, Payne was shown wearing a full beard. A later sculptor removed the beard at an unknown date to show how Payne actually wore his facial hair during his life.

→ **Exit the circular walk surrounding Payne's monument to the right.**

3 RENWICK CHAPEL

Just beyond the Payne monument is the Renwick Chapel, a Gothic Revival building from 1850 designed by James Renwick Jr., the architect who designed the Smithsonian Castle and the Renwick Gallery. The chapel is notable for its gem-like proportions within a small one-story rectangle; note the details of the chapel's buttresses, its pointed-arch windows decorated with tracery, the contrast between the Seneca red sandstone and the gray stone exterior, and its steeply pitched roofline. Sited at the highest point of land in the cemetery, the chapel was commissioned and paid for by W. W. Corcoran, the founder of the cemetery (see stop number 12 on this tour), and added to the National Register of Historic Places in 1972. Take the circular path on the right, which leads you around toward the back of the chapel, where a large stained glass angel dominates the rear window.

→ **At the start of the chapel's circular path, look for the Graham grave on your left.**

4 PHILIP GRAHAM AND KATHARINE MEYER GRAHAM GRAVE

Chapel Section, Lot 24

Philip Graham (1915–1963) was the publisher of the *Washington Post* from 1946 to 1963. He built the newspaper from a struggling local daily to a nationally recognized news source and led the Washington Post Company's expansion to include multiple other newspapers and radio and television stations. He served in the army, earned a law degree, and worked as a clerk for the US Supreme Court justice Felix Frankfurter. When he married the daughter of the *Post*'s owner, Eugene Meyer, he took over the family business. Philip Graham struggled with bipolar disorder and alcoholism and committed suicide at age forty-eight.

Katharine Graham (1917–2001) took over as president of the *Post* after her husband's death, making her the first female CEO of a Fortune 500 company. She published the newspaper for over two decades during its most influential period, when it published the Pentagon Papers and broke the Watergate story that led to the resignation of President Richard Nixon. Katharine Graham is the author of the memoir *Personal History*, which won the Pulitzer Prize in 1998. She was named a World Press Freedom Hero by the International Press Institute in 2000 and given a posthumous Presidential Medal of Freedom award by President George W. Bush in 2002.

The Graham mansion at 2920 R Street NW is located at the corner of Thirtieth Street NW, across the street from the cemetery's main gate. Built in 1784 for a female descendant of Ninian Beall (the original owner of the land that became Georgetown) and her husband (who was George Washington's great-nephew), this was one of several homes owned by the Grahams. It is known locally as the Beall-Washington House.

→ **Continue walking around the chapel and then take the first set of stairs to your right. Continue down the stairs. You will need to zigzag to the left at the second landing in order to continue to the top of the fourth landing. The next grave will be on your right.**

5 E. D. E. N. SOUTHWORTH GRAVE

Chapel Section, Lot 534

Emma Dorothy Eliza Nevitte Southworth (1819–1899) was a romance novelist who was so prolific that the exact number of her books is not known; the best guess is between sixty and seventy. Born in DC, she worked as a schoolteacher prior to her marriage to Frederick Southworth and the birth of their two children. He abandoned the family in 1844, but they never divorced, and she began writing to support her children.

Southworth was an advocate for women's rights and abolition. Her earliest short fiction was published in the abolitionist newspaper the *National Era.* (Most of her novels were serialized prior to being published in book form.) After 1857, all of her work in newspapers appeared in *The New York Ledger,* under the terms of an exclusive contract that secured her income for thirty years.

Books by Southworth were translated into German, French, Chinese, Spanish, and Icelandic. Most of her works feature a plucky heroine who balances feminine domestic virtues with a sense of adventure. Although extremely popular in her time, the books dated quickly, and most contemporary readers will find that their Victorian sensibilities make them nearly unreadable. Her most popular novel, *The Hidden Hand* (1859), sold nearly two million copies and was adapted into a play.

→ **Continue down the stairs to the end and then turn left on Chapel Avenue, taking the second right toward North Hill. Look for stairs leading up on the left. Take them to the circular walkway on the ridge of North Hill and turn left. Look for two flat grave markers on your left, one bearing a bronze plaque.**

6 JOHN ADLUM GRAVE

North Hill Section, Lot 133

Major John Adlum (1759–1836) served as a soldier in the Revolutionary War when he was just a teenager and also fought in the War of 1812. In addition, he worked as a surveyor and a judge. But he is best known as an early viticulturist and the developer of the Catawba grape, an American varietal.

Adlum moved to DC in 1814 with his wife and two daughters, and in 1816, he began farming in what is today the Cleveland Park neighborhood on a 220-acre plot of land. He set aside 22 acres for a vineyard, making him the owner of one of the first commercial wineries in America. While some of his earliest attempts at growing European vines failed, he found a number of hardy American varieties and was praised for his efforts by Thomas Jefferson, who wrote that American growers should follow Adlum's model "without losing our time & efforts in search of foreign vines, which it will take centuries to adapt to our soil & climate."

The Catawba is a hybrid grape native to North Carolina. Adlum made cuttings that he cultivated and shared widely with other growers across the East Coast, as far north as the Hudson River Valley of New York, and as far west as Cincinnati. His book *A Memoir on the Cultivation of the Vine in America and the Best Mode of Making Wine* (1823, republished in an enlarged edition in 1828) was the first book on winemaking published in the United States, and he also wrote *Adlum on Making Wine* (1826). A native climbing plant, *Adlumia fungosa,* is named in his honor, and the Williamsburg Winery in Virginia sells a John Adlum chardonnay.

Although he was known as the father of American viticulture, ironically, Adlum's own winemaking efforts were not particularly successful. Several factors may be to blame, including the high amounts of sugar he added and the high temperatures his batches reached during fermentation. Nevertheless, Adlum lobbied agricultural societies and the federal government for recognition of winemaking as a distinct scientific discipline, and he became known as a national expert on wine production.

→ **Look directly on the other side of this path to the center of the grassy circle for the next two graves.**

7 MADELEINE ALBRIGHT GRAVE

North Hill Section, Lot 103c

Madeleine Albright (1937–2022) served as the sixty-fourth US secretary of state from 1997 to 2001. She was the first woman to hold that post. In 1948, at age eleven, Albright immigrated to the United States with her family from what was then Czechoslovakia. After earning a PhD in political science from Columbia University, she began her career on the staff of the National Security Council. She moved to DC in 1962; in 1982, she was hired as a professor at Georgetown University, and she was appointed by President Bill Clinton as ambassador to the United Nations from 1993 to 1997. Although raised Catholic, Albright learned at age fifty-nine that her parents had converted from Judaism to avoid persecution and that dozens of her family members had been murdered in the Holocaust.

Albright was the author of the memoirs *Hell and Other Destinations* (2020), *Prague Winter* (2012), *Read My Pins* (2009), and *Madame Secretary* (2003) as well as the nonfiction books *Fascism: A Warning* (2018), *Memo to the President Elect* (2008), and *The Mighty and the Almighty* (2006). In 2009, she exhibited her personal jewelry collection at the Museum of Art and Design. Albright held honorary degrees from ten universities, was a Fellow of the American Academy of Arts and Sciences, and served on the boards of the New York Stock Exchange, the Council on Foreign Relations, the Truman Scholarship Foundation, the Council of Women World Leaders, the National Democratic Institute for International Affairs, and the Commission on Legal Empowerment of the Poor. Her funeral at Washington National Cathedral was attended by American presidents and world leaders.

8 VICTORIA POST SANT GRAVE

North Hill Section, Fowler Circle, Lots 3–5

Victoria Sant (1939–2018) was a philanthropist known for her service on boards in the arts (National Gallery of Art, Phillips Collection, the International Council of the Museum of Modern Art, and the Foundation for Art and Preservation in Embassies); the environment (World Wildlife Fund National Council, National Geographic); and the empowerment of girls and women (The National Campaign to Prevent Teen Pregnancy, the International Center for Research on Women). She was cofounder and president of the Summit Foundation and its successor, the Sant Foundation. She endowed the National Gallery of Art with a special fund to acquire works of visual art by women, and she funded the Smithsonian Museum of Natural History's Sant Ocean Hall. Sant also endowed staff positions, such as the National Symphony Orchestra's music director and a professorship in art and art history at Stanford University. A longtime resident of the Georgetown neighborhood, Sant was an avid private art collector, ranked several times among the Top 200 Collectors by *ArtNews*.

The Sant family commissioned Andy Goldsworthy to create the funerary art for this grave. Goldsworthy (1956–) is a Scottish sculptor famous for site-specific land art installations. Many of his sculptures are intended to be ephemeral, made with natural materials such as leaves, stones, sticks, snow, and ice. Permanent works are on display at Storm King Art Center, the Museum of Jewish Heritage, and the National Gallery of Art. In 2000 he was named an Officer of the Order of the British Empire (OBE). This grave marker is unusual in his oeuvre and a notable addition to Oak Hill's funerary art. His simple low arch is intended to symbolize the bridge from life to death.

→ **Continue around North Hill. Look for a Seneca red sandstone mausoleum on your left.**

9 LINTHICUM-DENT MAUSOLEUM

North Hill Section, Lot 150

This handsome red stone mausoleum resembles a miniature chapel; unfortunately, it has experienced some structural damage and is now clamped together with iron bars. Interred inside is Edward Magruder Linthicum (1797–1869), the former owner of Dumbarton Oaks. Linthicum owned a successful hardware business in Georgetown and was an avid amateur horticulturalist. Although the gardens for which Dumbarton Oaks is now famed were developed by subsequent owners, the Bliss family, Linthicum's addition of an orangery to the property still stands (among his other improvements). Today, Dumbarton Oaks, located a short distance from the cemetery at 1703 Thirty-Second Street NW, is administered by Harvard University as a museum and research center focused on Byzantine and pre-Columbian arts as well as garden and landscape studies.

→ **Continue on the circular path. When you are facing a mausoleum shaped like a Roman temple with "Eustis" engraved at the top (which will be stop number 12 on this tour), you should zigzag to your left to take the stairs with the iron railing down the slope to a series of mausoleums built into the hill. Turn left and walk to the second mausoleum on the left.**

10 SPENCER FULLERTON BAIRD MAUSOLEUM

North Hill Section, Lot 279

Spencer Fullerton Baird (1823–1887) was a naturalist who specialized in ornithology, ichthyology, and herpetology. In 1850, he was the first curator to be named to the Smithsonian Institution. He served as assistant secretary from 1850 to 1878 and secretary from 1878 to 1887—the second person, after Joseph Henry, to hold that post. (Henry is also buried here; see site 16.) In addition, Baird served as secretary of the American Association for the Advancement of Science and was the first commissioner for the US Fish Commission.

Among other scientific publications, Baird wrote *A History of North American Birds* (1874), *Geographic Distribution of North American Birds* (1865), *Mammals of North America* (1859), and *The Catalogue of North American Serpents* (1853). An unusually large number of animals have been named in his honor, including a genus of drumfish, a crab, a woodpecker, a sparrow, a sandpiper, a flycatcher, a beaked whale, a rat snake, and a tapir, among others. He was named a Knight of the Royal Order of St. Olav by the king of Sweden and was a founding member of the American Ornithologists' Union.

→ **Continue on the path to the very last mausoleum.**

11 CARROLL MAUSOLEUM

North Hill Section, Lot 292

William Thomas Carroll (1802–1863) was an attorney who served as one of the first professors of law at Columbian College, the forerunner to George Washington University, and a clerk of the US Supreme Court (1827–1863). He lived nearby at Dumbarton House, 2715 Q Street NW, one of the most significant Federal-era mansions in Georgetown and now the National Headquarters of the Society of the Colonial Dames of America. Carroll and his wife, Sallie, offered space in his family vault to President and Mrs. Lincoln after their son Willie's death from typhoid fever in 1862. Willie's remains stayed here until 1865, when Abraham Lincoln was assassinated;

the bodies of both father and son were then transferred by funeral train to Oak Ridge Cemetery in Springfield, Illinois. A bronze plaque inside the gates of the Carroll Mausoleum commemorates Lincoln's numerous visits to his son's casket.

Carroll is best remembered today for a different Lincoln connection: he purchased the Bible that Lincoln used for his swearing-in. Carroll certified that significant event with his signature on the flyleaf.

→ **Retrace your steps; once up the stairs you'll need to cut across the grass to the Eustis mausoleum (aka the Corcoran Mausoleum), shaped like a Roman temple, on your left.**

12 CORCORAN MAUSOLEUM

Corcoran Section, Lots 1–15

In 1848, William Wilson Corcoran (1798–1888) purchased fifteen acres, originally called Parrott's Woods, from George Corbin Washington (the great-nephew of President George Washington) to found this cemetery in honor of his wife, Louise, who died at age twenty-one. It was originally designated for whites only, although it was always nondenominational, accepting burials of people of all religions.

Congress approved the charter in 1849, and the grounds were dedicated on the Fourth of July. Corcoran hired George F. de la Roche to design the terraced grounds and supervise the grading and plotting of the complex site. He also paid for the construction of the Renwick Chapel on the grounds and personally arranged for the interment of John Howard Payne (see stop number 2 on this tour), paying all expenses to have his cremated body returned from Tunis to the United States. Corcoran's mausoleum, in the shape of a round Roman temple with eight Ionic columns, was designed by Thomas U. Walter

(1804–1887), who also served as architect of the US Capitol. (Corcoran's daughter Louise married George Eustis Jr., and the Corcoran Mausoleum holds the remains of members of both the Corcoran and Eustis families.)

Corcoran was born and raised in Georgetown, gaining his fortune as cofounder of Riggs National Bank and through investments in real estate. He supplemented this with war profits from the Mexican-American War, which he financed through the sale of millions of dollars of government bonds. After his retirement in 1854, he began to collect one of the nation's most ambitious personal art collections, which included a substantial amount of work created by American artists. He hired Renwick to construct a mansion to hold the collection (now the Renwick Gallery of Art in Lafayette Square), but as it neared completion, the Civil War broke out. Corcoran was, like many Washingtonians, a Confederate sympathizer—and he opted to sit out the war in exile in Paris. The US Army confiscated his mansion for use as a supply depot. Upon Corcoran's return to the District, he reclaimed his property and completed work on the mansion. It opened to the public as the Corcoran Gallery, DC's first art museum, in 1874.

Corcoran's philanthropy helped build or sustain several Washington institutions, including a retirement home for gentlewomen, the Louise Home; the George Washington University; the Church of the Ascension and Saint Agnes; and Mount Vernon.

Riggs Bank was taken over by PNC Bank in 2005. The Renwick Gallery of Art is now administered by the Smithsonian Institution and collects American fine crafts and decorative arts. Corcoran's personal art collection was transferred to a new Corcoran Gallery of Art in 1897; it was transferred again in 2014 into the collections of the National Gallery of Art.

→ **Continue across the grass and look to your left for a staircase and pathway leading downhill. At the end**

of the stairs, bear right and then left to get down to Central Avenue. Turn left onto Central Avenue, then stay left at the split in the road onto Carriage Avenue. Take the first path on the right (almost immediately after turning onto Carriage Avenue). Where this path forks, bear right to reach the higher trail. The next grave can be found on your right.

13 ALBERT PIKE GRAVE

Steuart Section, Lot 541 East

Why does Albert Pike have two graves? He has one here at Oak Hill, where he was originally buried, but that site now lies empty. His body was removed in December 1944 and entombed at the Scottish Rite Temple at 1733 Sixteenth Street NW, where the Masons also maintain a permanent exhibit on Pike's controversial life.

Albert Pike (1809–1891) was a journalist and newspaper owner as well as a soldier who served in the Mexican-American War, the Indian Wars, and the Civil War (on the Confederate side), where he rose to the rank of brigadier general. He was forced to resign his commission after his brigade was defeated in the Battle of Pea Ridge and his men were found scalping the bodies of the Union dead. Fellow officers also accused him of misappropriating funds; he was briefly incarcerated until President Andrew Johnson granted him a full pardon in 1866.

Strong anecdotal evidence supports allegations that Pike was a leader of the Ku Klux Klan in Arkansas. As a Freemason, he attained the rank of sovereign grand commander for the Southern Jurisdiction of the United States and wrote the book *Morals and Dogma of the Ancient and Accepted Scottish Rite of Freemasonry* (1871). His other numerous publications include books on religions of the Indian subcontinent, legal history, and such creative works as *Prose Sketches and Poems Written in the Western Country* (1834) and *Hymns to the Gods and*

Other Poems (1872). He claimed to be fluent in five languages (an assertion now questioned by modern scholars) and to have attended Harvard College (where he was never a student—but was awarded an honorary degree in 1859).

During his lifetime, Pike's poems were extremely popular, and his books sold well. A bronze statue of Pike stands in Judiciary Square, making him the only Confederate military officer to be honored with a statue in the capital. The statue was paid for by private funds but stands on federal land. It was toppled in 2020 by Black Lives Matter protesters. At the time, the Society for Architectural Historians released a statement, saying, "Confederate monuments do not serve as catalysts for a cleansing public conversation, but rather express white supremacy and dominance, causing discomfort and distress to African-American citizens who utilize the public spaces these monuments occupy."

The National Park Service reinstalled the statue in October 2025 in compliance with a contentious executive order issued by President Donald Trump. "Restoring Truth and Sanity to American History" states, in part: "Over the past decade, Americans have witnessed a concerted and widespread effort to rewrite our Nation's history, replacing objective facts with a distorted narrative driven by ideology rather than truth. This revisionist movement seeks to undermine the remarkable achievements of the United States by casting its founding principles and historical milestones in a negative light. Under this historical revision, our Nation's unparalleled legacy of advancing liberty, individual rights, and human happiness is reconstructed as inherently racist, sexist, oppressive, or otherwise irredeemably flawed."

The return of the Pike statue is alarming enough on its own. But the larger implications are even more disturbing: we devalue democracy when we sanitize or erase large parts of American history in order to present a glorified narrative.

→ **Continue on this path to where it meets Central Avenue and look immediately across the road for a grave topped with a statue.**

14 JOHN A. JOYCE GRAVE

Joyce Section, Lot 444 East

The grave of John A. Joyce (1842–1915) is topped with a bust of the author in bronze. Joyce is one of numerous Union soldiers interred at Oak Hill. He served as a colonel in the Union Army, with the 24th Kentucky Infantry, during the Civil War. Born in Ireland, he settled in DC after the war, earned a law degree, and worked for the Internal Revenue Service. He is the author of books of poems, memoirs, and criticism, including *A Checkered Life* (1883), *Jewels of Memory* (1895), *Complete Poems* (1900), and *Beautiful Washington* (1903), as well as studies of Edgar Allan Poe, William Shakespeare, and Robert Burns. Quotes from four of Joyce's poems are inscribed on each side of his grave marker. He lived in Georgetown, in a large brick house located at 3238 R Street NW. His obituary in the *Washington Times* states, "Hardly an event of importance occurred in the last quarter of a century that John A. Joyce has not sought to immortalize in a poem."

The bust's sculptor, Jerome Connor (1874–1943), was also born in Ireland. He established a studio in Washington, DC, from 1910 to 1915. Local commissions include the Nuns of the Battlefield Memorial (located south of Dupont Circle), portraits of Bishop John Carroll and Robert Emmet (on the grounds of Georgetown University and the Irish embassy, respectively), and *The Supreme Sacrifice*, a sculpture in the John A. Wilson Building commemorating District government employees who died in World War I. He is also thought to have helped the artist Roland Hinton manufacture the Court of the Neptune

Fountain, a complex sculptural group in front of the Library of Congress Jefferson Building.

→ **Take Bridge Avenue to the left. Look for a stone on your right, just a few gravesites down.**

15 MYRTILLA MINER GRAVE

Joyce Section, Lot 439 East

Myrtilla Miner (1815–1864) was an abolitionist and a national leader in the training of African American teachers. A white woman from New York, Miner moved to Washington, DC, in 1851 to open the Normal School for Colored Girls, at that time the only school in the city offering education to students of color beyond the elementary school level. Local opposition to the school was intense. After incidents of stoning, arson, and physical threats, Miner was forced to move the school three times within the first two years, and she slept with a gun under her pillow. Funds for the school came from Northern abolitionists, such as Harriet Beecher Stowe and the Reverend Henry Ward Beecher, as well as local supporters Gamaliel Bailey and Johns Hopkins. Miner's health, never robust, suffered under the stress. She gave up teaching in 1857, but the school continued—under the leadership of Emily Howland—until the Civil War. After the war, the school was reestablished as Miner Teacher's College, in association with Howard University, and it educated the majority of teachers of color in Washington's public schools between the 1870s and World War II. In 1955, the Miner school merged with the white Wilson Teachers College to form DC Teachers College, and in 1976, it merged with a couple of other educational institutions to form what would become the University of the District of Columbia.

An article in the *Journal of Negro History* from 1920 states, "For her noble character, her high ideals, her progressive methods in education, her struggles against opposition in the pursuit of her God-given task, her lasting contribution of an organized institution for the training of teachers in the spirit of the Master to serve all humanity, the citizens of the District of Columbia and especially the people of color must ever revere her memory."

Ellen O'Connor published *Myrtilla Miner: A Memoir* about the pioneering educator in 1885. (O'Connor is also buried at Oak Hill; see stop 23.) A plaque on the front of the School of Education at Howard University honors Miner, and Miner Elementary School, part of DC Public Schools, is named for her.

→ **Continue on Bridge Avenue and look for a four-sided red marble monument on your right, located on a rise. You will see a pathway on your right leading up to the top of the knoll.**

16 JOSEPH HENRY GRAVE

Henry Crescent Section, Lot 1

The first secretary of the Smithsonian Institution, Joseph Henry (1797–1878), was a physicist famed for his discovery of electromagnetism. Henry taught mathematics and natural history at The Albany Academy and the College of New Jersey (the forerunner of Princeton University) prior to his appointment to the Smithsonian, where he served from 1846 to the end of his life. From 1855 to 1878, Henry lived in upstairs quarters in the Smithsonian Castle with his family.

In addition to his pioneering experiments with magnetism and magnetic relays, Henry worked with other scientists to enhance fog signal acoustics for lighthouses, determine relative temperatures of the surface of the sun, and develop the field of aeronautics (including the inauguration of a US Army Balloon Corps during the

Civil War). Henry created the Smithsonian Press, editing its first publication, *Ancient Monuments of the Mississippi Valley*, by Ephraim G. Squier and Edwin H. Davis. He also promoted the creation of the US Weather Bureau and cofounded the National Academy of Sciences.

Henry's memory has been honored in a range of ways. A statue of him stands in front of the Smithsonian Castle, and another is included in the main reading room of the Library of Congress (where he joins Isaac Newton in representing science, one of the eight pillars of civilization). Schools in Albany, New York, and Washington, DC, were named for him (although the DC school was unfortunately demolished in the 1930s). A coast guard cutter was named for him, as were the university laboratories at Princeton. A mountain range in Utah has been given the name the Henry Mountains, and the standard unit of electrical inductance is known as the henry.

→ **Retrace your steps back down to continue on Bridge Avenue; look for a gravestone on your left. Facing Rock Creek, you'll be looking at the back of this grave, with its scroll design at the top. It is on a slope almost exactly across from the path you were just on.**

17 HENRY ULKE GRAVE

Rock Creek Section, Lot 483 East

Henry Ulke (1821–1910) was a photographer, painter, and avid amateur naturalist. Born in Prussia (now Germany), he moved to New York in 1852 and then to Washington, DC, in 1860. With his brothers Julian and Lee, he opened a photography studio at 1111 Pennsylvania Avenue NW (now part of the US Capitol grounds). Ulke also took commissions for painted portraits, specializing in paintings of noted politicians and scientists. His subjects included Edwin M. Stanton, Charles Sumner, James G. Blaine, Roger Brooke Taney, and Ulysses S. Grant.

Ulke lived in a boardinghouse across the street from Ford's Theater at 516 Tenth Street NW, now the Petersen House museum—and famous as the place where President Abraham Lincoln died. Ulke's most well-known photograph depicts Mary Lincoln in mourning.

Ulke amassed one of the largest collections of American beetles, which he donated to the Carnegie Museum of Natural History in Pittsburgh. He was active in the Megatherium Club, a group of DC-based scientists, many of whom were associated with the Smithsonian Institution. The club was named for an extinct giant ground sloth.

→ **Continue downhill on Bridge Avenue and take your first right to enter a crescent-shaped pathway. Midway down this path, look for a grave on the slope to your right.**

18 WILLIAM TYLER PAGE GRAVE

Amphitheater Section, Lot 635 East

William Tyler Page (1868–1942) is a direct descendant of President John Tyler. He worked at the US Capitol for sixty-one years, first as a page and later as clerk of the House of Representatives. He is famous for writing the American's Creed in 1917, a statement affirming loyalty to the United States that is used today as part of the naturalization ceremony to swear in new American citizens. Drawing from such sources as the Declaration of Independence, the Preamble to the Constitution, and Lincoln's Gettysburg Address, the creed is a two-sentence declaration originally written in response to the entry of the United States into World War I. It is printed in its entirety on a memorial stone next to the gravestone. Entered into a national competition, the creed was chosen over more than three thousand other entries and won the top prize of one thousand dollars for its author.

A public elementary school in Montgomery County, Maryland, is named in Page's honor.

→ **Turn around and look down the slope at the view toward Rock Creek.**

19 STONE BRIDGE AND WILLOW COLUMBARIUM

Rock Creek Section

A rugged stone bridge gives sweeping views down the valley toward Rock Creek Parkway. The large round structure you see is a modern columbarium. Since only a small amount of land in the cemetery is available for conventional burials, most modern burials at Oak Hill are now for cremated remains, such as those in the columbarium and those underneath pathways and staircase pavers. As cremation has become more accepted in the past decades, this has allowed the cemetery to remain in active use.

→ **Continue to your right and take the first pathway on your right; go up the hill to a templelike mausoleum placed at the highest point of land in this section.**

20 VAN NESS MAUSOLEUM

Van Ness Section, Lot 173 East

This imposing mausoleum, modeled after the Temple of Vesta in Rome, was designed by George Hadfield and located originally on H Street NW, between Ninth and Tenth Streets (now the site of the US Secret Service Headquarters). In 1870, the structure was moved to the top of this knoll at Oak Hill. Interred within are members of the Van Ness family. Marcia Burnes Van Ness (1782–1832), founder of the Washington Orphan Asylum, grew up in a house once located on what is today White House grounds, and her father sold the land to the government. Her husband, John Peter Van Ness (1769–1846), was a congressional representative from New York (1801–1803), major of militia for the District of Columbia (1803–1813), and the mayor of Washington, DC (1830–1834). He was also vice president of the Washington National Monument Society, president of the Commissioners of the Washington Canal, and president of the National Metropolitan Bank. He cofounded the Washington Jockey Club, which sponsored horse-racing competitions, and was a member of the Columbian Institute for the Promotion of Arts and Sciences. Marcia and John Van Ness were one of the most notable "power couples" of the early years of the city's history. The mausoleum was added to the National Register of Historic Places in 1982.

→ **Follow the path to the right of the mausoleum and look for a grave marker in the shape of a simple marble cube.**

21 JOHN NICOLAY AND HELEN NICOLAY GRAVE

Van Ness Section, Lot 273

Along with John Hay, John George Nicolay (1832–1901) was one of two personal secretaries to President Abraham Lincoln. Hay and Nicolay shared a second-floor bedroom in the northeast corner of the White House. The two later collaborated on a biography, *Abraham Lincoln: A History* (1890). Nicolay was named US consul in Paris, serving from 1865 to 1869, and marshal to the Supreme Court (1872–1887). He also wrote the book *The Outbreak of the Rebellion* (1881) and was a founding member of the Washington Literary Society.

His daughter, Helen Nicolay (1866–1954), was an author of children's books, painter, and linguist. Born in France, she moved to Washington, DC, in 1870. During World War II, she worked for the US State Department as an interpreter. In addition to such children's books as *The Boys' Life of Abraham Lincoln* (1906), *The Boys' Life of Ulysses S. Grant* (1909), *The Boys' Life of Lafayette* (1920), and *The Boys' Life of Alexander Hamilton* (1927), Helen Nicolay also wrote the guidebook *Our Capital on the Potomac* (1924) and a biography of her father, *Lincoln's Secretary* (1949). Helen Nicolay never married, and she cared for her father during his final years.

→ **Continue on this path and take the first right. Look for a grave on your right, partially obscured by large bushes.**

22 ADOLPH CLUSS GRAVE

Van Ness Section, Lot 161 East

The most influential and prolific architect in DC in the late nineteenth century, Adolph Ludwig Cluss (1825–1905) was born in Germany and immigrated to the United States at age twenty-three. He settled in the District in 1849, became a citizen in 1855, and began a private architectural practice in 1862, in the midst of the Civil War. He designed and built more than ninety buildings in the city of Washington between 1862 and 1887.

Cluss's beautiful and ornate red brick buildings included churches, schools, federal buildings, museums, hotels, commercial buildings, and private homes. Those still standing include the Smithsonian Castle and the Arts and Industries Building, Eastern Market, the Charles Sumner School, the Franklin School (now the Planet Word Museum), the Washington Arsenal at Fort McNair, Alexandria City Hall, the mansion in Dupont Circle known as Stewart's Castle, and Calvary Baptist Church. In addition, Cluss served as a DC city engineer and an inspector for the Board of Public Works. He married in 1859 and fathered seven children, but all four of his sons died young, predeceasing their father. Active in

Republican Party politics, Cluss served on the inauguration committee for President James A. Garfield.

→ **Continue further on this path. Look for two graves side by side on your left.**

23 GRAVES OF WILLIAM DOUGLAS O'CONNOR AND ELLEN TARR O'CONNOR CALDER

Amphitheater Section, Lot 88 East

When William O'Connor and his wife (who went by the nickname Nelly) moved to DC in the beginning of 1861, they joined a growing group of Civil War–era federal workers with literary ambitions and their spouses. William O'Connor and Walt Whitman shared the same publisher, and they were friends prior to Whitman's arrival in the city in December 1862. The O'Connors invited Whitman to live in the same boardinghouse where they were then living, and he stayed for over six months at an address on L Street near the intersection with Vermont Avenue. Whitman wrote to his mother that the O'Connors "won't listen to me leaving . . . I can never forget their kindness & real friendship & it appears as though they would continue the same, if it were for all our lives." The O'Connors were in mourning at that time, after the death of their two-year-old son Philip from smallpox. (An older daughter, Jeannie, was five at the time and living in the household.) Whitman seemed to fill an emotional void for Nelly during this difficult period, and he was soon helping her with household chores, including drawing water from a common outdoor pump each morning, as none of the houses had running water at that time. When Whitman finally moved out, his next boardinghouse on Sixth Street was close enough that he could continue to eat supper with the O'Connors daily, a practice he kept up through May 1864, when he moved to a location farther away in the city.

William O'Connor (1832–1889) is the author of one novel, *Harrington: A Story of True Love* (1860), and the nonfiction pamphlet *The Good Gray Poet: A Vindication* (1866), defending Walt Whitman's reputation. Whitman had been fired from a job at the Bureau of Indian Affairs when the secretary of the interior discovered that he was the author of *Leaves of Grass,* a book he considered indecent. O'Connor's pamphlet turned Whitman into a cause célèbre. (O'Connor also immediately found Whitman a new federal job in the Attorney General's office.) William O'Connor's uncollected short fiction appeared in journals and newspapers and addressed reform themes of prohibition, women's rights, the abolition of slavery, and spiritualism. One story, "The Brazen Android" (1891), is considered one of the earliest science fiction stories on robots. A book of nonfiction about lighthouse keepers, *Heroes of the Storm,* was published posthumously in 1904.

O'Connor was a journalist for the *Boston Commonwealth* and associate editor at the *Saturday Evening Post* in his earlier years. After coming to Washington, he worked as a corresponding clerk for the Lighthouse Board, a division of the US Treasury Department, and was promoted in 1873 to chief clerk. When the Life Saving Service was reorganized in 1878, O'Connor was appointed assistant general superintendent.

Ellen Tarr O'Connor Calder (1830–1913) also worked as a journalist. As a young woman, she worked as a mill hand in Lowell, Massachusetts, an experience that radicalized her. She became a feminist, socialist, vegetarian, and dress-reform advocate. She first moved to DC as a young woman to work as a governess in the home of the famed abolitionist Gamaliel Bailey (see site 24), and she began writing for his newspaper, the *National Era.* She also contributed to other progressive papers, including the *Liberator,* and a monthly paper on women's rights called *Una*. In 1855, she served as secretary for the New England Women's Rights Convention, and in 1870 she was vice president of the Women's Rights Washington Branch. She married William in 1856 and did not write or publish again until their separation, when she published *Myrtilla Miner: A Memoir* (1885), a book celebrating Miner's achievements in the education of African American students (see stop number 15). Nelly O'Connor reconciled with her husband at the end of his life, in time to nurse him through his final illness. After his death, in 1889, she edited two posthumous books of his: *Three Tales* and *Heroes of the Storm*. She subsequently moved to Providence, Rhode Island, and married Albert L. Calder in 1892. It is unclear why she ended up buried next to her first husband.

→ **Continue on the path and then take the staircase on the left to Eastern Avenue. Continue right onto East Gate Avenue, the higher of the two main roads (and the one closest to the amphitheater). You will see East Gate in front of you. Before reaching the gate, look for the second path on your right. Stay on this path for a short distance. Then take your first left onto a path that follows the fence line.**

24 GAMALIEL BAILEY AND MARGARET LUCY SHANDS BAILEY GRAVESITES

Reno Hill Section, Lot 701

In the Page family plot, the bodies of Margaret Lucy Shands Bailey and her husband, Gamaliel Bailey, are buried in an unmarked grave; they were disinterred from Congressional Cemetery in 1889. Charles and Virginia Page were related to Margaret Bailey, but it is unclear why the Baileys' bodies were moved here and why their new graves were never properly marked. They were among the most prominent white abolitionists in the nation during their lifetimes, and they deserve to be better remembered today for their activism.

Gamaliel Bailey (1807–1859) moved to Washington, DC, in 1847 to begin publication of the *National Era,* an abolitionist newspaper perhaps best remembered as the first to publish, in serialized form, Harriet Beecher Stowe's novel *Uncle Tom's Cabin.* The paper continued publication through 1860. In addition, Margaret Shands Bailey (1812–1888) founded an antislavery juvenile magazine, the *Youth's Monthly Visitor,* which she published from 1844 through 1852.

The Baileys' large downtown home (now the site of the Hotel Monaco on F Street NW) became a center for the region's white antislavery activists, a place where congressmen and white Northern abolitionists could meet, raise money to purchase people out of bondage, and plan actions to further support successful escapes, court cases, and the circulation of antislavery petitions to lawmakers. It is believed that their house was sometimes used as a stop on the Underground Railroad.

The Baileys had twelve children, half of whom died as infants. They hired a string of young radical Northern women as governesses, and many were also mentored as professional writers, getting their work first published in the *National Era.* At least three former governesses went on to careers as pioneering women journalists (including Ellen Tarr O'Connor; see site 23).

The Baileys were under constant scrutiny in a capital city whose residents were largely Southern sympathizers. Twice their presses were damaged by mobs of protesters. Once they had to flee the city, fearing for their lives.

Margaret volunteered as a literacy teacher to soldiers of African descent, and she ran a Saturday night salon of like-minded radicals in her home. She also wrote sentimental poems, including one, "The Blind Slave Boy," that was set to music and became popular on the national antislavery lecture circuit. The Baileys both supported educational efforts for students of African descent and helped raise funds to support Myrtilla Miner's Normal School for Colored Girls (see site 15). After Gamaliel's early death in 1859, Margaret briefly took over publication of the newspaper on her own.

→ **Continue on the path, then take the set of stairs on your right down to the parallel path just below. Turn left and look for the next gravesite on your right.**

25 WILLIAM WADDEN TURNER GRAVE

Chapel Valley, Lot 453

Born in England, William Wadden Turner (1810–1859) emigrated to New York in 1818 and developed an aptitude for languages early while working as a printer. He was fluent in French, German, Latin, Hebrew, and Arabic, and he had a working knowledge of Sanskrit, Yoruba, and several Native American languages. For ten years (1842–1852) he worked as a professor of oriental literature at Union Theological Seminary. He then moved to Washington, DC, to take a federal job as a librarian for the US Patent Office.

Turner is the author of *A Critical Grammar of the Hebrew Language* (with Isaac Nordheimer, 1838), *Chrestomathy: or A Grammatical Analysis of Selections from the Hebrew Scriptures, with an Exercise in Hebrew Composition* (1838), *Hebrew and Chaldee Concordance to the Old Testament* (1842), *Vocabulary of the Jargon or Trade Language of Oregon* (1853), and *Grammar and Dictionary of the Yoruba Language* (1858). He also translated, from German, *America and the American People* (1845), *Compendium of Modern Civil Law* (1845), and *Latin-German Lexicon* (1851).

Turner and his wife and sisters were part of a network of scholars in DC who gathered regularly at the home of Smithsonian secretary Spencer F. Baird (see site 10).

Jane Turner (also buried at this plot) prepared a catalogue of all the holdings of the Smithsonian Library, beginning in 1857.

→ **Retrace your steps up to the higher path. Continue on this path, which will lead you back past the Renwick Chapel to the Ellipse.**

26 BEN BRADLEE MAUSOLEUM

Cross Avenue, Lot F

Located in a prominent place in the middle of the Ellipse, you'll find the mausoleum of Ben Bradlee (1921–2014), executive editor of the *Washington Post* from 1968 to 1991 and famed as the man who oversaw the publication of the Pentagon Papers, documenting the Watergate scandal. Bradlee is the author of two books: *Conversations with Kennedy* (1975) and a memoir, *A Good Life: Newspapering and Other Adventures* (1995).

Bradlee worked as a communications officer for the US Navy during World War II, handling coded cables for the Office of Naval Intelligence. After the war, he worked as a journalist, as press attaché for the American embassy in Paris, and for the Office of US Information and Educational Exchange. As a reporter in the 1950s, Bradlee became close friends with John F. Kennedy. They lived near one another in Georgetown, had both graduated from Harvard University, and Bradlee's first wife, Jean Saltonstall, was related to Jacqueline Bouvier Kennedy. Bradlee was the Washington bureau chief for *Newsweek;* in 1965, he was hired as managing editor of the *Washington Post* by publisher Katharine Graham (see stop 4). He taught occasional courses in journalism at Georgetown University. Among other honors, Bradlee received the French Legion of Honor and a Presidential Medal of Freedom.

→ **Continue walking along the Ellipse to the far western end and follow the road as it bends to the right. At the intersection of Cross Avenue and Western Avenue, look for the large sculpted granite stone on your left.**

27 SPENCER FAMILY GRAVE

Montrose Section, Lot 970

The large angel with upraised arms sculpted in low relief on this massive granite stone was created by the Tiffany Company (better known for its work in stained glass). It is thought that Tiffany artists created this grave marker from a stone already on site.

Samuel Spencer (1847–1906) was the first president of the Southern Railway. Born in Georgia, he served in the Confederate cavalry during the Civil War. Spencer helped consolidate dozens of rail lines throughout the American South. He became president of the Southern Railway in 1894 and led the company during a period of unprecedented growth, doubling the miles of track and increasing ridership to nearly twelve million passengers a year. Ironically, he died in a collision on his own company's rail line on Thanksgiving morning while in his private railcar, traveling to his private hunting lodge. Spencer, North Carolina, was named in his honor.

→ **Return to the road and take Abelia Path, the first path on your right. Look for a tall grave, topped with a square column and a cross, on your left.**

28 SETH EASTMAN AND MARY HENDERSON EASTMAN GRAVES

Chapel Hill Section, Lot 652

General Seth Eastman (1808–1875) spent his career in the US Army, working as a cartographer and illustrator.

He spent two tours of duty at Fort Snelling, the northernmost post in Indian Territory in what is today Minnesota, where he learned the Sioux language and sketched scenes of Sioux and Ojibwa daily life. During his first posting (1830–1833), he married a Dakota woman, Wakan Inajin-win (or Stands Sacred), and they had a daughter, but Eastman abandoned them when he was reassigned to West Point, where he became a professor of drawing. During his second tour (1841–1849), he was accompanied by his second wife, Mary Henderson Eastman. They had five children together.

Seth and Mary Eastman moved to DC in 1849, and Seth Eastman collaborated with Henry Rowe Schoolcraft to create *Historical and Statistical Information Regarding the History, Conditions, and Prospects of the Indian Tribes of the United States,* a six-volume series published between 1851 and 1857. Schoolcraft, a former US Indian agent, wrote the text; Eastman created more than 275 pages of illustrations. Eastman's final army assignment was to create a series of paintings for the US Capitol. His nine paintings for the House Committee on Indian Affairs, and seventeen for the House Committee on Military Affairs, were completed in the 1870s, and many of them remain on display. In addition to his books with Schoolcraft, Seth Eastman is the author of a textbook on mapmaking, *Treatise on Topographical Drawing* (1837), and a posthumously published nonfiction book, *Memoir of General Seth Eastman, U.S. Army* (1875).

Mary Henderson Eastman (1818–1887) was a white woman born in Warrenton, Virginia, and raised in DC, where her father was stationed as assistant surgeon general of the US Army. She married in 1835 at age seventeen and accompanied her husband to his second posting in Indian Territory. She is the author of several books on Native American life, including *Dahcotah, or Life and Legends of the Sioux Around Fort Snelling* (1849, illustrated by her husband), *Romance of Indian Life* (1853), *The American Aboriginal Portfolio* (1853), and *Chicóra and Other Regions of the Conquerors and the Conquered* (1854). In these books she criticizes the treatment of tribes by the military and by religious missionaries. But she is best known as the author of the best-selling novel *Aunt Phillis's Cabin, or, Southern Life as It Is* (1852), a novel ardently defending slavery that was written in direct response to Harriet Beecher Stowe's *Uncle Tom's Cabin.*

A decade later, Mary Eastman had changed her position on slavery, perhaps based on the fact that her sons fought for the Union Army during the Civil War. Feeling remorse for her earlier novel, Eastman wrote *Jennie Wade of Gettysburg* (1864), a novel praising a Union heroine. Her other books of fiction include *Fashionable Life* (1856) and *Easter Angels* (1879).

→ **Return to Western Avenue and turn right. Look for the next grave on your left, by a metal bench.**

29 PAUL PELZ GRAVE

Montrose Section, Lot 992

Paul Pelz (1841–1918) was born in Silesia, now part of Poland, and moved to the District in 1867 to work as a civil engineer for the US Lighthouse Board. He is responsible for the design of a dozen lighthouses on both the East and West Coasts. After establishing an architectural firm, Pelz designed churches, homes, and commercial buildings, but he is best known as the first architect for the Thomas Jefferson Building of the Library of Congress, widely admired for its amalgamation of several different architectural styles into a cohesive whole.

Some of his other architectural commissions include Healy Hall and Riggs Memorial Library at Georgetown University, Grace Reformed Church and the Emanuel Swedenborg Center in DC, Randall Hall at the University of Virginia, and the Keepers Lodge at Antietam National Cemetery in Sharpsburg, Maryland.

30 BACK TO THE MAIN GATE

The *Washington Post* has called Oak Hill "practically the country club of the afterlife . . . where boldface Washingtonians come to rest." Despite its segregated status at its founding, by the 1960s, Oak Hill Cemetery had changed its policies and today accepts burials of people of all races and ethnicities. Listed on the National Register of Historic Places, the cemetery operates as a private, nonprofit organization and remains a popular place for walking.

Beginning in the 1830s, cities in the United States started to look at cemeteries in a new light: they were spaces that offered peaceful respite and served as public parks in a time before such parks existed. Oak Hill is the first cemetery in DC to be part of the rural cemetery movement, in which romantic ideas of landscaping and the fear of overcrowding and disease in the inner city combined to create a new aesthetic for burial grounds. Instead of treeless grids of headstones, this bucolic nineteenth-century ideal favored meandering footpaths and carriage roads, meticulous landscapes with varied vistas, and a range of monument styles. This type of cemetery was meant to be spiritually uplifting, a place to celebrate the memory of the deceased and to contemplate the rewards of the afterlife.

Oak Hill Cemetery publishes a quarterly online newsletter and hosts regular events, including guided tours, stone-carving classes, an annual Dog Days walk, and a book club. Services continue to be held in the little Renwick Chapel (which has even hosted wedding ceremonies). There are now nearly twenty thousand people interred in these historic grounds.

GLENWOOD CEMETERY (1854)

219 Lincoln Road NE, Edgewood neighborhood, DC

Glenwood Cemetery, located north of the center city in what was then a suburb in Washington County, was chartered by an act of Congress in 1854. It was the first for-profit cemetery in Washington, DC (before Georgetown was annexed), and among the first nationwide. Sited on just under fifty-four acres, the property features eight miles of serpentine, picturesque roadways leading past five circles, overlooking a number of historic Victorian and Art Nouveau–style funerary monuments. The cemetery is wedged on a polygon of land between two major streets: North Capitol Street and Lincoln Road. It was listed on the National Register of Historic Places in 2017.

The landscape design was created by civil engineer George F. de la Roche. De la Roche is better known as the designer of Oak Hill Cemetery (which he designed just prior to Glenwood and where he chose to be buried, along with his wife and two daughters). De la Roche was born in Germany. He lived in Baltimore and Philadelphia before serving as a sailing master for the US Navy in the War of 1812, attaining the rank of captain. He then opened his engineering and design office in DC, in the Georgetown neighborhood, and specialized in cemeteries. In addition to his two cemeteries in the District, he is known for his design of Oakdale Memorial Gardens in Davenport, Iowa. All of de la Roche's cemetery designs feature winding carriage lanes that follow the rolling topography of their sites, circular areas to break up the lines of graves, and generous plantings. De la Roche wrote that Glenwood was perfect for its new use as a cemetery, as the "tract is undulating, with hills and a dell,

Revelations chainsaw angel sculpture (5)

a considerable portion of it embellished with grand and towering native forest trees . . . giving it a rural, quiet, and secluded character."

Before You Go

https://www.theglenwoodcemetery.com
Open daily 6:00 am to 8:00 pm
Nearest public transportation: Rhode Island Avenue–Brentwood Station to bus
Parking and restrooms available

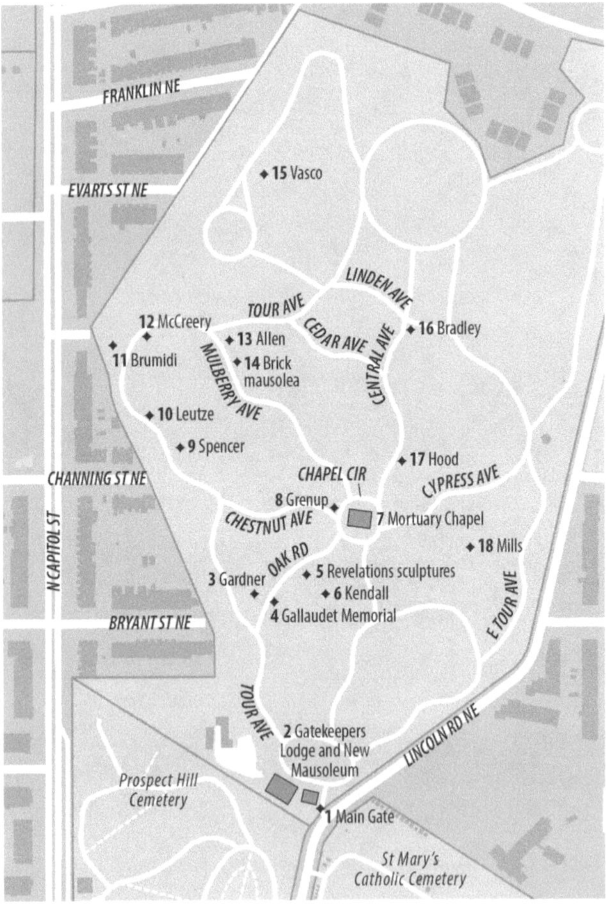

Glenwood Cemetery

1 MAIN GATE

Constructed in 1898 at the cemetery's southern boundary, the main gate spells out the cemetery's name in wrought iron capital letters arched between two limestone piers, each topped with cast-iron urns. This is the second gate in this location; an earlier design by de la Roche was replaced. The west side of the property has a steep drop in elevation, and de la Roche built a thick stone retaining wall, which can be seen from the Lincoln Road side.

Driving through the gate brings visitors to a circular drive, decorated with a series of cast angels, some blowing large horns. The creator is unknown. Despite the cemetery's purported nonsectarian mission, the website states that these statues "are symbolic of GOD'S grace to minister to his children even in death, to comfort the hearts of the weary and sad in heart, and to bring joy to HIS elect." The angels near the entrance have become symbols of the cemetery, used as images on all of their brochures. But the cemetery is famous as the final resting place of much more renowned and original visual artists than these welcoming angels would suggest. Highlights of this tour include the graves of Alexander Gardner, Emanuel Leutze, Constantino Brumidi, and Clark Mills.

2 GATEKEEPER'S LODGE AND NEW MAUSOLEUM

An attractive two-story Gothic Revival building to the left of the main gate once housed the cemetery superintendent and his family (and now holds the cemetery offices). Built in 1899 by the architectural firm of Freehold and Walsh, the Gatekeeper's Lodge is a brick building atop a limestone foundation with limestone lintels; its gable roofs are topped by limestone finials.

In stark contrast to the design of the Gatekeeper's Lodge, just to the right is the New Mausoleum, a postmodern building of large marble blocks with room for services, a receiving vault for bodies awaiting burial, and individual niches for cremated remains. Although it has no windows, ample light comes into the building through skylights and large glass doors. The New Mausoleum was built in 2011 and joins a few other modern improvements to the grounds, such as six smaller aboveground columbaria and a Zen garden, with a pagoda-like gazebo, in the midst of Freedom's Garden of Scattered Memories, where families can scatter cremains.

→ **Walk to the far side of the circle and take West Tour Road. Take your first right on Oak Avenue. Look for the next site on your left, a raised monument surrounded by a low stone enclosure.**

3 ALEXANDER GARDNER GRAVE

Section C, Lot 38

Alexander Gardner (1821–1882) is best known for his Civil War battle photographs and his portrait photographs of such notable figures as Abraham Lincoln and Walt Whitman. Born in poverty in Scotland, Gardner worked as a jeweler's apprentice and a journalist before joining the photographic studio of Mathew Brady in New York in 1856. By 1858, he had relocated to DC, where he managed Brady's gallery on Pennsylvania Avenue and convinced Brady to send him and other photographers out to battlefields to create some of the earliest frontline documentary photos.

Gardner broke with Brady in 1863 to open his own photo business, located on the corner of Seventh and D Streets NW through 1867. His two-volume *Photographic Sketch Book of the Civil War* (1866), although it sold poorly during his lifetime, is now considered a masterpiece of photojournalism. Gardner photographed Lincoln's funeral and made portraits of all of the conspirators. He also documented numerous Native Americans who visited the capital to negotiate treaties with the government, worked with the DC police to develop the first photo records of criminals, and documented western expansion for the Union Pacific Railroad Company.

→ **Continue on Oak Avenue. Look almost immediately to your right for a flat, modern memorial.**

4 GALLAUDET MEMORIAL

In 2006, a memorial was laid to mark the remains of four early students of what would become Gallaudet University as well as the niece of school's first superintendent, Edward Miner Gallaudet. All five individuals lived on the campus when it was known by its earliest name, the Columbia Institution for the Deaf and Dumb and Blind. Federally chartered by Congress in 1857 as the first higher educational institution for deaf and hearing-impaired students, the renowned university is located south of here, in the Trinidad neighborhood.

→ **Continue along the roadway a little further until you come to a brick pathway on your right. This path is surrounded by three chainsaw sculptures.**

5 REVELATION SCULPTURES

In 2008, the cemetery commissioned Dayton Scoggins (1965–) to transform four old-growth trees, then dying or heavily damaged by storms, into sculptures. One sculpture has since been damaged and removed, but three remain: a dragon and two angels, inspired by the Book of Revelation. The dragon sculpture, the largest of the three, is thirty feet tall. A bench near the dragon features biblical texts that served as inspiration to the artist. Scoggins is the owner of Artistry in Wood and creates chainsaw sculptures in competitions at fairs and festivals across the United States. He lives in Sandersville, Mississippi, and is a member of the Craftsmen's Guild of Mississippi.

→ **Behind the brick path, look for a tall, columnar monument.**

6 AMOS KENDALL GRAVE

Section B, Lot 176

Amos Kendall (1789–1869) served as postmaster general under two presidents, Andrew Jackson and Martin Van Buren. He is best remembered today, however, as a cofounder of the institution that would become Gallaudet University. Kendall purchased 102 acres of farmland in 1841 and named it Kendall Green. In 1857, he opened the Kendall School on the property, hired Edward Miner Gallaudet as the school's first superintendent, and assumed presidency of the board of directors. The two men built the grammar school into a national institution, which today educates deaf and hearing-impaired students with bilingual study (in English and American Sign Language) from kindergarten through graduate school. At Kendall's urging, Congress awarded the school a federal charter in 1864. The school remains on the site of Kendall Green.

Kendall was born in Dunstable, Massachusetts, where his family owned a prominent tavern. After study at Dartmouth College, he became a lawyer and established a legal practice in Kentucky. Kendall also worked as a journalist and editor on several newspapers. He moved to Washington, DC, in 1829, when he was appointed an auditor for the US Treasury Department. In that position, he uncovered embezzlement by his predecessor and became a close advisor to President Andrew Jackson, who rewarded him with an appointment as postmaster general (1835–1840).

→ **Continue on Oak Avenue to Chapel Circle.**

7 MORTUARY CHAPEL

The chapel was designed in 1892 by architect Glenn Brown (1854–1932) in the Romanesque Revival style.

The centerpiece of Glenwood Cemetery, it is the architect's most prominent accomplishment, with its massive geometric shapes giving the chapel solidity and an austere simplicity of form. Brown was secretary of the American Institute of Architects from 1899 to 1913 and is the author of a memoir, *Memories: A Winning Crusade to Revive George Washington's Vision of a Capital City* (1931), and the two-volume *History of the United States Capitol* (1900, 1903). Brown moved to DC in 1880 and, over fifty years, developed a well-respected and prolific architectural practice. He also advocated for the City Beautiful movement, which renewed DC's core around the National Mall. He was elected to the National Academy of Design in 1927.

The mortuary chapel was separately listed from the rest of the cemetery on the National Register of Historic Places in 1989. It is noted as a "one-story brick building . . . laid in flemish bond with walls that flare out to give the chapel a solid visual base for a massive slate roof."

→ **Walk to the back side of the chapel (the side facing west) and look for a monument enclosed by a wrought iron fence painted silver, with three bright red fire hydrants posted at each fence corner.**

8 BENJAMIN C. GRENUP MEMORIAL

Benjamin C. Grenup (1832–1856) was one of the first firemen killed in the line of duty in Washington, DC. His unusual memorial depicts the dramatic manner of his death in grisly detail in bas-relief. Grenup was twenty-four years old when the Columbia Fire Company wagon, en route to a burning stable, collided with a lamppost on Pennsylvania Avenue. Grenup was thrown to the ground underneath the axles and crushed to death by the water wagon. In this artistic depiction, his fellow firemen react to the accident: one raises his arms in the air in alarm, while others fight to no avail to stop the wagon.

The monument was sculpted by Charles Rousseau (?–1903), a Belgian-born artist who designed a number of grave monuments (mostly for Congressional Cemetery). In addition to the central tableau, you can also find images of a fire hose with two nozzles and a fire axe, torch, and spanner wrench held together by rope. The inscription on the side states that "a truer, nobler, trustier heart, more loving or more loyal, never beat within a human breast."

Grenup was a member of Columbia Fire Company #1, now known as DC Fire Department Engine Company #3. The modern company continues the tradition of sending new recruits annually to the monument to ensure that Grenup's sacrifice will never be forgotten.

→ **Pass the Grenup Memorial and take Chestnut Avenue (the next road off Chapel Circle). Pass a road on your left and continue straight. (You have now reentered Tour Avenue.) Look for an obelisk on your right.**

9 SARA ANDREWS SPENCER MEMORIAL

Section D, Lot 58

Notice the design on the shaft of the obelisk, which represents the gates of heaven opening to receive the dead. Sara Andrews Spencer (1837–1909) was an activist for women's suffrage. She was one of seventy-two women who attempted to register to vote in 1871 and then sued the government when they were refused. Her case, *Sara J. Spencer v. Board of Registration,* went all the way to the US Supreme Court but was ultimately unsuccessful. Spencer was a prominent activist and a popular public speaker for the suffrage movement during its dramatic first decade. She served as secretary of the National Woman Suffrage Association (1874–1881) and president of the Woman

Franchise Association of the District of Columbia (1871–1876). She was chief lobbyist for the 1878 woman's suffrage amendment in Congress.

Spencer was the author of two books, *The Woman Question* (1871) and *Thirty Lessons in the English Language* (1873). Spencer also advocated for other radical reforms, most notably for welfare for former prostitutes (or, as she wrote, "the rescue of outcast girls"). She addressed the Republican Convention of 1876, held in Cincinnati—the first woman to speak at a major party political convention. She promoted women's service as nurses through work with the American Red Cross. With her husband, she cofounded and ran the Spencerian Business College in DC, a coeducational, desegregated business school.

Today, Spencer is less remembered than her cohorts Belva Lockwood, Mary Ann Shadd Cary, and Clara Barton; that was not true during her active life. Note that she is listed on the memorial as "consort" to her husband, although she was undoubtedly the more famous of the pair—and that her first name is misspelled on her grave marker.

→ **Continue on Tour Avenue. Just before the road makes a right turn, look to your right for a gravestone by a small tree. The text of the stone has worn badly and is only barely readable.**

10 EMANUEL GOTTLIEB LEUTZE MEMORIAL

Section D, Lot 53

Emanuel Leutze (1816–1868) is best known for his painting *Washington Crossing the Delaware (1851).* Born in Germany, Leutze was brought to the United States as a child in 1825. He was raised in Fredericksburg, Virginia, and Philadelphia, and he returned to Europe in 1840 to study art, traveling to Munich, Venice, Rome, and Düsseldorf, where he became president of the Düsseldorf

Artists' Association. He returned to the United States in 1859 and divided his time between New York City and Washington, DC, painting portraits of eminent men and elaborate patriotic scenes. In 1860, he was commissioned by the US Congress to paint *Westward the Course of Empire Takes Its Way* for the Capitol building (sometimes referred to as *Westward Ho!*). Leutze was a member of the Union League Club of New York and the National Academy of Design. His best works, now in the collections of the Metropolitan Museum of Art, the Museum of Fine Arts in Boston, and the National Gallery of Art, created iconic, romantic imagery that idealized American history.

→ **Continue on Tour Avenue, going downhill. You will see the backs of houses on North Capitol Street on your left. Look on your left for a fenced plot with a hanging sign.**

11 CONSTANTINO BRUMIDI GRAVE

Section Q, Lot 70

Constantino Brumidi (1805–1880) was born in Rome and studied at the Italian Academy of Arts. He emigrated to the United States in 1852, settling in New York City. He was granted citizenship in 1857 and worked on commission, painting altarpieces and murals in churches. In 1854, he put forth a proposal to decorate the interior of the new US Capitol with a series of murals and frescoes, and he was hired by Quartermaster General Montgomery C. Meigs. For the next twenty-five years, Brumidi dedicated his life to the project, creating *The Apotheosis of Washington* inside the great dome's rotunda, the allegorical *Frieze of American History,* and the Brumidi Corridors in the Senate Wing, among other great works. Brumidi was influenced by frescoes from ancient Rome and Pompeii; he worked in the Classical Revival style to create a distinctly American fusion. Although he died before his work could be completed, other artists carried out his designs, finally finishing the Capitol's murals in 1953.

Brumidi is buried in the same family plot as his son Lawrence. Lawrence was apprenticed to his father and helped him work on some of the Capitol frescoes, but his clinical depression became so debilitating that his mother later had him committed to St. Elizabeths Hospital, where he lived for the last four and a half years of his life, dying at age fifty-nine. Next to Lawrence is his mother, Lola Germon Clover Walsh Kirkwood—who, despite what her grave marker says, was never legally married to Constantino Brumidi. Brumidi considered Lola his muse. Their relationship began when she was still a child, perhaps fourteen years old, and he was fifty-six. They lived together briefly until the birth of her son Lawrence, and then again two more times, between her marriages (two of which ended in divorce, and the last one taking place after Brumidi's death). All three joined Lola's parents in the Germon family plot.

It should be noted that Lola served as the model for some of Brumidi's paintings and frescoes. Most famously, hers is the face of the allegorical figure of Freedom in *The Apotheosis of Washington,* wearing armor and brandishing a sword, standing next to an eagle with outstretched wings. She is prominently placed just underneath the depiction of George Washington and is the largest figure in the entire fresco.

When Brumidi was buried at Glenwood, Lola could not afford a grave marker, and his plot remained unmarked for seventy-two years. A capital tour guide and author, Myrtle Cheney Murdock (1885–1980), who was the wife of an Arizona congressman, raised the money to rescue him from obscurity and finally honor him at his gravesite. Among her other books, Murdock wrote *Constantino Brumidi, Michelangelo of the United States Capitol* (1950). For her efforts, Murdock was awarded the Order of the Star of Italian Solidarity from the Italian government. Brumidi was posthumously awarded the Congressional Gold Medal in 2008 by President George W. Bush.

→ **Continue on Tour Avenue as it turns to the right. Look for a black marble headstone inscribed with a stanza of poetry on your right.**

12 JOHN LUCKEY MCCREERY GRAVE

Section D-4, Lot 1

John McCreery (1835–1906) was born in rural New York State, the son of a poor Methodist minister. He had little formal schooling. At age seventeen, he was apprenticed to a printer in Illinois, and at age twenty-one, he became an editor of the *Dubuque Times* in Iowa. He moved to DC in 1878 to take a job as a clerk in the Department of the Interior and stayed for the remainder of his life.

McCreery published a single book of poems, *Songs of Toil and Triumph* (1883). His fame as an author rests on a single poem, "There Is No Death," which was written in the spring of 1863. The poem was reprinted in newspapers across the United States and set to music by several composers. It's not hard to imagine why this poem would become such a sentimental favorite during the carnage of the Civil War. His tombstone reprints the first stanza. The full poem is printed below.

There is no death! the stars go down
To rise upon some other shore,
And bright in Heaven's jeweled crown,
They shine forevermore.

There is no death! the dust we tread,
Shall change, beneath the summer showers,
To golden grain, or mellow fruit,
Or rainbow-tinted flowers.

The granite rocks disorganize
To feed the hungry moss they bear;
The forest leaves drink daily life
From out the viewless air.

There is no death! the leaves may fall,
The flowers may fade and pass away;
They only wait, through wintry hours,
The coming of the May.

There is no death! an angel form
Walks o'er the earth with silent tread;
He bears our best-loved things away,
And then we call them dead.

He leaves our hearts all desolate,
He plucks our fairest, sweetest flowers,
Transplanted into bliss, they now
Adorn immortal bowers.

The birdlike voice, whose joyous tones
Made glad the scene of sin and strife,
Sings now its everlasting song
Amid the trees of life.

Where'er he sees a smile too bright
Or soul too pure for taint or vice,
He bears it to that world of light
To dwell in Paradise.

Born into that undying life,
They leave us but to come again;
With joy we welcome them the same
Except in sin and pain.

And ever near us, though unseen,
The dear, immortal spirits tread—
For all the boundless universe
Is Life—there are no dead!

→ **Continue to the next intersection, marked with rows of mausolea. Turn right on Mulberry Avenue to see the next two sites.**

13 ALLEN FAMILY TOMB

This granite Classical Revival mausoleum was built around 1900. A rough-cut base supports two Ionic columns on either side of a circular arch. A look through the decorative bronze gate reveals two marble sculptures, a mosaic ceiling, and stained glass windows. The marble figure of a woman standing by the raised tomb is particularly graceful. The artist is unknown. Of the fifteen private mausolea at Glenwood, this is the most beautiful.

14 ROW OF BRICK MAUSOLEA

Five red brick mausolea were constructed in the mid- to late nineteenth century in the Romanesque Revival style. All are set into the hillside; they have similar facades with arched doors and a central bay that rises approximately two feet above the rest of the structure. Decorated with corbeled arches in the cornices, each has a blind arched niche on either side of a simple iron door. A survey of the five reveals small differences in the design of each, but they were likely built by the same builder and constructed simultaneously. They make a striking grouping along this quiet roadway.

→ **Retrace your steps to the intersection and turn right on Tour Avenue. At the first intersection, bear left, and at the second intersection, make a sharp left. You will come to a circle. Stay to the right, passing the circle and a small triangle of land just beyond the circle. Look to your right for the carved figure of a girl in a rocking chair.**

15 TERESINA VASCO MONUMENT

Section F, Lot 225

The Teresina Vasco Monument by DC-based sculptor Andrea Sichi portrays a two-year old girl in a rocking chair. This life-sized marble portrait of Teresina Vasco (1911–1913) was commissioned, as the marker indicates, by her "inconsolable parents." The figure wears a dress with a lace collar, and her curly hair is held back by bows. She is often accompanied by grave offerings of toys and teddy bears placed by modern visitors.

Andrea Sichi was born in Florence, Italy, and emigrated to Washington, DC, in 1900. He was a master stonecutter employed to create the gargoyles and other decorative features at the National Cathedral. Sichi was part of a lively Italian immigrant community in the city, where he likely met Teresina's parents. This is his only known commission of funerary art.

→ **Retrace your steps, staying to the left as you go around the circle and making your first left (still retracing your steps). At the intersection, go straight on Linden Avenue. At the next intersection, turn right on Central Avenue and look to your left at the first monument, an obelisk marked "Kennedy." On the other side of the obelisk, you will see the name "Bradley."**

16 PHINEAS BRADLEY MEMORIAL

Section M, Lot 48

The burial of Dr. Phineas Bradley (1769–1845) predates the creation of this cemetery. Bradley was born in Litchfield, Connecticut, and was a practicing physician before gaining federal employment. He moved to the District in 1801 to help supervise the transfer of the Post Office Department from Philadelphia to the new capital; he later was appointed second assistant postmaster general. Bradley purchased the land that would become Glenwood Cemetery and named it Clover Hill. He is buried alongside his wife, twice-widowed daughter, and two sons-in-law (the Reverend Levin I. Gilles and attorney John Clements Kennedy, whose names are more prominently displayed on the obelisk than his). Bradley held onto this land until 1839, after which time it went through a series of shorter-term owners before being chartered as a cemetery. This gravesite was the original family plot when this was still farmland.

→ **Continue on Central Avenue, heading back toward the Mortuary Chapel. (You will pass Cedar Avenue on your right.) As the road begins to bend, look to your left for the next two graves. One is a small raised obelisk, and the other is a marker flush with the ground.**

17 EDWIN MILTON HOOD AND GRETCHEN HOOD GRAVES

Section M, Lot 100

Edwin Milton Hood (1858–1923) was the chief of the Associated Press Washington Bureau, covering the White House and the Department of State, where he reported on diplomatic affairs. He covered a wide range of major news events, including the assassination of President Garfield, the Spanish-American War, the opening of the Panama Canal, and the World War I Peace Conference in Paris in 1919, which he attended while traveling with President Woodrow Wilson. Hood cofounded the National Press Club, which now offers an annual award for excellence in journalism named after him. He was friends with eight US presidents as well as scores of other prominent political figures, and he was known as

Washington's dean of newspaper correspondents for five decades.

Hood married and had one daughter, Gretchen Hood (1886–1978), who is buried next to him. Gretchen Hood was an opera singer who performed professionally in Paris, London, Brussels, and New York. After she returned to DC, she gave private voice lessons to students in her home.

A prominent socialite, Gretchen Hood was known for her exploits: dancing at a party with the future King Edward VIII, performing for Calvin Coolidge and First Lady Lou Hoover, playing piano accompaniment for Pearl Bailey on a radio show, drinking in public during Prohibition. She hosted parties in her home for Presidents William Howard Taft and Warren G. Harding as well as Secretary of State William Jennings Bryan.

Hood married as a young woman, but the union lasted only one month and ten days and was annulled (after which she reverted to her maiden name). She had romantic ties to a wide range of men, from composer Jerome Kern to Mayor Fiorello LaGuardia of New York and Winston Churchill, the British prime minister. Her most famous liaison was with the writer H. L. Mencken, with whom she corresponded and whom she dated for ten years. (Her selected correspondence with him was posthumously published in 1986; he wrote that she was "completely incomparable.") Hood's social life was widely covered by gossip columnists, and the home she shared with her father was filled with memorabilia, much of which she bequeathed to the National Press Club after his death.

→ **Behind the Hood graves, cut across the grass, crossing Cypress Avenue. Continue toward the fence line, looking for a cedar tree. The next grave is a large piece of marble flush with the ground near the base of the tree.**

18 CLARK MILLS GRAVE

Section O, Lot 132

Clark Mills (1815–1883) was a self-taught sculptor known for patriotic statues that are famous landmarks in Washington, DC. He created the giant bronze allegorical figure of Freedom that stands atop the dome of the US Capitol (working with designs initiated by another artist, Thomas Crawford) as well as the equestrian statue of George Washington that sits in the middle of Washington Circle. He also made a life cast of Abraham Lincoln's head in 1865 and 124 portrait busts, including a series of Native Americans. But his gravestone mentions only one sculpture: his equestrian statue of Andrew Jackson, the first equestrian statue designed by an American and cast in America.

Although he had never previously made a statue of a horse, Mills decided to make his Jackson statue on a horse reared back on only two legs, a particularly difficult engineering challenge. He depicts Jackson as a major in the War of 1812, reviewing troops at the Battle of New Orleans in 1815. (The War of 1812 did not officially end until Congress ratified a peace treaty in 1815.) Mills's statue of Jackson, now in a place of honor in the middle of Lafayette Square, facing the White House, was so popular that he won commissions for replicas in three other cities: Nashville, Tennessee; Jacksonville, Florida; and New Orleans. A total of six castings were made of the statue.

Mills operated his own foundry on Bladensburg Road in Maryland. He employed eleven enslaved men as artist's assistants, including the master craftsman Philip Reed (ca. 1820–1892), whose skills in bronze casting were instrumental to Mills's success. (See site 1 in the National Harmony Memorial Park tour on page 263 for Reed's grave.) Mills purchased Reed as a youth in Charleston, South Carolina, for $700. Reed worked for over twenty years while enslaved, first as an apprentice and then as the lead artisan in the bronze foundry. His training included engineering, plasterwork, and casting in bronze and steel. Reed was not recognized in his lifetime but is now credited for his work at the US Capitol Visitor Center. He was freed in the District of Columbia Compensated Emancipation Act of 1862 at approximately age forty-two. Mills received a payment of $350.40 to release Reed from bondage; Reed was one of 3,185 enslaved people who were emancipated by government decree prior to the Emancipation Proclamation. The District was the only place in the nation where this experiment with compensated emancipation took place—and the only time former owners were paid for the release of their human "property." After emancipation, Reed remained in DC.

Mills's foundry operated until 1903, long after his death. Today he is recognized as a better engineer than sculptor, someone who pioneered the use of plaster for life masks and developed bronze casting techniques that are still in use today.

→ **Continue to the farthest road (running alongside the Lincoln Road fence line), which is East Tour Road. Turn right and head back toward the entrance.**

19 BACK TO THE ENTRANCE GATE

Three notorious figures connected to very public murders were given unmarked graves at Glenwood—but only the bodies of two still remain. Frederic de Frouville murdered his estranged wife, Andrea Wolstrup de Frouville, in April 1883 before committing suicide. De Frouville was a federal employee who had been dismissed from posts in the Signal Corps and the Coastal Survey (the forerunner to the US Coast Guard) due to his alcoholism. His wife, originally from Denmark, worked as a translator for the US Post Office but resigned after becoming pregnant. When their only child died soon after birth, Andrea initiated divorce proceedings, stating that her husband was physically abusive and making threats on her life. The story of her tragic death was covered extensively in the *Washington Evening Star* newspaper. Her body was buried in Congressional Cemetery; Frederic, aged thirty-three, was laid in an unmarked grave somewhere on the grounds of Glenwood.

One of the Lincoln conspirators was also buried at Glenwood: George Atzerodt, who plotted with John Wilkes Booth to take down the elected government. Atzerodt's assignment was to kill Vice President Andrew Johnson at his home in April 1865 while Booth murdered President Abraham Lincoln at Ford's Theater. Atzerodt lost his nerve, but he was hanged as a traitor all the same. Later, family members had his body disinterred and moved to St. Paul's Cemetery in Baltimore, where they buried him under the pseudonym Gottlieb Taubert.

Another man associated with Lincoln's assassination is also interred in an unmarked grave on these grounds: John Frederick Parker, one of four DC police officers assigned to guard the president at Ford's Theater. Parker was not in the theater box when Lincoln was shot, and he was charged with neglect of duty. His case was later dismissed. Parker remained on the police force until 1868, when he was fired for another dereliction: sleeping while on duty. Police records show that this was a pattern of behavior: Parker had numerous infractions, including being drunk on duty, visiting houses of prostitution while on duty, using "intemperate language," and "conduct unbecoming an officer." After finally being fired, he worked as a carpenter until his death from pneumonia.

Another story of strange interest connected with Glenwood comes from Paul E. Sluby, the author of *Bury Me Deep* and one of the most respected historians of area cemeteries. (See site 4 in the National Harmony Memorial Park tour on page 271 for Sluby's grave.) In a conversation with an earlier superintendent, he found that the cemetery "perhaps is the site of the only vertical interments in the District. On June 30, 2001, six bodies were buried in a standing position because the prepaid area was too small for regular interments." When I tried to confirm this with the current cemetery superintendent, he seemed mystified. He had never heard the story.

Glenwood Cemetery was designed to be nonsectarian, unconnected to a specific religious or civic group. Several groups, however, have favored it for their members. Thus, there are sections of the grounds filled with Masons, members of the Presbyterian Home and the Methodist Home, and members of the Association for the Blind. There are also a number of burials of former DC policemen on these grounds and US representatives from several states, including Louisiana, New York, North Carolina, South Carolina, Virginia, and Washington (when it was still a territory, not yet a state).

Glenwood was originally only open to interments of white people. By 1950, that policy was changed, and burial plots were made available to people of all races and ethnicities. The cemetery has been in active use continuously since its founding in 1852 and contains over forty-eight thousand burials.

MOUNT OLIVET CEMETERY (1858)

1300 Bladensburg Road NE, Trinidad neighborhood, DC

Mount Olivet Cemetery was founded in 1858 by the Roman Catholic Archdiocese of Baltimore (which then covered the District of Columbia) when it purchased the forty-acre Fenwick Farm. The cemetery has since expanded to eighty-five acres, making it the largest Catholic burying ground in Washington. (It is now administered by the Archdiocese of Washington.) Although surrounded by heavily trafficked roads, the location alongside the National Arboretum gives this section of the city one of its largest swaths of open green space.

Notably, the property has been racially integrated since its founding. That was a rarity for a pre–Civil War cemetery—and makes it all the more ironic to see how many of the sites on this tour bring up issues of slavery and American race relations. The other major theme of this tour is how the experience of war brings out some of the best and worst aspects of human nature.

Mount Olivet also administers a smaller Catholic cemetery in DC, St. Mary's Cemetery on Lincoln Road NE (across the street from Glenwood Cemetery).

Before You Go

Administered by the Archdiocese of Washington
https://ccaw.org/mount-olivet-cemetery
Open daily 7:30 am to 5:00 pm
Nearest public transportation: NoMa–Gallaudet University Station to bus
No restrooms; parking available

James Hoban Monument (11)

1 MAIN GATE

A semicircular entry drive leads to a main gate facing Bladensburg Road, with stone piers topped with urns and a cast-iron fence. Just inside the gate on the left, a gray stone lodge holds administrative offices (where free maps of the cemetery are available). The property holds the remains of over one hundred thousand people, some moved from earlier cemeteries once surrounding Catholic churches in the center of the city. Because those

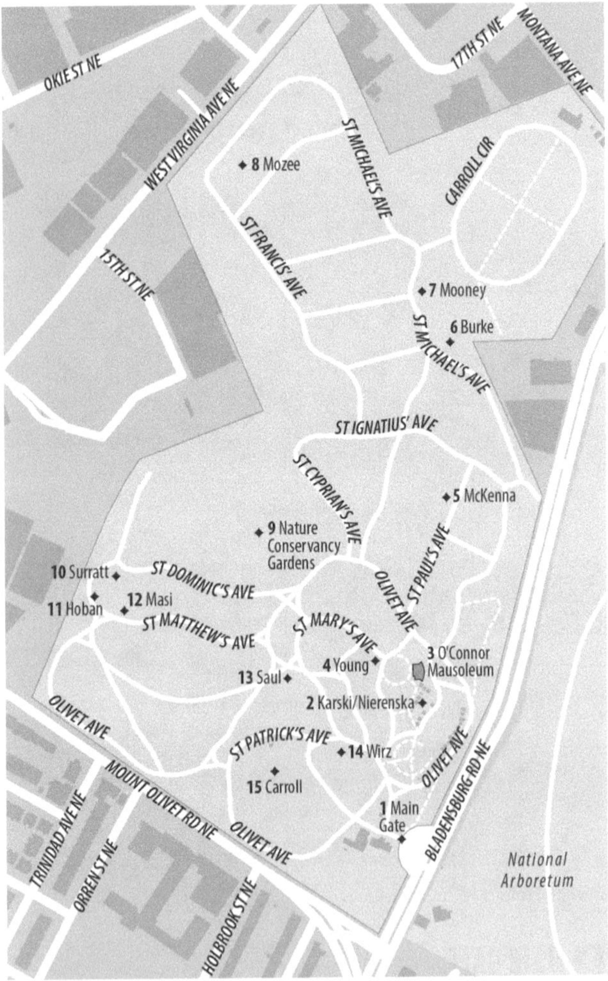

Mount Olivet Cemetery

church cemeteries were nearly full, and because of the 1852 ordinance that barred the creation of new cemeteries anywhere within the downtown area, a new "rural" cemetery further out was deemed necessary. Father Charles I. White, then the priest of St. Matthew's Roman Catholic Church, was the primary advocate for this new burial ground. It was named after the Mount of Olives in Jerusalem.

Mount Olivet's winding carriage roads (named for saints) and its changes of elevation, which afford expansive views across the city, make a stroll through the grounds quite scenic. Several sections are circular, an emblematic feature of rural cemeteries, which contrasts with uniform rows of gravestones. Other sections are shaped like uneven ovals, and the rows of the graves follow the orientation of each oval section rather than being lined up the same way over the whole property. This arrangement makes each section feel distinct and creates a pleasing visual variation.

→ **Take Olivet Avenue to the right of the entrance. Stay to the right of the flagpole, and you will see a circular section, numbered 38-A. Enter the footpath on your left, crossing the circle and continuing uphill. Cross the road into Section 40. Behind the first row of mausolea, cut across the grass and look for a simple modern grave marker on your right.**

2 JAN KARSKI AND POLA NIRENSKA-KARSKI GRAVE

Section 40

Jan Karski (1914–2000) was a resistance fighter in Nazi-occupied Poland during World War II. He began his career as a Polish diplomat and held posts in Romania, Germany, Switzerland, and Great Britain. At the start of World War II, he joined the Polish army and was captured, but he managed to escape from a German POW camp. His fluency in other languages, knowledge of geography, and remarkable memory were assets when he became a courier in the underground resistance movement. His firsthand reports on the mass transport of Jews to killing centers was a turning point in British and American intelligence.

Karski emigrated to the United States in 1952 to complete a PhD at Georgetown University and join the faculty there, teaching international affairs and comparative government for forty years. Karski was featured in the film *Shoah* (1985), a documentary on the history of the Holocaust, and in the short documentary *The Karski Report* (2010). He returned to Poland on a Fulbright Fellowship in 1974; in 1989 he was awarded the Order of the White Eagle, Poland's highest civilian decoration. Other honors include a Wallenberg Medal from the University of Michigan, a Presidential Medal of Freedom, and a memorial tree on the Avenue of the Righteous Among the Nations at Yad Vashem in Israel. Statues of Karski have been erected at Georgetown University, at Tel Aviv University, and in New York City, at the corner of Thirty-Seventh Street and Madison Avenue. He is the author of *The Great Powers and Poland, 1919–1945: From Versailles to Yalta* (1985) and *Story of a Secret State* (1944).

Pola Nirenska (1910–1992) was a modern dancer, choreographer, and dance teacher who began her career in Poland, escaped rising antisemitism in 1935, and spent fourteen years in England before migrating to the United States in 1949. Much of her choreography directly addressed the Holocaust and her flight from Nazism. She was the only member of her family to escape murder by Nazis. Nirenska performed at Jacob's Pillow Dance Festival, the Boston Conservatory, the Kennedy Center, and Carnegie Hall, among other places, and after 1952, she taught at DC-area private schools and formed the Washington Dance Company. Until her suicide, she was considered a major force in the District arts community and the grand matriarch of DC's modern dance. Nirenska and Karski were married from 1965 to 1992.

→ **Continue across the grass to the road, and then take a right on St. Teresa's Avenue and look at the first mausoleum on your right.**

3 JOHN J. O'CONNOR MAUSOLEUM

Section 40, Mausoleum Site 7

John Joseph O'Connor (1904–1978), buried inside this site with other members of his family, was a sociologist and historian specializing in American social justice and race relations. Born in the District, he spent his teaching career at Georgetown University, with the exception of seven years at St. John's University and two years serving in the US Army in World War II. O'Connor founded the Catholic Interracial Council of Washington. Among his honors, he was awarded the James Hoey Award from the Catholic Interracial Council of New York, the Edith Stein Award and the Brotherhood Award, both from the National Conference of Christians and Jews, and the President's Medal from Georgetown University. O'Connor was the author or coauthor of *Twenty-Five in Ireland* (1932), *Catholic Revival in England* (1942), and the textbooks *Sociology* (1940) and *Social Order* (1941).

→ **Turn to your right and walk north on Olivet Avenue, past the modern columbarium. Take your first left, then turn again at the first left onto St. Mary's Avenue, passing the small circular section marked 39. In Section 32, look for the next site, a simple white obelisk with a wreath carved on one side.**

4 GEORGE WASHINGTON YOUNG MONUMENT

Section 32

George Washington Young (1796–1867) came from one of the largest landholding families in Washington and was one of the wealthiest men in the city prior to the Civil War. His primary plantation, Giesboro Manor (sometimes spelled Giesborough), comprised 624 acres of land along the confluence of the Potomac and Anacostia Rivers, now the location of the US Navy and Air Force's Joint Base Anacostia-Bolling. Young also owned Nonesuch Plantation, a property of 150 acres along Oxon Run, now the site of the Hillcrest neighborhood (a part of which, located just over the DC line in Suitland, Maryland, is operated as Cedar Hill Cemetery).

Young's primary crop at both plantations was tobacco, a labor-intensive product that was managed through the forced toil of ninety-one individuals, according to the 1850 Slave Schedule of the census—giving Young the shameful distinction of being Washington's largest slaveowner. Although other crops were grown for the use of Young's family, tobacco was exported to European markets and was the basis of his massive wealth. He also harvested trees and sold the wood from land he owned that is now part of St. Elizabeths Hospital.

Young rented part of his property along the Potomac River to the Union Army during the Civil War for use as a cavalry depot headquarters (holding up to thirty thousand horses at a time) and a garrison called Fort Carroll. In 1862, when the federal government enacted the Compensated Emancipation Act in DC, Young was the largest beneficiary. He received a total of $17,771.85 for the mandatory release of the remaining sixty-nine men, women, and children whom he had held in bondage, ranging in age from three months to two men aged seventy. (Ironically, his petition for compensation provides the best written documentation we have of many formerly enslaved families, as he was required to provide full names, ages, family relationships, and other identifying information about each person for whom he requested compensation.) Young lived until 1867 and left his extensive landholdings to his heirs, who slowly sold off the properties.

→ **Backtrack along St. Mary's Avenue to where it deadends. Turn left on Olivet Avenue, then take your first right onto St. Paul's Avenue. Cross St. Cecilia's Avenue, continuing on St. Paul's, then look to your left. In**

the sixth row of Section 50, look for a large upright grave marker with carved oak leaves and ivy vines surrounding a round cartouche. The name "McKENNA" can be seen prominently carved on the stone's raised base.

5 JOSEPH MCKENNA GRAVE

Section 50

Justice Joseph McKenna (1843–1926) served in all three branches of the US government. He was admitted to the bar in California, served four terms in the House of Representatives, and then was appointed to the Ninth Circuit Court of Appeals by President Benjamin Harrison and as attorney general by President William McKinley. He is best remembered as a conservative US Supreme Court justice; in that role, he served from 1898 until 1925, when he retired after suffering a stroke. Among his most notorious rulings was *Williams v. Mississippi,* which upheld voting restrictions that disenfranchised nearly every African American in the state of Mississippi through poll taxes and literacy tests.

→ **Continue on St. Paul's Avenue until it ends. Cut directly across the grass to the next road and turn left on St. Michael's Avenue. Follow the fence line. Just before the next intersection, look for a modern, reddish stone on your right in Section 53.**

6 MAJOR JOHN M. BURKE GRAVE

Section 53

John Burke (1842–1917) was the publicist and press agent for Buffalo Bill Cody's Wild West Show from 1883 through 1917. The company was founded in New Jersey, and Burke was its first employee (initially with the title

General Manager). He was among the first to make use of such publicity techniques as celebrity endorsements, product placements, billboards, and newspaper op-eds (under false names), which contributed to the success of the show—and built the field of publicity. His advertisement campaigns included printed programs, handbills, and advertising booklets; he arranged photo opportunities and planted copy with local newspapers along the tour routes, racking up extravagant expense accounts. Burke also served as a location scout and talent scout for the show.

Born in New York City, Burke was orphaned as an infant and raised by relatives in Maryland and Delaware. He is the author of the biography *Buffalo Bill from Prairie to Palace* (1893), which was released to drum up ticket sales when the Wild West Show was scheduled to play Chicago at the same time as the 1893 World's Fair. Friends described his preference for fine cigars and his capacity for imbibing large amounts of alcohol. Despite being called a "major," he never served in the military. Likewise, despite his nickname of "Arizona John," he had no association with that state. When he died in Washington, DC, in 1917, he was buried in an unmarked grave at Mount Olivet Cemetery. This marker was erected in 2017, a hundred years after his death, by a modern admirer.

→ **Continue on St. Michael's Avenue. At the turn in the road, just before it intersects with St. Bernard's Avenue, look to your right, still in Section 53, for the next grave. It has a stylized flower and vine pattern at the top, just above an engraved cross.**

7 JAMES MOONEY GRAVE

Section 53

James Mooney (1861–1921) was an ethnographer who conducted studies of Southeastern Native American tribes as well as some tribes of the Great Plains. He lived for several years among the Cherokee. After the death of Hunkpapa Lakota leader Sitting Bull, Mooney documented the rise of the Ghost Dance, a spiritual movement that prophesied the removal of white people from Native lands. Mooney's books *The Sacred Formula of the Cherokees* (1891), *The Ghost-Dance Religion and the Sioux Outbreak of 1890* (1896), *Calendar History of the Kiowa Indians* (1898), *Myths of the Cherokee* (1900), and *Indian Missions North of Mexico* (1907) were all published by the Smithsonian Institution.

Mooney began working for the Smithsonian in 1885 and compiled a list of over three thousand Native American tribes. Artifacts that he collected during his fieldwork are now held at the Smithsonian Institution in Washington, DC, and the Field Museum of Natural History in Chicago.

→ **Continue on St. Michael's Avenue. The road will bear left, then take the first right (still on St. Michael's Avenue). Continue on this road all the way to the end, where it bears to the left, following the edge of the property as it parallels the fence line and West Virginia Avenue. Look to your left, in the middle of Section 62, for a metal grave marker flush with the ground. You will find it in the sixth row in, near other markers also flush with the ground.**

8 LOUISA HARRIET MOZEE GRAVE

Section 62

Born Louisa Harriet Marshall in London, the performer known as Sadie Johnson or Sadie Crawford (1885–1965) was a singer and dancer of the early Jazz Age. She began her career as a teenager and almost immediately began passing as mixed-race, or creole, although she was white. She performed in a touring review with the degrading name *A Trip to Coontown* that traveled throughout the major cities of Europe. She subsequently worked in vaudeville music halls in Europe, taking advantage of the newest "jazz craze" to perform in Russia, Scandinavia, Berlin, Paris, Australia, and Brazil. She made her only known recordings with Pathé Records in 1923 as part of Gordon Stretton's Orchestra Syncopated Six. She moved to the United States in 1929 to join a review called *Blackbirds*.

Mozee married twice, both times to American men of African descent. Her public persona as a person of color made these marriages socially acceptable. Her first husband was a saxophonist, Adolph Crawford, with whom she toured Europe. They were married for eleven years, until Crawford's death in Paris in 1929. Her second marriage was to Frank Mozee, a chauffeur who was sixteen years younger. After they wed in 1930, Mozee ended her stage career (at age forty-four) to settle in Washington for the last thirty-five years of her life. She is remembered in London with a historic plaque on her childhood home, naming her a "jazz pioneer," and a music scholarship in her name at a London high school.

→ **Continue uphill on the road, which has now changed its name to St. Francis' Avenue, heading back south toward the entrance. At the third intersection, enter the grass and follow the tiered garden up the hill.**

9 NATURE CONSERVANCY GARDENS

The cemetery began a partnership with the Nature Conservancy in 2018 to build bio-retention areas and replace some of the original carriage roads on the property with grassy swales and flower beds. The project helps mitigate problems with water runoff on permeable surfaces, which lessens pollution in groundwater and helps control the cemetery's large water bills. The largest section replaces most of St. Cyprian's Avenue with a tiered garden designed by landscape architect Gwen Wolfgang. This garden commemorates enslaved men and women buried on the property in unmarked graves. In honor of their memory, Wolfgang makes ample use of yucca plants—one of the plants traditionally used by enslaved communities as grave markers.

→ **Continue up the hill, following the gardens and taking in the views of surrounding neighborhoods as you get high in elevation. Turn right on St. Jerome's Avenue, and at the next three-way intersection, stay to the right to turn onto St. Dominic's Avenue, looking to your left at Section 12. At the far end of this section, just before the road turns left to follow the fence line, look for a simple modern headstone with a rounded top on your left.**

10 MARY JENKINS SURRATT GRAVE

Section 12

Mary Elizabeth Jenkins Surratt (1823–1865) was the owner of the boardinghouse where the plot to assassinate President Abraham Lincoln was developed. Although she maintained her innocence until her death by hanging in 1865, her boardinghouse was known for hosting Confederate sympathizers, and the conspirators John Wilkes Booth, George Atzerodt, and Lewis Powell were regular visitors. Booth had arranged to stop by the boardinghouse on his escape from DC to pick up rifles and binoculars she was holding for him, creating a strong circumstantial case against her. Her son John, a Confederate spy and another member of the Lincoln conspiracy group, was the only one to escape conviction: he fled to Canada, and from there to Europe. By the time he was arrested and extradited from Egypt, the statute of limitations had expired on most of the charges, and he was never tried. His mother was not so lucky. Although she pleaded for clemency from President Andrew Johnson because of her age and her sex, she was the first woman to be executed by the US government.

Surratt was initially buried in the prison yard of the Washington Arsenal (now the site of Fort McNair). In February 1869, President Johnson agreed to release her remains to her family, and she was disinterred and buried at Mount Olivet. An earlier headstone was badly defaced; it was replaced by a second granite stone, proclaiming that she was swept "from obscurity to the limelight of a military trial and inglorious death on a scaffold" and that her "guilt in the conspiracy is still questioned." That stone was also removed (and is now on display at the Surratt House and Tavern Museum in Clinton, Maryland). This small marble stone, marked simply "Mrs. Surratt," is the third in this spot. Two of her children are buried next to her in unmarked graves.

→ **Continue on St. Dominic's Avenue. At the far end, where the road begins to loop back, look for a large brownstone monument topped with a stone cross and decorated with several classical elements. A modern plaque is placed in front of the monument.**

11 JAMES HOBAN MONUMENT

Section 12

James Hoban (1755–1831) was born in Kilkenny, Ireland, and was apprenticed as a boy to learn the crafts of wheelwright and carpenter. Although of modest means (his father was probably a tenant farmer), Hoban showed enough skill to win a scholarship to the Dublin Society School of Architectural Drawing. He emigrated to the United States after the Revolutionary War, settling in Philadelphia in 1785 and later moving to Charleston, South Carolina, to open a private architectural practice.

Hoban is best remembered as the architect who provided the winning design for the White House. He moved to DC to oversee construction, which took place over an eight-year period. After the White House was damaged by fire during the War of 1812, Hoban was hired again to restore the residence over a three-year period. Hoban was also a supervising architect for several other notable buildings in DC: the US Capitol, the Octagon House, the Treasury Building, and several roads and bridges. He was appointed superintendent of all of Washington's public works projects.

Hoban was a prominent civic leader in Washington's early growth: he was one of twelve members of the city council from 1802 (when DC was granted limited home rule) for most of the rest of his life. He was captain of a local militia company. Hoban was also a leader in the Roman Catholic community, involved in the development of several Catholic institutions in the city, including Georgetown University, St. Patrick's Parish, and Georgetown Visitation Monastery, and in a social service organization called the Sons of Erin, which provided housing, food, and medical attention to needy Irish immigrants.

Although in favor of the abolition of slavery, Hoban was himself a slave owner. Three of the enslaved men he owned worked as carpenters who built the White House. Records only provide their first names: Ben, Daniel, and Peter.

→ **Continue on the roadway as it wraps around Section 12, where it changes its name to St. Matthew's Avenue. Look to your left for a tall, tapering grave monument topped with a carved stone urn.**

12 SERAPHIM MASI MONUMENT

Section 12

Seraphim Masi (1797–1884) was born in Frascati, Italy, and moved to the United States, earning his citizenship by serving in the War of 1812. He worked in Washington, DC, as a silversmith, jeweler, and watchmaker from 1822 until his retirement in 1870. He owned a shop on Pennsylvania Avenue that sold silver, spectacles, jewelry, and (according to a listing in the *Washington Directory*) "a variety of other fancy goods." Some of his coffee and tea services, chalices and baptismal bowls, and other ceremonial pieces are in the collections of the National Archives, the DAR Museum, the Metropolitan Museum of Art, Winterthur Museum, the Department of State, and the National Park Service. Masi is best remembered as the designer of the second Treaty Seal of the United States. Created in 1825, it was used for making pendant seals in red wax on all official treaties issued by the government until 1871, when the federal government discontinued the use of wax seals. Masi was also the official horologist for the US Senate, regulating and maintaining all the Senate's clocks for nearly fifty years.

→ **Bear right at the next intersection, and at the second three-way intersection, look to your right in Section 19 for a large rough-hewn gravestone topped with a rusticated stone cross.**

13 JOHN HENNESSY SAUL MONUMENT

Section 19

John Hennessy Saul (1819–1897) was born in Cork, Ireland, the son of a country estate gardener. He emigrated to the United States in 1851 to take a landscaping job with Andrew Jackson Downing, improving the grounds of the National Mall, Lafayette Square, and the Smithsonian Museum. When the Washington Parks Commission was founded in 1854, Saul was named the first chairman. Among his accomplishments in this position was his extensive enhancement of the city's tree canopy, and he remained on the board until his death at age seventy-seven.

Saul ran a successful nursery and seed business, eventually operating twenty greenhouses and gardens on eighty acres and creating numerous new cultivars of plants and trees through hybridization and grafting. Several of his varieties are named for his wife and won national horticultural awards. He supplied customers nationwide; one regular client was Frederick Law Olmsted, the designer of Central Park and Prospect Park in New York and the US Capitol grounds in DC. Saul was a regular contributor to the national journal the *Horticulturalist.*

→ **Continue on St. Matthew's Avenue, past another complex intersection, bearing to the right. Where the road dead-ends, you will see Section 27 in front of you. Enter this section and look just past a magnolia tree for a small Maltese cross of black metal near the ground.**

14 CAPTAIN HENRY WIRZ GRAVE

Section 27

The grave of Captain Henry Wirz is marked by a Confederate States of America metal cross and plaque claiming him as a "Confederate Hero-Martyr." Born in Switzerland as Hartmann Heinrich Wirz (1823–1865), he worked as a translator and homeopathic physician before the outbreak of the Civil War. He was a slave overseer on a plantation in Louisiana at the time of his enlistment. Wirz then was assigned as commandant of Camp Sumter near Andersonville, Georgia, a notorious prisoner-of-war camp where nearly thirteen thousand Union soldiers died of disease, starvation, and exposure.

The Andersonville facility was originally planned as a temporary prison, with wooden barracks. The barracks were never constructed, however, and men were held prisoner in a large open-air stockade. The camp was infamous for severe overcrowding, unsanitary conditions, infectious diseases, lack of potable water, and lack of medical supplies and food. At its height in August 1864, thirty-two thousand prisoners were held on 16.5 acres.

Wirz ran the camp for fourteen months, during which approximately 28 percent of the Union soldiers held there died. After the end of the Civil War, he was convicted by a military court of conspiracy and murder, with ten counts of personal cruelty. He claimed in court that he was simply following orders, but nearly 150 guards, former prisoners, and medical staff testified that he withheld supplies, punished prisoners for minor transgressions, and issued orders that directly resulted in the deaths of soldiers. He was hanged—and is one of the few men tried, convicted, and executed for war crimes during the Civil War. Despite the overwhelming evidence of his war crimes, Wirz remained a polarizing figure, celebrated by some as a Lost Cause martyr (as can be seen with the plaque here at his gravesite). A large monument celebrating the memory of Wirz was erected in the town of Andersonville in 1909. But the law stipulated that all prisoners of war must be given access to the same supplies available to troops in the field—and Wirz's violations of that law are clear. After his hanging, President Andrew Johnson ordered a halt to all further military tribunals.

→ **Take St. James' Avenue as it bends to the left. On your right, enter Section 18. Across the grass, look for a small, flat gravestone with the name "Carroll" on the side and "Little Nelly" engraved on top. This small stone is hard to see, but look for the two adjacent stone crosses, one of which has a broken top (so it looks more like a T); the Carroll stone will be to the left of the crosses.**

15 DANIEL CARROLL OF DUDDINGTON GRAVE

Section 18

Daniel Carroll (1764–1849) was one of the major landowners in Washington, DC, when the city was formed: he owned all of what is now Capitol Hill. When he began construction of a grand new mansion in 1791, he placed it on land that Pierre Charles L'Enfant had mapped as a roadway—the future New Jersey Avenue SE—and L'Enfant retaliated by having the house razed in the middle of the night. Carroll, who belonged to a socially prominent family (his first cousin was a signer of the Declaration of Independence), complained directly to President George Washington. As a result, Carroll was awarded $4,000 in compensation and L'Enfant was fired. (Carroll did, however, move his house foundations when rebuilding to accommodate the road as originally mapped.)

Carroll was one of sixteen landowners who sold over five thousand acres to the federal government to create the city. He sold more land, in fact, than any of the other proprietors: approximately 1,400 acres. He served as the president of the first bank in Washington and owned a brickmaking business. In 1800, Carroll enslaved twenty-five people, who raised crops on his properties, built houses for his real estate business, and labored in his brick factory. He donated the land for St. Peter's Church, which still stands on Second Street SE. He married and was widowed twice and had eight children. In his later years, he became a recluse, rarely leaving his (rebuilt) mansion.

→ **Continue on Olivet Avenue back to the main gate.**

16 A FINAL UNMARKED GRAVE

No one knows for sure how many bodies interred at Mount Olivet are in unmarked graves. I will end with the story of one of them. Josephina Guerrero (1917–1996) was born in the Philippines in Quezon Province. Orphaned at an early age, she was raised by the Sisters of the Good Shepherd and survived childhood tuberculosis. In 1941, she was diagnosed with Hansen's disease, also known as leprosy; her husband subsequently abandoned her and permanently separated Guerrero from her two-year-old daughter as well.

When Japanese troops invaded the Philippines in 1942, Guerrero lost access to medications to treat her condition. Fearing that she would die, she was determined not to die in vain, and she tracked down members of the resistance movement in order to volunteer as a spy. Because of her worsening skin lesions, Japanese soldiers avoided searching her as she traveled, and she was able to transmit secret messages, supplies, and weapons by hiding items in her hair and clothes. She mapped out Japanese gun emplacements and minefields and reported them to American allies. In the Battle of Manila, Guerrero heroically treated wounded civilians and soldiers in the midst of active gunfire.

After the end of World War II, Guerrero sought treatment, first at Tala Leprosarium in the Philippines and later at Carville National Leprosarium in Louisiana. Because her case was so advanced, it took nine years of treatment at Carville to cure her. She was finally discharged in 1957.

Guerrero was awarded the Medal of Freedom by the US government in 1948. She was granted US citizenship in 1967 and spent the last thirty years of her life in Washington, DC.

US SOLDIERS' AND AIRMEN'S HOME NATIONAL CEMETERY (1861)

21 Harewood Road NW, Petworth neighborhood, DC

This site invites visitors to think more deeply about the two wars in which Americans fought, captured, tortured, and killed other Americans: the Civil War and the Indian Wars. These conflicts still reverberate in our nation's race relations.

At just under sixteen acres, this cemetery is roughly triangular in shape, tucked between North Capital Street, Rock Creek Church Road, and Harewood Road NW, a one-way side street. The nation's first military cemetery, it predates Arlington National by thirteen years. The first interment here took place in August 1861, during the Civil War. The National Cemetery System, which determines norms for military burials, was formally established in 1862.

The cemetery, one of 115 national cemeteries across the United States, is still in active use. Currently, approximately fourteen thousand veterans are buried here. Under the National Cemeteries Act of 1973, the US Congress transferred the jurisdiction of eighty-two out of a total of eighty-four national cemeteries to the Veterans Administration. Only Arlington National Cemetery and the US Soldiers' and Airmen's Home National Cemetery (sometimes referred to as the Old Soldiers' Home Cemetery or the Armed Forces Retirement Home Military Cemetery) remain under the auspices of the US Army.

Among the national military cemeteries, this small plot has always been a "special case."

The Main Entry Gate is permanently closed. Entry

is now through the Lodge Gate, a double iron gate with stone piers located on Harewood Road. A 24-pounder flank howitzer, forged in 1844, faces the Lodge Gate; the cannon sits atop a concrete plinth placed in a flower bed. To the right of the gate is the Lodge, with a first floor of red sandstone blocks and a wood-frame second floor, built to house a gatekeeper and his family.

Before You Go

Administered by Arlington National Cemetery
https://www.arlingtoncemetery.mil/Explore/Soldiers-and-Airmens-Home-National-Cemetery
Open daily from 8:00 am to 5:00 pm
Nearest public transportation: Georgia Avenue–Petworth Station to bus
Parking available; no restrooms

1 SECTION A: CIVIL WAR SOLDIERS

A walkway between the Lodge and its attendant garage takes visitors to the oldest section of the cemetery, where the stark white stones of Civil War dead are lined up in precise rows under the shelter of mature trees. Each tombstone is numbered, with the name and home state of each soldier listed underneath. Only a few give the additional details of rank and date of death. Note that some stones are being slowly swallowed by tree roots. A few families opted to pay the additional cost for larger gravestones, but most stuck with the standard-issue stones that create long sight lines following the dips and gentle slope of the topography. In 1873, the secretary of war formalized features of all stones in military cemeteries, based in part on practices that were already in place in the US Soldiers' and Airmen's Home National Cemetery. He designated cambered rectangular headstones in marble as the norm, laid out in a geometric pattern to recall the way tents were lined up in military camps.

Section A: Civil War Soldiers (1)

Although traffic on North Capital Street can be heavy at certain times of the day, this small plot of land still exudes calm. I've even seen deer feeding in the early morning under the maple, holly, and white oak trees. The landscaping and design features follow the suggestions made by noted landscape architect Frederick Law Olmsted, who advised Quartermaster General Montgomery C. Meigs on the design of military cemeteries in 1870. Olmsted wrote of the importance of creating "a *sacred* grove, sacredness and protection being expressed in the enclosing wall and in the perfect tranquility of the trees within."

The original cemetery was a mere six acres, and following the Battle of Bull Run, it quickly reached capacity at 8,000 burials. By 1864, the army sought other locations to bury Civil War soldiers and opened Arlington National Cemetery. (Since some soldiers were reinterred elsewhere, it is estimated that the number of Civil War veterans in these grounds today number about 5,200.) The US Soldiers' and Airmen's Home National Cemetery was expanded to sixteen acres in 1883 and began accepting burials once again. In the late nineteenth century, the cemetery was reorganized to create a more consistent alphanumeric grave system. Most of the gravestones seen today bear only a sketchy relation to the site of underground remains.

→ **Retrace your steps back to the main gate, then look for the series of gravestones along the fence line that runs parallel to Harewood Road. (Don't worry about looking at the big mausoleum on the other side of the paved path yet! We will come back to it.)**

2 SECTION O

In a raised sarcophagus grave, look first for Brevet Brigadier General Samuel Beckley Holabird (1826–1907). Holabird trained at West Point and was assigned to frontier duty in Texas for nearly a decade, serving as a scout and regimental quartermaster. During the Civil War, he participated in battles in Maryland and Virginia, including the Battle of Antietam, before being posted to New Orleans as chief quartermaster of the Department of the Gulf. In the Indian Wars, he served tours of duty in the Dakota Territories, Texas, Missouri, and California. From 1883 to 1890, Holabird was quartermaster general of the US Army. He retired in 1890 after forty years in the military.

Just past the Holabird grave, look for a small stone

flush with the ground with the name of Agnes von Kurowsky Stanfield (1892–1984). A World War I nurse with the American Red Cross, Kurowsky is the basis for the character of Catherine Barkley in Ernest Hemingway's semi-autobiographical novel *A Farewell to Arms.* She trained as a librarian and worked for the DC Central Library before attending Bellevue Nurses Training Program in New York. Kurowsky took postings in Milan, Italy (where she tended to Hemingway, then a wounded nineteen-year-old ambulance driver), as well as Romania and Haiti. Kurowsky married twice after refusing to marry Hemingway. Hemingway described Catherine Barkley as a "quite tall" blonde with "tawny skin and gray eyes. I thought she was very beautiful." Later, when the narrator in his novel removes Barkley's hairpins, he describes it as being "inside a tent or behind a falls"—although Barkley shows her independence by telling him she plans to cut her hair short. Throughout the book, her character is praised for bravery and idealism. *A Farewell to Arms* was Hemingway's first best-selling novel.

Seek out the tall grave marker topped by an angel grasping an anchor. This sentimental statue marks the remains of Brevet Major General Benjamin William Brice (1809–1892). Brice trained at West Point and was serving in the Paymaster Department of the US Army when the Civil War broke out. He served as paymaster general from 1864 to 1872, rising through the ranks from colonel to brigadier general to major general.

Further along the row, there are two larger stones bearing the name Henry Hunt. The one to the right marks the grave of Brevet Major General Henry Jackson Hunt (1819–1889). Hunt served as chief of artillery for the Army of the Potomac in the Civil War; considered a great tactician and strategist, his artillery tactics influenced the outcome of some of the most significant battles of the Civil War, including Antietam, Fredericksburg, and Gettysburg. Hunt was trained at West Point and served in the Mexican-American War, where he cowrote a manual, *Instructions for Field Artillery.* After the Civil War, he held various commands until his retirement from the army in 1883. He served as governor of the US Soldiers' and Airmen's Home National Cemetery from 1883 to 1889. Fort Hunt Park in Fairfax County, Virginia, is named in his honor.

Another large stone bears a bas-relief cross for Brigadier General John C. Kelton (1828–1893). Kelton trained at West Point; during the Civil War he served as assistant adjutant general of the Department of the West and the Department of Mississippi, and he saw battle during the Siege of Corinth. After the war's end, he was posted to the Division of the Pacific and the Adjutant General's Department in Washington, DC. He was then appointed governor of the Armed Forces Retirement Home, where he remained until his death. His gravestone is notable for its testament to him as "The Soldier's Friend." Note the brass sword encircled by a wreath that lies at the stone's base.

To the right, a group of stones marks the graves of the Stanley family. General David Sloane Stanley (1828–1902) was awarded the Medal of Honor during the Civil War for action at Franklin, Tennessee. His citation reads, "At a critical moment rode to the front of one of his brigades, reestablished its lines, and gallantly led it in a successful assault."

Just beyond the group of larger graves, you'll find rows of smaller identical white tombstones. Seek out the one for Sergeant Louis Gedeon (1878–1950). Gedeon served in the infantry in the Philippines. He was awarded a Medal of Honor for single-handedly defending "his mortally wounded captain from an overwhelming force of the enemy."

Despite this cemetery's modest size, it is the final resting place of a remarkable number of Medal of Honor recipients. Twenty-one soldiers in this cemetery hold the nation's highest military decoration. For those who want to seek out more Medal of Honor awardees, a full list is appended to the end of this tour.

→ **At the corner of Rock Creek Church Road and Harewood Road, you will see the main gate.**

3 MAIN GATE

Although always kept locked, this gate impresses with its high arch supported by eight Doric columns. Each column is inscribed with the name of an American general from the Revolutionary War through the Civil War. Facing outward toward the intersection of Rock Creek Church Road and Harewood Road are the names Grant, Jackson, Washington, and Scott. From the inside of the cemetery, you can see the names Taylor, Greene, Brown, and Meade.

The main gate was constructed in 1883, when the cemetery expanded from six acres to sixteen. Materials used in the creation of the main gate were salvaged by Quartermaster General Montgomery C. Meigs from the US Patent Office Building after it burned in 1879.

→ **Retrace your steps back to the large mausoleum across from the Lodge Gate.**

4 LOGAN MAUSOLEUM

As you come back toward the gate, you'll find the major attraction of this cemetery on your left: the impressive mausoleum of General John A. Logan (1826–1886). The mausoleum was designed by Alfred Mullett (1834–1890), the former supervising architect of the US Treasury. Made of granite in the Anglo-Norman style, the mausoleum has stained glass windows and holds the remains of Logan and his wife, daughter, and two grandsons.

Mullett is best known as the designer of the Eisenhower Executive Office Building (formerly called the State, War, and Navy Building) located next to the White House, the finest example of French Second Empire–style architecture in the country.

The best time to visit this cemetery is the morning of Memorial Day, when the Logan tomb is opened to the public. An honor guard is sent from Arlington National Cemetery, and an official reads aloud Logan's "Memorial Day Order" of May 5, 1868, made when Logan was commander-in-chief of the Grand Army of the Republic (GAR). As the annual ceremony always draws residents of the Armed Forces Retirement Home and their families, this gives visitors a tangible link between the past and the present.

The "Memorial Day Order" is reprinted on a plaque in front of the mausoleum. Originally called Decoration Day, the federal holiday honors military personnel who died while serving. Logan's original order reads, in part, that the day is intended "for the purpose of strewing with flowers or otherwise decorating the graves of comrades who died in defense of their country during the late rebellion, and whose bodies now lie in almost every city, village, and hamlet churchyard in the land."

Although the custom of decorating graves long predates Logan's Order Number 11, the GAR proclamation made the holiday date an official, nationwide, annual ceremony. Many cities had held earlier commemorations. One of the earliest and most significant was organized by a group of formerly enslaved people at the Washington Race Track in Charleston, South Carolina, less than a month after the end of the war in 1865. After exhuming a mass grave to reinter Union soldiers in a new formal cemetery, these freed laborers organized a parade that drew a crowd of ten thousand to hear speeches and songs in their honor. This is generally considered by historians to be the first collective celebration of what was then called Decoration Day—and Logan used it as a model.

In response to Logan's Memorial Day Order, observances on May 30, 1868, were conducted in twenty-seven states and the District of Columbia at a total of 183 cemeteries. Thousands of Americans attended. Memorial Day celebrations helped Americans change how they thought about their beloved dead. Because the losses in the Civil War were so great—it was by far the most devastating military conflict in American history—the holiday helped transform the act of mourning from something intensely personal to a shared, national ritual.

Logan, nicknamed "Black Jack" by his troops for his dark eyes and hair, began his military career in the Mexican-American War but is best known as a general in the Union Army in the Civil War, where he rose through the ranks to become commander of the Army of the Tennessee. Logan trained as a lawyer, and after the war he was elected to the House of Representatives (1867–1871) and the Senate (1871–1877 and 1879–1886). From 1868 to 1871, he also served as commander-in-chief of the Grand Army of the Republic. He wrote two books about the Civil War: *The Great Conspiracy: Its Origin and History* (1886) and *The Volunteer Soldier of America* (1887).

Logan is well celebrated in DC. In addition to this mausoleum, a traffic circle at the confluence of Rhode Island Avenue, Vermont Avenue, P Street, and Thirteenth Street NW is named for him. The park inside the circle, 1.8 acres in size and planted with oak trees, centers on an equestrian bronze statue of Logan, sculpted by Franklin Simmons, on a bronze and granite base. The base is decorated with two bas-reliefs depicting moments in Logan's life and was sculpted by Richard Morris Hunt.

5 BACK TO THE LODGE GATE

Daily at 11:45, the bell tower at the Armed Forces Retirement Home plays five recorded songs, the themes for each of five branches of the military. (Although the Space

Force has had an official theme song since 2022, that has not yet been added to the repertoire.) "The U.S. Air Force" (also known as "Wild Blue Yonder") is played first, followed by the "Marines' Hymn" ("From the Halls of Montezuma, to the shores of Tripoli"), "Anchors Aweigh" for the navy, "The Army Goes Rolling Along" for the army, and "Semper Paratus" for the coast guard. If you can time your visit for the mid-morning, it is pleasant to wander the grounds while listening to the bells.

A tour of the US Soldiers' and Airmen's Home National Cemetery can be combined with a tour of Rock Creek Church Cemetery, which is located just across the street. Alternatively, I'd suggest combining this excursion with a tour of President Lincoln's Cottage, which gives visitors access to the grounds of the Old Soldiers' Home through Eagle Gate, around the corner at 140 Rock Creek Church Road NW. The Lincoln Cottage was opened as a museum in 2008 by the National Trust for Historic Preservation. Lincoln summered at the Old Soldiers' Home; its higher elevation meant cooler temperatures, and it provided a quiet respite from the White House. The cottage was where Lincoln wrote the Emancipation Proclamation, and the accompanying museum traces Lincoln's evolution in his thinking about slavery. While in this summer residence, Lincoln was attending to the national crisis of war while mourning the loss of his third child, Willie, who died in February 1862. During Lincoln's first season at the cottage that year, 1,255 burials took place in the cemetery, an average of more than eight per day. Lincoln could see the cemetery from the veranda of the cottage, and he was known to walk among the graves of Civil War dead interred in the cemetery during times of deep reflection. The proximity of the cemetery certainly reinforced for him the human cost of war.

→ **Visitors could end their tour here. For those who want to learn more about this site, particularly about soldiers honored for their service in the Indian Wars,**

follow the paved path that leads around the rest of the cemetery, making a large circle bisected in the middle by another paved path. Sections J and I can be found near the brick utility shed and chain-link enclosure. Sections L and K are inside the farther half of the circle, with K closest to North Capital Street. Section M is outside the paved path, near Rock Creek Church Road. Gravestone numbers can be found at the back of each stone.

6 THE INDIAN WARS: ALL THE REMAINING MEDAL OF HONOR RECIPIENTS IN THE CEMETERY

The Indian Wars were a series of conflicts that took place west of the Mississippi River, primarily in Arizona, Texas, and New Mexico, from the 1860s through the 1890s. Although the nation does not classify these battles as genocide, the purpose of the wars was to wrest land from Indigenous Americans and to exterminate tribal populations—or at least to decimate the number of Native Americans and relocate the remaining survivors to reservations. By reading the citations given to the twenty US soldiers listed below, we are forcefully reminded of those not honored. This is a place not only to honor those who served but to contemplate whose lives are valued above others and whose stories have been deemed worthy of telling by our government. In addition to remembering the unnamed Native American warriors who died in these conflicts, we must remember, too, that the vast majority of those killed were Native noncombatants.

The Indian Wars, like the Civil War, left the country with an unresolved racial reckoning that continues to deeply affect the daily life of Americans of color.

THOMAS LITTLE, SECTION I-5637. Little (1830–1880) was born in the West Indies and served as a bugler with the cavalry in the Arizona Territory during the Indian Wars, where he was awarded a Medal of Honor for bravery. He is one of only forty musicians known to have been awarded the highest medal.

SERGEANT THOMAS BOYNE, SECTION J-5859. Born enslaved in Prince George's County, Maryland, Boyne (1849–1896) served in the Second Colored Light Artillery during the Civil War and as a "Buffalo Soldier" in one of six all-Black regiments formed to serve mainly on the western frontier following the Civil War. (African American cavalry and infantry soldiers were given the nickname of Buffalo Soldiers by Native American tribes.) Boyne was awarded the Medal of Honor for bravery in action in New Mexico. Supporting his nomination, Major Albert B. Morrow wrote, "I have seen him repeatedly in action and in every instance he distinguished himself. I cannot speak too highly of his conduct." After he developed health issues during his service in Oklahoma and the Dakota Territory, Boyne was discharged with a disability pension and lived the rest of his life at the Armed Forces Retirement Home. He died of tuberculosis.

SERGEANT JAMES DOWLING, SECTION J-6352. Dowling (1846–1891) was born in Ireland and served in the US cavalry in 1868 during the Indian Wars. He was awarded a Medal of Honor for bravery as a scout in the Arizona Territory and lived at the Armed Forces Retirement Home at the end of his life.

SERGEANT THOMAS MURRAY, SECTION K-6502. Murray (1836–1888) was born in Ireland and worked as a laborer until enlisting in the Civil War. He was severely wounded in the left hand during the Battle of Williamsburg in New York. He reenlisted during the Indian Wars and was wounded again during the Battle of Little Bighorn; he was awarded the Medal of Honor for resupplying troops under heavy fire. Murray later worked for the cavalry as a farrier in the Dakota Territory. After his discharge with a diagnosis of chronic bronchitis, he resided at the Armed Forces Retirement Home.

SERGEANT WILLIAM OSBORN, SECTION K-6512. Osborn (1837–1876) served in the cavalry in the Arizona Territory during the Indian Wars and was awarded the Medal of Honor for bravery during battles with Apache warriors.

SERGEANT CORNELIUS DONOVAN, SECTION K-6721. Donovan (1839–1895) was born in Ireland and served in the cavalry during the Indian Wars. He was awarded the Congressional Medal of Honor for gallantry during his service in the Arizona Territory; he lived his final years at the Armed Forces Retirement Home.

SERGEANT RICHARD BARRETT, SECTION K-6765. Born in Ireland, Barrett (1838–1898) was awarded the Medal of Honor for "conspicuous gallantry in a charge upon the Tonto Apaches" in the Arizona Territory in 1872 during the Indian Wars. He moved to Washington, DC, after his retirement from military service.

SERGEANT CHARLES TAYLOR, SECTION K-6851. Taylor (1840–1899) was born in Baltimore and served in the cavalry in the Arizona Territory during the Indian Wars. He was awarded a Medal of Honor for a battle at Big Dry Fork, where, surrounded by White Mountain Apache warriors, he scaled a canyon for a better offensive position and, according to his citation, "advanced far ahead of his comrades and in a cool and deliberate manner picked out one hostile Indian after another, firing with great effect." Three others were also awarded Medals of Honor for this battle, the last major battle between the US Army and the Apaches. The battle ended with the outgunned Apache warriors retreating on foot under cover of darkness.

CORPORAL JOHN JAMES, SECTION K-6991. Born in England, James (1838–1902) served in the infantry in the Indian Wars and was awarded a Medal of Honor for "gallantry in action" in Texas for defending the Lyman Train, a group of thirty-six supply wagons, against a war party of Kiowa and Comanche warriors in 1874. The Lyman Train defenders are famous for holding out against continuous gunfire for almost a week—in temperatures that soared, at times, to one hundred degrees—before reinforcements arrived and the Native Americans were outnumbered. James was a resident at the Armed Forces Retirement Home at the end of his life.

CORPORAL JOHN DENNY, SECTION K-7020. Denny (1846–1901) was born in New York and served as a Buffalo Soldier in New Mexico. He was awarded a Medal of Honor for saving a wounded comrade under heavy fire during an engagement with Apache warriors in New Mexico. His medal citation was not issued for twelve years; finally, at the urging of his commanding officer, he was recognized in 1891. Denny retired in 1897 and moved to Nebraska. He was a resident of the Armed Forces Retirement Home for the last two years of his life.

SERGEANT WILLIAM D. EDWARDS, SECTION K-7023. Edwards (1849–1903) worked as a plumber in New York State until enlisting in the US Army in 1870. While serving in the infantry in Dakota Territory, he joined the first Chartered Masonic Lodge in what is now North Dakota, becoming a Master Mason in 1872. He then served in Montana, where he was awarded the Medal of Honor for bravery during the Battle of Big Hole in 1877—a battle with Nez Perce warriors led by Chief Joseph. Just two months later, Chief Joseph would surrender about forty miles from the Canadian border, after a journey of almost two thousand miles from the traditional lands of the Nez Perce in northeastern Oregon. The Nez

Perce fought continuously with the much larger, better-supplied troops of the US cavalry throughout a three-and-a-half-month journey over rough and mountainous terrain, today considered one of the greatest military retreats in history. (The Nez Perce, unlike the soldiers, also traveled with women, children, the elderly, and the wounded.) Edwards served in the Wyoming Territory as well. After his medical discharge, he moved to the Armed Forces Retirement Home.

RICHARD J. NOLAN, SECTION K-7179. Born in Ireland, Nolan (1848–1905) served as a farrier in the cavalry during the Indian Wars. He was awarded the Medal of Honor for bravery during a battle in the Dakota Territories.

SERGEANT JOHN CONNOR, SECTION K-7258. Born in Ireland, Connor (1845–1907) served in the Indian Wars and was awarded a Medal of Honor for gallantry during an engagement with Kiowa warriors in Texas in 1870. Part of the rear guard when his unit formed a defensive square, Connor was noted for "rapid and accurate" rifle fire in a battle in which a bullet grazed his forehead and his horse was shot out from under him; he was pinned underneath the horse before other soldiers pulled him to safety. After two months in the hospital recovering from injuries, Connor reenlisted and served in artillery units in Maryland, Washington, DC, Georgia, Alabama, Florida, and Massachusetts. After his discharge in 1890, he married and lived with his wife in Alexandria, Virginia. Connor spent the last two years of his life at the Armed Forces Retirement Home.

PRIVATE THOMAS SMITH, SECTION K-7492. Smith (1847–1909) served in the cavalry in the Arizona Territory during the Indian Wars. He is one of two soldiers named Thomas Smith awarded the Medal of Honor (the other Smith served in the navy).

SERGEANT BENJAMIN BROWN, SECTION K-7519. A Buffalo Soldier and expert rifleman, Brown (1859–1910) was awarded the Medal of Honor for his engagement with bandits during the Wham Paymaster Robbery in the Arizona Territory in May 1889. Brown was part of a twelve-man escort of two mule-drawn carriages, traveling from one military fort to another, that was ambushed. A total of $28,345 in gold and silver coins was stolen—and never recovered. Brown sustained injuries to his abdomen and both arms in the resulting two-hour-long fight and lived the rest of his life carrying bullets in his body. A committee on military affairs in the US House of Representatives concluded that Brown and his fellow soldiers "displayed unusual courage and skill in defense of the Government's property." Brown would serve a total of seven tours of duty, five of them after the Wham Paymaster Robbery. After a stroke in 1904, Brown retired from the service and spent the remainder of his life in residence at the Armed Forces Retirement Home. In 2015, the Spotsylvania African American Heritage Trail in Pennsylvania installed a historic marker in his honor.

SERGEANT RUDOLPH STAUFFER, SECTION K-8132. Born in Switzerland, Stauffer (1836–1918) settled in Cincinnati prior to his enlistment. He served in the cavalry in the Arizona Territory during the Indian Wars, where his gallantry as a scout earned him a Medal of Honor. Stauffers Butte, a mesa outside Camp Verde, Arizona, was named for him; it's the site of a successful battle he led against Apache warriors. He spent his last forty years, from 1878 to 1918, in residence at the Armed Forces Retirement Home.

HENRY WILLIAM BIGLER MECHLIN, SECTION L-8861. Mechlin (1851–1926) served as the company blacksmith for a cavalry unit at the Battle of Little Bighorn. He was awarded a Medal of Honor as one of three marksmen who volunteered to cover a party of eleven canteen bearers who secured water from the Little Bighorn River for army troops. Mechlin lived in Pennsylvania after completing his enlistment, and from 1911 until his death he was a resident at the Armed Forces Retirement Home, where he died of broncho-pneumonia and chronic myocarditis.

PRIVATE JAMES BROPHY, SECTION L-9086. Born in Ireland, Brophy (1846–1929) served during the Indian Wars in the cavalry in Arizona, where he was awarded the Medal of Honor for bravery as a scout.

SERGEANT JOHN A. KIRKWOOD, SECTION L-9102. Kirkwood (1851–1930) served in the cavalry in the Dakota Territory and was awarded the Medal of Honor for his actions in a conflict against Sioux warriors in 1876 known as the Battle of Slim Buttes, during which he was shot in the abdomen. This battle was the first victory for the US Army after the major defeat of the Battle of Little Bighorn. Kirkwood's medal was donated by family members and is on display at the Soldiers and Sailors National Military Museum and Memorial in Pittsburgh, Pennsylvania.

SERGEANT JEPTHA L. LYTTON, SECTION M-9370. Lytton (1849–1932) served in the infantry in Nebraska and was awarded a Medal of Honor for gallantry during a "charge on hostile Sioux" in 1876.

ALEXANDRIA NATIONAL CEMETERY (1862)

1450 Wilkes Street, Alexandria, VA

This military cemetery holds the remains of approximately 4,000 Civil War soldiers who died in battle or in one of Alexandria's twenty-six Union hospitals. Burials include 229 soldiers of the United States Colored Troops and 123 unknown soldiers. This was the first military cemetery to bury Black soldiers alongside white ones.

Alexandria National Cemetery, the second-oldest national cemetery in the United States, is one of 14 original national military cemeteries established in 1862. There are now 131 national cemeteries administered by the Department of Veterans Affairs. The property, on slightly over five acres, is surrounded by a well-wrought red Seneca sandstone wall topped with bluestone coping. The cemetery is considered full and was closed to new casket interments in 1967. It was added to the National Register of Historic Places in 1995.

Before You Go

Administered by the US Department of Veterans Affairs, under the supervision of the Director of Quantico National Cemetery

https://www.cem.va.gov/cems/nchp/alexandriava.asp

Open daily from dawn to dusk; office open weekdays, 7:30 am to 4:00 pm

Nearest public transportation: King Street Station

No parking or restrooms

Rostrum (3)

1 ENTRANCE GATE

This set of cast-iron gates was added in 1892, thirty years after the cemetery opened, to replace an earlier wooden arch over the road. The gates measure twelve feet wide and are decorated with familiar military symbols: eagles, flags, and cannons. Identical gates can be seen at several other national cemeteries.

2 SUPERINTENDENT'S LODGE

The third building to stand on this site, the Lodge was designed in the Second Empire style by Quartermaster General Montgomery C. Meigs. The building is an exact match for the one at Battleground National Cemetery on Georgia Avenue NW in DC, using locally quarried Seneca sandstone. A version of Meigs's design in stone or brick was used at fifty-five of the national cemeteries across the United States. The Lodge served as both an office and a residence for a superintendent and his family. Note the toolhouse behind the Lodge, which was added in 1887 for storage of equipment and public toilets; today it is used as a maintenance shed.

3 ROSTRUM

A central oval-shaped section with a flagpole, plaza, and rostrum for services was added in 1945. Constructed of marble, the rostrum is unique to this military cemetery.

4 SECTION A

A rough stone monument was dedicated in 1922 to the four civilians who died in pursuit of John Wilkes Booth after his assassination of President Lincoln. All four—Peter Carroll, Samuel N. Gosnell, George W. Huntington, and Christopher Farley—were employees of the Quartermaster Corps and died by drowning in the Potomac River. They are buried in Section A, graves 3174 through 3177.

5 SECTION B

L'Ouverture Hospital was built in 1863 as a Union military hospital for African Americans and was named for the Haitian revolutionary leader Toussaint L'Ouverture. The hospital site originally filled the entire block bounded by Prince, Duke, S. Payne, and S. West Streets in downtown Alexandria, and it included barracks, a cookhouse, linen room, office, sutler's store, morgue, and dispensary. Only one original building remains: the private residence at 219 S. Payne Street was the hospital administration headquarters. During its operation from 1864 to 1865, L'Ouverture served approximately 1,400 African American patients (troops as well as contraband civilians). The hospital was built to accommodate 600 patients at a time but was chronically overcrowded.

The city created a new burial ground for those people of African descent who died as self-emancipated slaves, or "contrabands," in nearby encampments as well as those who died at L'Ouverture. The city had originally planned to bury only white soldiers at Alexandria National Cemetery, but 443 soldiers at L'Ouverture Hospital signed a petition demanding that they be buried with the same honors as their white counterparts. Captain J. C. G. Lee approved this request, making Alexandria the first American military cemetery that was not segregated by race.

There were, however, 118 soldiers already buried at Freedmen Cemetery. The Contrabands and Freedmen Cemetery Memorial is preserved as a park at 1001 S. Washington Street, a mile away. Although no above-ground remnants of graves can be seen, approximately 1,800 remains have been identified as being buried at this site, over half of whom are children under the age of sixteen. All the 118 soldiers originally buried there were disinterred and reburied with honors in marked graves at Alexandria National Cemetery in 1865.

The Contrabands and Freedmen Cemetery Memorial features a large statue by C. J. Howard. Six figures swirl upward in a spiral of muscular proportions, topped by a bronze hoop that reads simultaneously as a halo and a crown of thorns, imagery suggesting heavenly redemption. In addition, the park has four bas-relief panels with information on the enslaved residents of Alexandria and the city's Civil War schools for newly emancipated residents, among other material. Much of the site remains open land, covered with grass. The area was abandoned after 1939 and was subsequently the site of a gas station, office building, brick factory, and parking lots. As a result, many graves were lost or disturbed over the ensuing years. The memorial opened in 2014, and a visit can easily be paired with this tour. (See additional information in the Other Sites of Interest listings on page 292.)

Of the 443 signers of the L'Ouverture Petition, 23 Civil War soldiers of color are buried at Alexandria National Cemetery in Section B.

Row 13
William A. Jackson, B-3218
Daniel Thomas, B-3221
John Smith, B-3234
William Wood, B-3247

Row 14
John Green, B-3312
John H. Hall, B-3320

Row 15
Peter Julius, B-3572

Row 16
Levi Mapp, B-3453
Peter Dyer, B-3457
Daniel Barrett, B-3461
David Jones, B-3466
William H. Clay, B-3477
Tobias Trout, B-3478
Joseph Carr, B-3479

Row 17
James Neal, B-3484
Oscar Gregory, B-3485

John H. Wills, B-3487
Asa Carr, B-3492
George Jones, B-3497

Row 18
John Thompson, B-3540
Charles Lewis, B-3547
William Burke, B-3554

6 CONFEDERATE GRAVES

At one time, thirty-nine white Confederate prisoners of war who died in nearby prison camps were buried in the cemetery. All were later disinterred and buried elsewhere—the majority, thirty-four of them, in the nearby Christ Church Cemetery, where they were placed in 1879 by the United Daughters of the Confederacy. The cemetery's oldest graves now hold only the remains of Union soldiers from the Civil War.

Christ Church Cemetery is one of thirteen adjoining private cemeteries in what is today known as the Wilkes Street Cemetery Complex. Nine of the burial grounds are still in active use. When the city set aside these burial grounds in 1803 after a yellow fever epidemic that killed over three hundred people, this spot was considered far enough outside of the town not to adversely affect the health of residents: city leaders believed at the time that decomposing corpses would spread yellow fever through well water, and this site was downriver from the city's water supply. As a health precaution, city leaders purchased a former farm, the 82-acre Spring Garden Farm, because an already existing burial ground, Penny Hill, had been established on its edge in 1795—a "potter's field" where the city's poor and indigent residents were buried in paupers' graves. Today the Wilkes Street Cemetery Complex is surrounded by modern housing, and a highway abuts one end of the complex.

Alexandria National Cemetery is part of the original Spring Garden Farm plot. Originally 4 acres, this cemetery was later expanded when an additional 1.5-acre plot was purchased by the US government from a private landholder, John H. Baggett. The small size of the cemetery meant that it filled to capacity only two years after it was established.

7 BUFFALO SOLDIERS

Buffalo Soldiers were African American troops who fought in military engagements from the Civil War through World War II in segregated units led by white officers. Most of these soldiers served during the Indian Wars. Six Buffalo Soldiers are buried at this site, all in Section B.

Row 14
Conny Gray, B-3587

Row 15
Lorenzo Foster, B-3565

Row 16
John T. Stevenson, B-3592

Row 18
Lewis J. Cook, B-3560
George Foster, B-3565
Joseph F. Whelen, B-3606

George and Lorenzo Foster were brothers. Only Lewis J. Cook was not a resident of Alexandria; all the others had strong connections to the town. Prior to enlisting, Conny Gray and his wife taught at a freedmen's school in Alexandria, known first as the Hallowell School and later as the Parker-Gray School.

8 BURIALS OF WOMEN

There are also three women buried here who attained the rank of yeoman during World War I—the first conflict that allowed women to enlist in the military outside the Nurse Corps. Lillian Estelle Edwards (D-14), Lulu Mae Hogue (B-5076), and Rosalie Myrtle Smith (C-18) were all yeomen in the US Naval Reserves.

BATTLEGROUND NATIONAL CEMETERY (1864–1936)

6625 Georgia Avenue NW, Brightwood neighborhood, DC

Just a single acre in size, this cemetery for veterans of the Battle of Fort Stevens (July 11–12, 1864) is one of the smallest of the national cemeteries in the United States. Administered by the National Park Service, it's a place to remember the role of the capital during the Civil War and the only battle site in which a commander-in-chief came under direct fire. Our tour will start at the site of Fort Stevens and then proceed to the cemetery. A second cemetery, in Silver Spring, Maryland, is an optional additional stop.

Before You Go

Administered by the National Park Service as part of the Civil War Defenses of Washington
https://www.nps.gov/places/battleground-national-cemetery.htm
Open daily 8:00 am to 6:00 pm
Nearest public transportation: Takoma Station to bus
No parking or restrooms

1 FORT STEVENS PARK, 6001 THIRTEENTH STREET NW

Washington's defenses during the Civil War consisted of Union Army fortifications surrounding the capital on all sides: 68 enclosed forts, 93 prepared batteries for field guns (which remained unarmed but ready in case of battle), 7 blockhouses, 1,501 field gun emplacements, and twenty miles of rifle pits. This giant ring—in what

Marble rostrum with excerpt from "Bivouac of the Dead" (5)

is today Montgomery and Prince George's Counties in Maryland and Arlington, Fairfax, Alexandria, and Falls Church, Virginia, as well as in DC proper—made the capital one of the most fortified cities in the world. The forts were built in 1861 under the direction of Major General John G. Barnard on strategic heights, overlooking roads, rail lines, and bridges. Most of the 22 surviving fort sites are now administered by the National Park Service.

Traces of the original earthwork fortifications can be seen at only a few surviving sites, and only two—Fort Ward in Alexandria, Virginia, and Fort Stevens in DC—

are well interpreted. Soldiers at the manned ring forts were generally inexperienced rear-echelon troops. They built the forts by digging up massive amounts of soil by hand to create rammed earth walls surrounded by dry moats. The ramparts were lined with fallen trees to hold the dirt more firmly in place, and a perimeter of abatis, trees whose branches pointed outward like swords, provided further disincentive to attack. Within the fort, parts of the walls were lined with wood to create bombproofs (rooms to shelter gun crews) and hold the embrasures, where guns were placed in notches facing outward. Today you can see this structure (part original, part re-created) at Fort Stevens. Earth was used not only because it was readily available but also because it was stronger than brick or stone when absorbing the impact of projectiles.

2 THE BATTLEMENTS

On July 11 and 12, 1864, Confederate troops under the command of Lieutenant General Jubal A. Early reached this site—the only time that Confederate forces tried to break through the defenses of Washington. At this late point in the war, few soldiers were assigned to Fort Stevens, or, in fact, to any of the ring forts. Most of the soldiers placed at Fort Stevens earlier in the war had been reallocated to the front lines in Virginia. As Early's troops advanced over the Monocacy River into Rockville, Maryland, defense of the capital was cobbled together with men who worked as government clerks, retired veterans from earlier wars, and wounded soldiers from area hospitals. Skirmishes took place over the course of a day and a half, and the Confederates finally withdrew during the night of July 12.

3 THE LINCOLN PLAQUE

A metal plaque set into a large stone commemorates Lincoln's attendance at this battle. It was not uncommon for daring civilians to come out to watch the action during the Civil War, and carriages of Washingtonians arrived on July 12 to witness the battle on the second day. The most notable witness was the president, who was not content to watch from the sidelines but actually entered the fort. Standing on the parapet to better see Confederate sharpshooters, Lincoln became the only sitting president in history to come under direct fire. Witnesses reported that several soldiers tried to convince Lincoln to be more careful. A young officer finally told him, "Get down, you damned fool!" That soldier, Oliver Wendell Holmes Jr., would later serve as a justice on the US Supreme Court.

The Lincoln plaque was placed at the park in 1920. The other monument at the park is a relief map of the fort, designed by John J. Early and dedicated by the Grand Army of the Republic in 1936.

The original owner of this land was Elizabeth Proctor Thomas (ca. 1820–1830), an African American woman, and her siblings. Because of its strategic site along the Seventh Street Pike (today's Georgia Avenue), the land was the major approach to the capital from the north. In September 1861, Union troops took possession of her land and destroyed her home, barn, orchard, and garden to build the fort. Thomas was a young mother with a six-month-old baby at the time. She continued to live in the neighborhood after the end of the war, fighting the government for compensation for her lost land and property. In 1911, she was present at the dedication of the first monument to President Lincoln located at the site (no longer extant). She was finally awarded $1,835 from the government as compensation in 1916—one year before her death.

The park today is on just over four acres of land. Grass has grown over the parapets, and the site remains free of trees. The cannons are modern replicas, and the recreated bombproofs and embrasures are made of concrete (styled to look like wood). Once a year, on the

Saturday closest to the dates of July 11 and 12, a day of commemoration is held at Fort Stevens, with reenactors, speakers, period music, and children's activities. Fort Stevens Day is hosted by the Alliance to Preserve the Civil War Defenses of Washington, a nonprofit group.

Most of the ring forts were dismantled or abandoned at the end of the Civil War. Only decades later, in 1902, was their preservation addressed as part of the McMillan Plan (most famous for creating the modern design of the National Mall). We now move a few blocks north, to the actual cemetery.

4 BATTLEGROUND NATIONAL CEMETERY

Battleground National Cemetery is unique for its single intent: it was established in 1864 exclusively for the remains of Union soldiers who took part in the battle at Fort Stevens, and all forty-one of the soldiers were able to be identified by name. Located on a busy street between houses, the site is small enough to almost be overlooked by the thousands of commuters who use this route along Georgia Avenue NW daily.

In 1864, this land was originally an orchard. The cemetery is reached by a short set of blue flagstone stairs between two small, black 6-pounder smoothbore cannons that were actually used to defend Fort Stevens in the battle. The path leads to a circle of graves surrounding a flagpole, whose base is decorated with eagles. President Abraham Lincoln spoke at the opening ceremony for the cemetery. The final interment took place in 1936, when the last survivor of the battle, Major Edward R. Campbell, was laid to rest.

5 BIVOUAC OF THE DEAD

Three signs placed among the graves reprint excerpts from a poem by Theodore O'Hara (1820–1867) called

"Bivouac of the Dead." O'Hara was a lawyer and journalist originally from Kentucky. He was a veteran of the Mexican-American War and the Civil War—but in the Civil War he fought for the Confederacy, which makes the wide use of his most famous poem a strange addition to so many Union cemeteries. At one time, nearly every national military cemetery contained plaques reprinting a couplet from the poem placed at strategic points. Visitors continue to see the poem reproduced in the smallest cemeteries (like this one) to the largest, such as at the entrance to Arlington National Cemetery. How did O'Hara's elegy become such a universal favorite? And why was a poem written about an earlier conflict embraced by those mourning the losses of the Civil War? The answer lies with Quartermaster General Montgomery C. Meigs, who recognized the poem's popularity and shared in its admiration. Meigs ordered the cast-iron tablets to be fabricated at the Rock Island Arsenal in Illinois, managed by the War Department, "to take the place of notices, verses, &c., on painted signboards which had become unsightly." The excerpts used at Battleground Cemetery, as at all other military cemeteries, are not attributed to O'Hara.

O'Hara was a DC resident who was admitted to the bar in DC in 1845 and worked for the US Treasury Department from 1845–46. He practiced law in DC after the end of the Mexican- American War, from 1848 to 1851, during which time he published "Bivouac of the Dead." At the beginning of the Civil War, in 1861, O'Hara joined the Confederate Army as lieutenant colonel in the 12th Alabama Regiment and fought in the Battle of Shiloh and the Battle of Stones River, among other actions. He would rise through the ranks to colonel.

The full text of the poem is as follows (with the lines excerpted at the cemetery marked in italics):

The muffled drum's sad roll has beat
The soldier's last tattoo;

No more on life's parade shall meet
That brave and fallen few.
On Fame's eternal camping-ground
Their silent tents are spread,
And Glory guards, with solemn round,
The bivouac of the dead.

No rumor of the foe's advance
Now swells upon the wind;
No troubled thought at midnight haunts
Of loved ones left behind;
No vision of the morrow's strife
The warrior's dream alarms;
No braying horn nor screaming fife
At dawn shall call to arms.

Their shivered swords are red with rust,
Their plumèd heads are bowed,
Their haughty banner, trailed in dust,
Is now their martial shroud.
And plenteous funeral tears have washed
The red stains from each brow,
And the proud forms, by battle gashed,
Are free from anguish now.

The neighing troop, the flashing blade,
The bugle's stirring blast,
The charge, the dreadful cannonade,
The din and shout are past;
Nor war's wild note, nor glory's peal
Shall thrill with fierce delight
Those breasts that never more may feel
The rapture of the fight.

Like the fierce northern hurricane
That sweeps the great plateau,
Flushed with the triumph yet to gain,
Came down the serried foe;
Who heard the thunder of the fray

Break o'er the field beneath,
Knew well the watchword of that day
Was "Victory or death."

Long had the doubtful conflict raged
O'er all that stricken plain,
For never fiercer fight had waged
The vengeful blood of Spain;
And still the storm of battle blew,
Still swelled the gory tide;
Not long our stout old chieftain knew,
Such odds his strength could bide.

'Twas in that hour his stern command
Called to a martyr's grave
The flower of his beloved land,
The nation's flag to save.
By rivers of their fathers' gore
His first-born laurels grew,
And well he deemed the sons would pour
Their lives for glory too.

Full many a norther's breath has swept
O'er Angostura's plain—
And long the pitying sky has wept
Above her moldering slain;
The raven's scream, or eagle's flight,
Or shepherd's pensive lay,
Alone awakes each sullen height
That frowned o'er that dread fray.

Sons of the Dark and Bloody Ground,
Ye must not slumber there,
Where stranger steps and tongues resound
Along the heedless air.
Your own proud land's heroic soil
Shall be your fitter grave;
She claims from war his richest spoil—
The ashes of her brave.

Thus 'neath their parent turf they rest,
    Far from the gory field,
Borne to a Spartan mother's breast
    On many a bloody shield;
The sunshine of their native sky
    Smiles sadly on them here,
And kindred eyes and hearts watch by
    The heroes' sepulcher.

Rest on embalmed and sainted dead!
    Dear as the blood ye gave;
No impious footstep shall here tread
    The herbage of your grave;
Nor shall your glory be forgot
    While Fame her record keeps,
Or Honor points the hallowed spot
    Where Valor proudly sleeps.

Yon marble minstrel's voiceless stone
    In deathless song shall tell
When many a vanquished age hath flown,
    The story how ye fell;
Nor wreck, nor change, nor winter's blight,
    Nor Time's remorseless doom,
Shall dim one ray of glory's light
    That gilds your deathless tomb.

The columned marble rostrum at the rear of the cemetery was designed for Memorial Day services.

6 THE SUPERINTENDENT'S BUILDING

The superintendent's combined office and residence was designed in the Second Empire style by Quartermaster General Montgomery C. Meigs using locally quarried Seneca sandstone. Meigs worked diligently to regularize the appearance of military cemeteries across the nation, providing plans for everything from ornamental gates to toolsheds, walls, and the layout of graves. This house is an exact match for the one at Alexandria National Cemetery (see page 202 of that tour). A plaque on the side of the building facing Georgia Avenue reprints Lincoln's Gettysburg Address. The only civilians buried at this site are four members of the Armbrecht family: the wife and three children of Augustus Armbrecht, the first superintendent. The house is still in use for a resident employee of the National Park Service. Two separate entrances—one public (to the office) and one private (to the residence)—open out to a front porch.

7 COMMEMORATIVE MONUMENTS

A series of stone monuments faces outward toward Georgia Avenue, erected by state governments to commemorate those who participated in the Battle of Fort Stevens. The inscriptions list those soldiers who were wounded and recovered as well as the names of those who died. The soldiers who participated in the battle include infantry and cavalry troops from New York, Ohio, Pennsylvania, Maine, Massachusetts, Rhode Island, and Vermont.

8 GRAVEYARD AT GRACE EPISCOPAL CHURCH

9115 Georgia Avenue, Silver Spring, MD

Just shy of three miles north, on the corner of Georgia Avenue and Grace Church Road in Silver Spring, a Confederate monument was erected to the seventeen unknown Confederate dead who fell in the Battle of Fort Stevens. The unknown soldiers have been moved twice. After initial burial in the fields near Fort Stevens, they were exhumed in 1874 by the rector of Grace Church and buried in a common grave in the church cemetery. When the road was widened in 1896, they were moved to their current location. The church's website states, "The Grace

Episcopal Church community condemns racism in any form." It continues, "The members of Grace join countless others who continue to raise concerns about statues and memorials to the Confederacy," but they continue to maintain the memorial as "a reminder of our painful past of slavery and division and how far we have often fallen from God's plan for us." The tablet sits on the corner closest to the road but is now obscured from view by a large sign that seems to be in continued conversation with those Southern troops. It reads, in capital letters, "BLACK LIVES MATTER."

ARLINGTON NATIONAL CEMETERY (1864)

1 Memorial Avenue, Arlington, VA

Because this site is so large, even a tour of the highlights can be quite long. This tour could be done in a single day but can also easily be divided in two, with a first visit taking you through Arlington House and a second visit continuing with the rest of the tour. Visitors should note that they will be required to go through a security check to enter the grounds. There is no food available for purchase, and only water can be brought on the site.

Before You Go

Administered by the US Department of the Army
arlingtoncemetery.mil
Open daily 8:00 am to 5:00 pm
Nearest public transportation: Arlington Cemetery Station
Parking, restrooms, and gift shop available

1 WELCOME CENTER

Arlington National Cemetery is a place to think more deeply about the way our country valorizes military service and how the legacy of slavery continues to echo—in federal policies and protests for civil rights—through the generations since the Civil War. Located on 639 acres in Arlington, Virginia, on the former site of Arlington Plantation, its placement directly across from the National Mall and its large number of major monuments mark the cemetery as a place always balanced precariously between mourning (both private and communal) and tourism.

The cemetery is divided into seventy sections. Cemetery maps and guidebooks are available at the Welcome Center and online. As the best-interpreted cemetery in DC—perhaps in the world—Arlington offers the visitor multiple approaches toward understanding what is often referred to as "these hallowed grounds." I found myself challenged by many of the official narratives, and this tour reflects that tension. And yet perhaps that is only appropriate. Tension, a sense of being pulled simultaneously in two directions, was built into the landscape right from the cemetery's founding. It is part of what makes the experience of visiting Arlington feel so American.

→ **The Welcome Center includes exhibits, restrooms, and a gift shop. Exit at the back of the building to take the path from the Welcome Center into the cemetery. Follow the pedestrian walkway, turn right on Eisenhower Drive, and walk through a set of gates to the plaza.**

2 WOMEN IN MILITARY SERVICE FOR AMERICA MEMORIAL

Honoring the three million women who have served in the armed forces (or in supporting roles with the military) since the nation's founding, this monument includes a Court of Valor, with a fountain and reflecting pool, and an education center with a research library, Hall of Honor, and exhibitions. Located prominently at the western end of Memorial Avenue at the cemetery entrance, the structure was designed by McKim, Mead and White and built in 1932 as part of the Memorial Bridge project. Shaped as a handsome neoclassical

John Wesley Powell grave (18)

ceremonial hemicycle entrance gate, it was never completed or used as intended, and in 1988 it was redesigned and dedicated as a Women's Memorial. Constructed of reinforced concrete with granite cladding, the memorial includes six circular niches and a central arch inlaid with Texas red granite.

It is notable that women are honored in such a prominent position on a ceremonial axis with the US Capitol, considering how long a struggle they had to endure just to get the right to enlist. Women have participated in every American conflict, openly (in civilian supporting jobs) or covertly (as spies or by disguising their gender). Yet it wasn't until 1948 that a law made women a

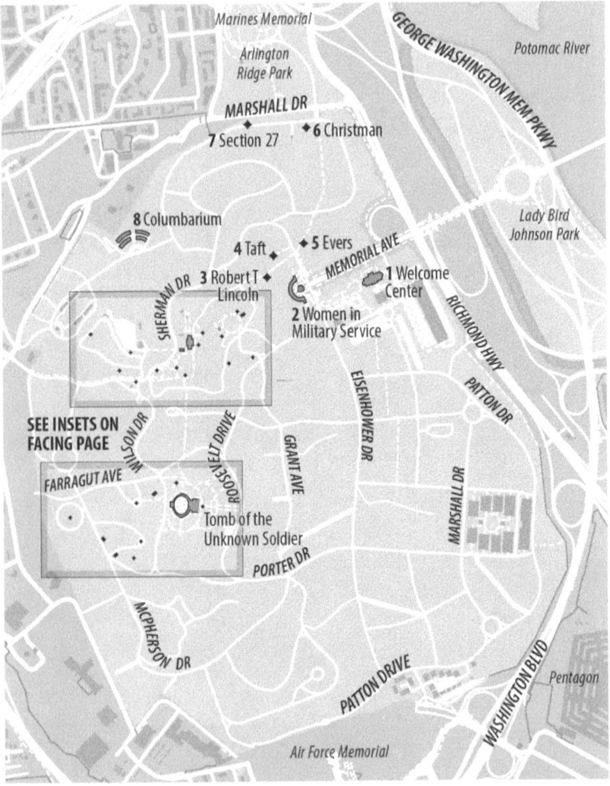

Arlington National Cemetery overview

permanent part of the military—and it wasn't until 1976 that women were allowed to be trained at US military academies.

The original hemicycle was built as part of the McMillan Plan (1902), which created the National Mall's core design, with the US Capitol on one end and the Lincoln Memorial (which would be built between 1914 and 1920) on the other. The grand new Memorial Bridge was built across the Potomac River to link Arlington House (in actuality but also symbolically) with the Lincoln Memorial. But the hemicycle was built outside of the military's landholdings, as it marked the far edge of the National

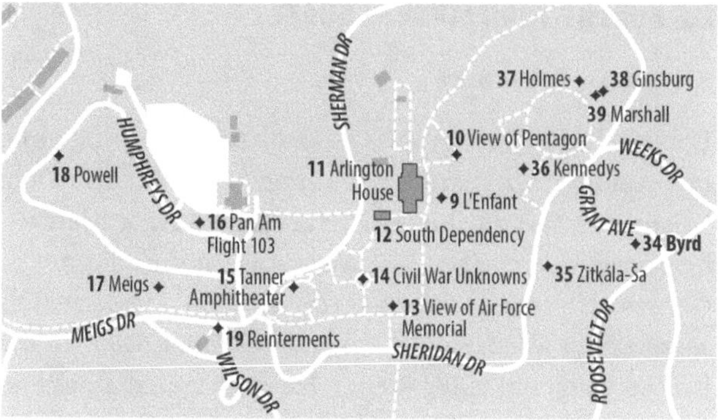

Arlington National Cemetery north

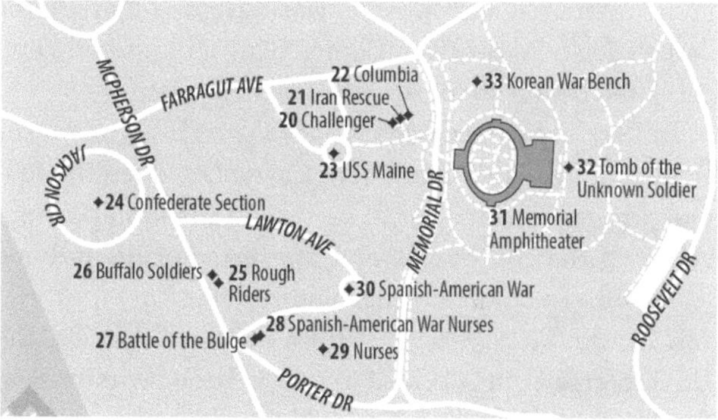

Arlington National Cemetery south

Mall on federal land. This explains its deteriorated condition prior to its redesign by architects Marion Weiss and Michael Manfredi.

→ **You can enter the Women's Memorial and look at the exhibits or choose to stay on the outside. When you are finished, cross the plaza and go through the ceremonial gates on the other side of the memorial. You will be on Schley Drive; from there, take the first left on Custis Walk. Go to the top of the stairs and look for a path on your left leading to a large raised sarcophagus.**

3 ROBERT TODD LINCOLN GRAVE

Section 31, Grave S-13

Robert Todd Lincoln (1843–1926) was the only child of President Abraham Lincoln and Mary Todd Lincoln to survive to adulthood. A Harvard-educated lawyer, he served during the Civil War as assistant adjutant to General Ulysses S. Grant. After the war, he served as secretary of war (1881–1885) and US ambassador to the United Kingdom (1889–1893). He maintained a successful private law practice in Chicago and became president of the Pullman Car Company (1897–1924). His handsome memorial sarcophagus was designed by sculptor James Earle Fraser from Connecticut pink granite, and it is sited on a brick plaza with two benches.

In 1877, upon the death of Mary Custis Lee (the wife of Robert E. Lee), her oldest son, Custis Lee, sued the federal government for illegal seizure of his family's land, claiming that he was denied the terms of his father's legal will. (For more on this history, see stop 11, Arlington House, on page 233.) After a series of appeals, the US Supreme Court decided in Custis Lee's favor in 1882. By this time, Arlington National Cemetery was the site of thousands of graves as well as a military installation, so Lee agreed to transfer title for the land in exchange for $150,000. Ironically, this final dispensation of the land was handled by Robert Todd Lincoln while he was secretary of war.

→ **Retrace your steps to Schley Drive. Turn left, then make an immediate left onto the next pathway, and go to the end.**

4 PRESIDENT WILLIAM HOWARD TAFT MEMORIAL GRAVE

Section 30

William Howard Taft (1857–1930), the twenty-seventh US president, was the first president to be buried at Arlington National (of only two). He also served as the tenth chief justice of the US Supreme Court (and is one of fourteen Supreme Court justices buried here). He is the only person to have served in both of these high offices. His accomplishments as president include amending the federal income tax system, initiating eighty antitrust lawsuits, and strengthening the Interstate Commerce Commission. But Taft always stated that he preferred law to politics. His accomplishments as chief justice include the formation of the League to Enforce Peace and his advocacy for reforms to the high court, leading to the establishment of the Judicial Conference of the United States.

Taft is buried with his wife, Helen Herron Taft (1861–1943), known to her friends as Nelly. She is the author of *Recollections of Full Years* (1914), the first memoir published by a former first lady. Nelly Taft is also remembered for arranging for the planting of three thousand Japanese cherry trees around the Tidal Basin (an idea first promoted by author Eliza Ruhamah Scidmore). Nelly Taft was also fluent in French, served as a president of the Cincinnati Symphony Orchestra, and played a large role in advising her husband on his presidential campaign, even writing some of his public speeches.

→ **Return to Schley Drive and turn right, then make an immediate left onto Custis Walk. Go almost to the bottom of the steps; the next site will be on your right. Find the first gravestone in the fourth row.**

5 MEDGAR EVERS GRAVE

Section 36, Grave 1431

It is impossible to forget that this land was reclaimed from a plantation, where human beings were held in bondage, raped, sometimes murdered, and sometimes sold away from their families as punishment or to pay off debts incurred by their white "masters." Perhaps no other grave symbolizes that reclamation—and the irony of an idealized corrective story of democracy—more than that of Medgar Evers (1925–1963).

Evers served as an army sergeant during World War II and participated in the post–D-Day invasion into Normandy, France, where he earned two Bronze Stars. Denied admission after the war to the University of Mississippi Law School based on his race, he worked with the NAACP in an unsuccessful attempt to force desegregation. He then began employment as the first state field secretary for the NAACP in Mississippi, emerging as a prominent civil rights leader. In this role, he organized voter registration drives and boycotts and investigated crimes against African Americans, including the murder of Emmett Till in 1955.

Evers escaped two attempts on his life before his murder in front of his home in 1963. It took three trials—and thirty-one years—for his killer to be convicted in 1994. Evers's death increased national awareness and support for federal civil rights legislation. He was awarded the NAACP Spingarn Medal; in addition, Medgar Evers College in Brooklyn was established in 1969, and an airport in Mississippi and a navy cargo ship have also been named for him.

Evers's funeral service was broadcast nationally on the radio. While he was buried as an American military hero, speakers referred to him repeatedly throughout the service as a fallen soldier for the civil rights movement.

→ **Continue following Custis Walk (crossing over Ord & Weitzel Drive, named for two Civil War Union generals) until you reach the Ord & Weitzel Pedestrian Gate. Note the white columns topped by urns. These columns, built in 1879, once adorned the War Department but today mark the entrance closest to the Netherlands Carillon and the Iwo Jima Memorial. Pass through the gate and turn left onto Ord & Weitzel Drive. Follow it to Section 27, which you will see on your left and right.**

6 WILLIAM H. CHRISTMAN GRAVE

Section 27, Grave 19

The first military burial took place in this section, which you can find in the first row on your left, twelve graves in, just after you turn onto Ord & Weitzel Drive. Private William Henry Christman (1844–1864) was a white laborer from Easton, Pennsylvania, buried at Arlington one month before it was officially designated. Christman died of peritonitis in a Washington hospital two months after his enlistment, before ever seeing combat. A manual laborer before the war, he volunteered with the 67th Pennsylvania Infantry and was buried on May 13, 1864, with no ceremony or family in attendance.

On June 15, 1864, Secretary of War Edwin Stanton designated two hundred acres, including the Custis-Lee family's "mansion and grounds immediately surrounding it," to be appropriated for a military cemetery. While Christman was buried in a location not visible from Arlington House, Stanton wished to make a political statement and ensure that future burials of white Union soldiers would be prominent and conspicuous.

→ **Continue to walk up Ord & Weitzel Drive. You will pass the Netherlands Carillon as the road follows along the edge of a stone fence on your right, marking the edge**

of the cemetery. Where the right side of Section 27 narrows, stop to look at the civilian gravestones.

7 SECTION 27

The furthest northern section of the cemetery was originally known as a "contraband cemetery" (whose headstones are marked "civilian" or "citizen"). More than 5,000 African Americans were buried in this section between 1864 and 1867 under the direction of the federal Bureau of Refugees, Freedmen, and Abandoned Lands. Most were self-emancipated; they found their way north to Washington, DC, as internal refugees and could not afford private burials. Although details of their lives were often lost in the chaos of war, it's notable that their graves were not labeled "slave" or "contraband." These individuals lived through the transition from enslavement to freedom and won the right to be called citizens.

This section continued to be used after the Civil War as a segregated burial section for African American soldiers, and today, approximately 1,500 men of the US Colored Troops are also found in Section 27. The burial of African American citizens and soldiers would continue at this furthest-north location until 1899.

Also known as the "lower cemetery," this section was over half a mile away from the main cemetery, separated by woods and a stream. It was so separate, in fact, that through the war and Reconstruction, this section had its own sexton. Despite complaints by prominent African American citizens, including Frederick Douglass, that white Confederate soldiers were better honored by placement in the main cemetery than these African American soldiers who had died for the Union cause, the cemetery's policy of segregation remained strictly enforced. Rather than giving better treatment to soldiers of color, the War Department chose instead to disinter Confederate soldiers, moving the remains of 89 Confederate soldiers to Hollywood Cemetery in Richmond, Virginia, in 1871.

The other three segregated burial areas for soldiers of color can be found in Sections 19, 23, and 25. The cemetery was not desegregated until 1948, when President Harry S. Truman issued Executive Order 9981 ordering the desegregation of all armed forces—including the dead.

→ **Continue following Ord & Weitzel Drive. Pass a maintenance yard on your right. Just before the road curves to the left, look to your right for Section 79, a recently added columbarium.**

8 COLUMBARIUM

Look to your right for a cement structure atop a tiered stone base. Beginning in 1980, Arlington National Cemetery began opening sections for cremated remains of military personnel, reflecting a greater public acceptance of the practice of cremation—but also opening more room for burials as the cemetery fills to capacity. This is the second columbarium added to the cemetery; a larger one fills Section 63.

The cemetery is quickly running out of available burial space. It has responded to this challenge by changing eligibility criteria, accommodating only combat heroes, battle casualties, and notable dignitaries (although there are looser criteria for cremated remains). With approximately seven thousand individuals interred in a typical year, the cemetery is racing to stay ahead of need. The new, more exclusive rules, coupled with a planned expansion at the south end of the cemetery grounds (surrounding the Air Force Memorial), may allow Arlington National to remain an active cemetery for another century.

→ **Continue on Ord & Weitzel Drive as it curves to the left. Where it intersects with Lincoln Drive, bear right to continue uphill on Ord & Weitzel for one more block. Turn right on Sherman Drive and follow the road up to the mansion. This is an uphill climb, and as there are no sidewalks along the winding road, pedestrians must stay alert for traffic. At the top of the hill, look for a staircase on your left, which will lead you to the rear of Arlington House. Walk around to the front, facing toward the Potomac River and the National Mall.**

9 PIERRE CHARLES L'ENFANT MONUMENT

Section 2, Grave S-3

Pierre Charles L'Enfant (1754–1825) is most famous as the city planner who designed Washington, DC. Born in Paris, L'Enfant served in the American Revolution in the Continental Army Corps of Engineers. He remained in the United States after the war, working as a civil engineer and architect in Philadelphia and New York before his appointment by President George Washington to create a grand urban design for the new US capital.

L'Enfant cofounded the Society of the Cincinnati and was a Freemason. He was a professor of engineering at West Point Academy from 1813 to 1817. Among his honors, two ships, a Washington Metro station, and L'Enfant Plaza, a complex of office buildings, were named for him. Since 2022, his statue—representing Washington, DC—resides in the US Capitol as part of the National Statuary Hall Collection. The American Planning Association gives an annual award named in his honor.

L'Enfant's "Plan of the city intended for the permanent seat of the government of the United States" showed his genius for creating a built environment using monumental spaces to reinforce democratic ideals. Unfortunately, his difficult temperament and his insistence on the integrity of his design brought him into increasing conflict with the three commissioners tasked to provide oversight on a limited budget. He was dismissed in 1792, after a year of service, and his plans were carried out by others. By the time of his death, he was living in poverty at a friend's farm in Chillum, Maryland, where he was originally buried in a family plot. His reputation was restored during the execution of the McMillan Plan, whose 1902 redesign of DC's central core reestablished some of his unfinished ideas. In 1909, L'Enfant's remains were exhumed and he was given a state funeral, with his casket on display in the Capitol rotunda. This monument was dedicated in 1911, two years after his reburial. Atop a table pedestal is an engraved portion of the map he designed. L'Enfant now lies in a place of honor with a scenic view over the city he helped create.

→ **Walk to the west end of the plaza and look for a set of stairs leading down the ridge. Go halfway down the stairs until you can see the Pentagon in the distance on your right.**

10 VIEW TOWARD THE PENTAGON

The Pentagon is the headquarters of the US Department of Defense and the world's second-largest office building. The land surrounding the Pentagon (including some of the land that is part of the building's modern footprint) was once the nation's first Freedman's Village.

In May 1863, a federally authorized contraband camp was laid out near the plantation's former slave quarters. Initially housed in tents, the residents of Freedman's Village were soon moved into a series of over fifty identical wooden structures, surrounded by farmland. Each wooden house was a story and a half tall, divided down the middle for occupancy by two families.

During the Civil War, thousands of people escaped slavery and traveled to Washington, DC, following troops of soldiers or on their own. The federal government established the Freedman's Village to manage this influx of internal refugees, trying out new policies for the provision of literacy education, job training and placement, and early ideas of welfare, especially for those who were too young, old, sick, or disabled to provide for themselves. Freedman's Village was managed by the military and the American Missionary Association, with input and donations from other charitable organizations.

Villagers paid rent, maintained (and sometimes added to or embellished) their houses, planted vegetable plots, formed three church congregations, and created mutual-aid societies and clubs. Some residents were hired to farm plots of land on what is today the site of the Pentagon and Columbia Pike. There were also communal structures built: a hospital, laundry, two schools (one to teach industrial trades), and a shared kitchen. One building was set aside for the care of elderly residents. In May 1864, *Harper's Weekly* described the village as "quite lively, having a large number of children in it. . . . The principal street is over a quarter of a mile long, and the place presents a clean and prosperous appearance at all times."

Although the federal government intended residence to be temporary at Freedman's Village, residents built strong community ties and resisted evictions from the land. The first unsuccessful evictions date to 1868. In 1887, the federal government finally began to pay compensation and evicted the last residents in 1900, which allowed the army to annex 142 acres. This addition to the cemetery—the first of several expansions—enlarged its original footprint from 200 acres to 342.

The three churches formed at Freedman's Village reestablished themselves in nearby neighborhoods, and parishioners followed, settling within walking distance of their houses of worship. Those constitute Arlington County's historic African American neighborhoods: Hall's Hill, Johnson's Hill (also known as Arlington

View), and Nauck (also known as Green Valley). An additional community, Queen City, was begun at the same time. The Queen City site is now the location of a cloverleaf highway structure leading onto Columbia Pike, just west of the Pentagon—and its residents, direct descendants of Freedman's Villagers, were subject to a new round of displacement in 1941 when Pentagon construction commenced.

The cemeteries for Freedman's Village and Queen City were also lost in expansions to Arlington National Cemetery and the Pentagon's transportation corridors. They remain unmarked.

→ **Retrace your steps up to the front of the mansion.**

11 ARLINGTON HOUSE

In 1778, John Parke Custis (1754–1781), the stepson of George Washington, bought 1,100 acres of this land. Jacky, as he was known, served as an aide to Washington during the Revolutionary War and died of "camp fever"—probably dysentery or typhus—during the Battle of Yorktown (1781). His two children were raised by George and Martha Washington at Mount Vernon.

Jacky's oldest son, George Washington Parke Custis (1781–1857), known as Wash, inherited the estate in 1802 along with two other plantations and a large number of enslaved people. Determined to create a shrine to his step-grandfather (who had died in 1799), Wash commissioned architect George Hadfield, former superintendent of the US Capitol, to provide a design for a grand mansion (see Hadfield's grave in site 31 in the Congressional Cemetery tour on page 86). Built entirely by enslaved labor between 1802 and 1818, Arlington House is one of the earliest Greek Revival houses in the nation, with a two-story "temple" supported by eight enormous Doric columns and flanked by one-story wings. The house is built of brick but faced with stucco painted to resemble marble and stone. It was placed at the highest elevation on the property, with direct sight lines across the Potomac River to the US Capitol.

Wash Custis filled the mansion with china, furniture, and other memorabilia and personal belongings inherited from his famous step-grandfather, turning half of the first floor into a museum. He was also a playwright, publishing *The Indian Prophecy; or Visions of Glory* (1828), and *Pocahontas; or The Settlers of Virginia* (1830). His biographical essays, collected as *Recollections and Private Memoirs of Washington,* were posthumously printed in 1860. In 1811, his enslaved laborers completed an eight-acre site with a covered reception area and pier called Arlington Spring. Day-trippers from Washington, DC, could take a ferry to the area and purchase light refreshments (or bring a picnic) and hear Wash lecture on George Washington and his own youth. This became a popular amusement. The mansion was open every day but Sunday during the spring and summer months.

Although historically presented as a "good master," Wash was known during his lifetime for providing insufficient food and housing to enslaved people, especially on his outlying plantations, Romancoke and White House, and allowing such harsh punishments that some enslaved people were drowned or whipped to death. His wife, Mary Lee Fitzhugh Custis (1788–1853), was a supporter of the American Colonization Society, which promoted the relocation of freeborn African Americans and emancipated slaves to Africa, believing that their integration into American society was impossible. Under the aegis of the society, Mary created a Sunday school at Arlington to teach enslaved people to read the Bible. This was against Virginia law and was interpreted in her time as dangerously liberal.

Mary and Wash had four children, but only one, Mary Anna Randolph Custis (1807–1873), lived to adulthood. When Wash Custis died in 1857, he left the mansion and its grounds to his daughter for use during her lifetime. Mary married her third cousin Robert E. Lee (1807–1870) in 1831. The estate would subsequently be inherited by her oldest son, George Washington Custis Lee (1832–1913), known as Custis. Wash's other two plantations were left to his other grandsons, and his granddaughters were to receive a cash inheritance of $10,000. Wanting to follow the model of his famous step-grandfather, Wash also stipulated in his will that all 196 enslaved people in his possession at the time of his death be freed within five years of his passing. Because of his bad management and enormous debts, the terms of his will were more aspirational than realistic.

Robert E. Lee never owned Arlington House. The man most associated with the property also rarely lived there. But Lee certainly was the recipient of the economic benefits that plantation slavery conferred. When he married Wash's daughter, she and their children, who eventually numbered seven, lived in the mansion for over thirty years while he was stationed at various military posts. Robert E. Lee became executor of the estate upon the death of his father-in-law and tried to offset Wash's debts and fulfill his wishes for cash inheritances by wringing as much labor as possible from the enslaved people at Arlington House before the end of the five-year period. He did so by greatly increasing workloads and breaking up families. Some of these included his relatives: we know that Wash raped and fathered numerous children with enslaved women he owned.

Warned repeatedly about approaching Civil War troops, Mary Anna Randolph Custis Lee finally abandoned the mansion in May 1861 with some of her prized possessions. A few days later, the grounds became a camp for two Union regiments from New York. Mary would never return—although, to the end of her days, the property became her obsession and the focus of bitter resentment.

Tours of the house are self-guided on weekdays, and a

more extensive guided tour is offered on Saturdays and Sundays. In 1955, in a misguided attempt to glorify an enemy, the US Congress designated the house as a permanent memorial to General Robert E. Lee. In 1933, the house came under the jurisdiction of the National Park Service, creating a Park Service "island" in the midst of the military cemetery. The mansion was added to the National Register of Historic Places in 1966.

→ **Walk through the mansion or, if you wish, you can choose to stay outside and walk around to the rear.**

12 SOUTH DEPENDENCY

Two symmetrical buildings remain at the rear of the mansion. The south one contains a re-creation of the slave quarters of Selina Norris Gray (1823–1907), Mary Lee's personal maid and housekeeper (as well as a skilled seamstress), and her husband, Thornton, and eight children. When Mary Lee escaped Union troops and left Arlington House, she left behind a large community of enslaved people and an overseer who had to restructure their lives with the chaotic presence of an army encampment. The Grays, who had previously been confined to one-third of the South Dependency (the part furthest from the mansion's back door), saw an opportunity to improve their living conditions. Thornton Gray cut internal doors into the two other spaces, originally a smokehouse and locked storage area, and took over the entire South Dependency.

The Grays were some of the many enslaved people who chose to stay at Arlington throughout and after the war. They were joined by dispersed enslaved people who returned, sometimes by foot over great distances, to rejoin family. Selina Gray has been portrayed as the "keeper of the keys"—the person to whom Mary Lee entrusted the safety of the plantation in her absence.

When Selina and her husband cut doors into the other parts of the South Dependency, they were able to access dry goods and slave rations and, in the confusion of the military occupancy, provide for themselves and for other enslaved people living in cabins closer to the Potomac River. Whether she was instructed by Mary Lee to take charge in this way or she took on the responsibility herself is unknown. But it's clear that Selina was already determining different claims on the spaces of the plantation than she had access to under Mary Lee's watch.

Selina Gray reported to the military commander, General Irvin McDowell, when she discovered that soldiers had broken into locked storage areas of the mansion and stolen or damaged some of the "Washington Treasures," items Wash had preserved that once belonged to President George Washington. McDowell sent the remaining items to the US Patent Office for safekeeping, where they were put on display throughout the war in an exhibit called "Captured from Arlington." They were later added to the collections of the Smithsonian Institution. These items included pieces from a formal china set, Revolutionary War field tents, and the blanket under which Washington died.

Since the 1990s, Selina Gray's role in saving the Washington Treasures has made her the most celebrated of Arlington's enslaved people. She is praised for her faithfulness to her owners, as a proto-preservationist, and as an example of shared patriotism across racial lines.

In 1863, when Mary Custis Lee sent her cousin to pay her property bill of $92.70 to the federal government, the payment was refused on the grounds that the tax must be paid in person by the legal owner. By this time, Mary was debilitated by arthritis, which required the use of a wheelchair. The federal government declared the property critical to the war effort and officially claimed it for use as a military encampment and quartermaster corrals.

Mary Lee spent the rest of her life trying to reclaim her mansion and belongings. She even initiated a correspondence with Selina Gray, who responded with a remarkable four-page letter in 1872. Although she could read, the letter may have been dictated. The largely unpunctuated letter begins, "Arlington it is a most lovely place now everywhere around it look beautiful there is not a tree to be seen except in the cemetery the whole of it is rented to the freemen they have little huts all over that beautiful place and besides that they have a large military school of signal co and the place is changed so you wold hardly know it."

By this time, Selina and Thornton Gray were no longer living at Arlington. She writes, "I am very happy that I have got a comfortable home of my own now down by the factory a bout half way to Alexandria we have ten acres of land it is very poor but we hope in time to improve it." She reports that her family is doing well, even giving the exact wages her daughter earned as a laundress and her son and husband earned working for the new military graveyard—which must have been pointed information to provide to a former mistress. She continues, "Harry has grow to be quite a larg man he is just 21 and as big and tall as father he is very steady and quite a working young man and is a great help to his father his father and him has been working up at Arlington all the summer each getting 45 dollars a month."

Selina reiterates that she doesn't know what happened to Mary's family belongings and asks her to pass along her regards to the Lee children. She also, thoughtfully, includes a pressed rosebud from the grave of Mary's mother. She closes her letter, "no more from your humble servant Selina Gray."

Under the auspices of the National Park Service, both the North and South Dependencies are now used as spaces to interpret the lives of enslaved people on the plantation.

→ **Vegetable gardens can be found to the right of the mansion, along with restrooms, water fountains, and**

a National Park Service bookstore. To the left of the mansion, enter the flower gardens and take the path all the way to the white picket fence at the other end.

13 VIEW TOWARD THE AIR FORCE MEMORIAL

Construction on a south parcel of 50 additional acres began in 2023, which, when completed in 2027, will raise the size of Arlington National Cemetery from 639 to 689 acres. That southern end will surround the existing Air Force Memorial, dedicated in 2006: three stainless steel spires 270 feet high, designed by James Ingo Freed to resemble jets' contrails.

→ **Walk to your right, following the picket fence around to a white picket side gate on your left. Take that path to the next site.**

14 CIVIL WAR UNKNOWN SOLDIERS MONUMENT

Section 26

In October 1865, the War Department undertook a major effort to locate, identify, disinter, move, and rebury hundreds of thousands of Union soldiers whose remains were scattered across former battlefields, military encampments, and roadways. Those found within thirty-five miles of Washington, DC, were moved from their temporary burial sites in Maryland and Virginia to Arlington. Of those, approximately 42 percent were unable to be identified, and Montgomery C. Meigs ordered the army to construct a collective tomb for the unknowns as well as "scattered bones and disorganized remains" that were not intact.

This altar tomb, dedicated to the "noble army of martyrs," contains approximately 2,111 soldiers from the Battle of Bull Run and those found along the nearby railroad tracks and trenches on the route to the Rappahannock River. Only the remains of white soldiers were included in this group, but it's likely that some remains were from Confederate soldiers. Placed in the mansion's former rose garden, the monument was dedicated in September 1866. On the first Decoration Day in 1868, former Union general James A. Garfield (then a congressman, but later elected president) gave an address on the portico of Arlington House and then led a procession of orphans to this tomb, where they sang, accompanied by a military band, while the tomb was decorated with garlands and flowers.

→ **Continue along the path.**

15 JAMES TANNER AMPHITHEATER

Dedicated in 1873, this wood and brick amphitheater features a circular pergola of Ionic columns supporting a trellis of wisteria vines, which surrounds seating for up to 1,500. Seats face a raised rostrum inscribed with the phrase "E Pluribus Unum," the Latin motto of the United States, meaning "out of many, one." It replaced a temporary amphitheater in the same spot that had been built in 1868 for the first Decoration Day ceremonies. Now overshadowed by the larger and grander Memorial Amphitheater, this older site is less visited, its partly shaded colonnade less often walked.

The old amphitheater was built on the former site of Mary Lee's Slave School House. Mary Anna Randolph Custis Lee was well educated for a Southern woman, learning Greek and Latin, and she read widely. She learned to paint landscapes and oversaw a garden (maintained, of course, by enslaved people) where eleven varieties of roses were cultivated.

Mary Lee was a devout Episcopalian, maintaining a family tradition of prayer readings in the parlor twice a day, after breakfast and dinner. Her School House, open on Sundays, was an outgrowth of her religious beliefs. Its goal was to teach enslaved people enough literacy to be able to read the Bible on their own. This did not mean, however, that Mary Lee supported emancipation. She fervently believed in the myth that enslavement was a benefit to a lower race of people who should be grateful for their paternal care and moral uplift through association with enlightened white owners such as herself.

In 2014, in honor of the cemetery's 150th anniversary, the old amphitheater was renamed to honor Corporal James R. Tanner (1844–1927), who lost both legs from gunshot wounds sustained in the Second Battle of Bull Run. Tanner, a stenographer, was present at Lincoln's deathbed and during the trial of the conspirators behind the assassination, and his notes are considered the most comprehensive records of both those events. He subsequently studied law and held jobs as tax collector for the city of Brooklyn, register of wills for the District of Columbia, commissioner of pensions, and commander in chief of the Grand Army of the Republic, a postwar fraternal organization. He also served on the executive committee of the American Red Cross.

→ **Take Meigs Drive, behind the amphitheater, and turn right on Humphreys Drive. Head toward the National Park Service ranger station, a white columned outbuilding. Take the second left and look for the next memorial on your right.**

16 PAN AM FLIGHT 103 MEMORIAL / LOCKERBIE MEMORIAL CAIRN

Section 1

In a 1988 terrorist bombing, 270 people died aboard an airplane over Lockerbie, Scotland, while en route from Germany to New York. The 259 passengers and crew, and the 11 people on the ground who died, were citizens of twenty-one countries; 190 were Americans, including 25 who were either active military personnel or veterans. This cairn, consisting of 270 blocks of red Scottish sandstone (one for each person who died), was quarried from a source near the flight path, the same quarry that provided the stone for the base of the Statue of Liberty. The monument was a gift from the people of Scotland, financed entirely through private donations.

The Lockerbie Memorial Cairn is one of several recent monuments and graves at Arlington that honor the victims of terrorist attacks in the post-Vietnam era. Others include the Pentagon Group Burial Marker (also known as the September 11th Memorial), the Attack on the USS *Cole* graves, the Iran Rescue Mission Memorial, and the Beirut Barracks Memorial. While not memorializing wars or military actions, these monuments are loosely gathered together under the rubric of the War on Terror and emphasize American victimization, often at the hands of what is characterized as "Islamic aggression."

→ **Retrace your steps to turn right on Meigs Drive. In Section 1, look to your right for a raised white sarcophagus on a base of rough granite blocks, about five rows in.**

17 MONTGOMERY C. MEIGS GRAVE

Section 1, Grave 1-EH

Montgomery C. Meigs (1816–1892) established Arlington National Cemetery while serving as quartermaster general of the US Army during the Civil War. Meigs graduated from West Point and served in the Army Corps of Engineers, supervising several important infrastructure projects in DC (including the wings and dome of the US Capitol and the construction of the Washington Aqueduct) until the Civil War broke out. He attained the rank of brevet major general and was widely praised for devising a complex supply system that got food, weapons, ammunition, and other supplies to troops in the field. He was responsible for overseeing military transportation, constructing telegraph lines, building a fleet of ironclad ships, instituting public bidding of government contracts, and managing military budgets. His logistics and leadership are considered key factors in the Union victory.

In addition to his war service, Meigs was a regent of the Smithsonian Institution, a member of the National Academy of Sciences and the American Philosophical Society, and an avid reader and watercolorist. He held more than a dozen patents for inventions and was one of the first engineers to employ photography to record his projects. Among the buildings he worked on in Washington, DC, are the Post Office Building (now Hotel Monaco), the roof truss for the Arts and Industries Building of the Smithsonian Institution, and the Pension Building (now the National Building Museum). Among other honors, three ships have been named for Montgomery C. Meigs, and Camp Meigs in Massachusetts was named for him as well.

Meigs designed Arlington National Cemetery's early layout and continued to implement changes during the fifteen years after the end of the Civil War. When selecting the site, the fact that it was wrested from Robert E. Lee was part of the cemetery's appeal: Meigs considered Lee's actions treasonable, and his property was therefore a valuable political asset. The Civil War Unknowns Monument, McClellan Gate, and James Tanner Amphitheater were built to Meigs's designs.

Meigs is buried with his wife, grandfather, uncle, and son. His son John's grave, topped by a bronze sculpture, is particularly moving: Meigs designed it to show how he died, shot in a Union battle near Harrisonburg, Virginia, at age twenty-two.

→ **Walk across the grass to the next road, Humphreys Drive, and turn left, following the road around a sharp right curve. On the right-hand side, look for a large granite stone with a bronze cartouche. The bronze image shows a bas-relief of John Wesley Powell's head, with his long beard.**

18 JOHN WESLEY POWELL GRAVE

Section 1, Grave 408

John Wesley Powell (1834–1902) was the first person to explore the Grand Canyon. He was director of the US Geological Survey (1881–1894) and the first director of the Smithsonian Institution's Bureau of Ethnology (1879–1880). Powell cofounded a number of scientific organizations in Washington, DC, including the Geological Society of America and the National Geographic Society.

Powell served in the US Army during the Civil War, attaining the rank of major, and lost his lower right arm as a result of gunshot wounds sustained during the Battle of Shiloh. After the war, Powell was a professor of geology at Illinois Wesleyan University, curator of the Museum of the Illinois State Natural History Society, and a lecturer at Illinois State Normal University and Columbian University in Washington, DC. He led a series of federally funded expeditions in the American West, exploring the Rocky Mountains and the Green and Colorado Rivers.

Powell is the author of *Report on the Lands of the Arid Regions of the United States* (1878) and *The Exploration of the Colorado River and Its Canyons* (1875). While working at the Smithsonian, he contributed to the Bureau of Ethnology's classification of Native American languages. His honors include the naming of the John Wesley Powell National Conservation Area in Utah; the Powell Federal Building at the USGS National Center in Reston, Virginia; Lake Powell, a reservoir on the Colorado River;

Mount Powell in the Sierra Nevada mountains of California; and the town of Powell, Wyoming. He was depicted on a US postage stamp, awarded two honorary degrees, and elected to the National Academy of Sciences, the American Association for the Advancement of Science, and the Anthropological Society of Washington.

→ **Retrace your steps to Meigs Drive. At the intersection of Meigs and Wilson Drives, you'll see a statue of Major General Phil Kearney on horseback. This is the boundary between Sections 1 and 2 of the cemetery.**

19 REVOLUTIONARY WAR AND WAR OF 1812 REINTERMENTS

Sections 1 and 2

Eleven Revolutionary War veterans who survived the war and died years later were reinterred at Arlington National Cemetery between 1892 and 1911, moved from the Presbyterian Burial Ground in Georgetown after that land was earmarked for new development. In 1905, construction workers at the Marine Barracks in Washington discovered the remains of fourteen unknown soldiers from the War of 1812; they were also moved to Arlington National Cemetery. As a result, the cemetery can claim to represent military personnel from every American war. (Although Congressional Cemetery in DC can make that same claim, Arlington is the only official *military* cemetery that has remains from every war.) These soldiers are buried in scattered plots in Sections 1 and 2.

→ **Take Wilson Drive down the hill. You will cross Farragut Drive and see Memorial Amphitheater in front of you. Don't enter the amphitheater yet! Instead, take the walkway directly across from the amphitheater entrance on your right. A spur off this walkway will lead you to three memorial plaques.**

20 SPACE SHUTTLE *CHALLENGER* MEMORIAL

Section 46

The *Challenger* exploded seventy seconds after takeoff in 1986, killing all seven crew members, including Christa McAuliffe, who had been selected from more than eleven thousand applicants to become the first teacher in space. The commingled cremated remains of the astronauts are buried here. The back of the memorial displays a poem, "High Flight," written in 1941 by a Royal Canadian Air Force pilot, John Gillespie Magee Jr.

21 IRAN RESCUE MISSION MEMORIAL

Section 46

Dedicated in 1983, this memorial commemorates the eight Americans who died when their helicopter collided with a transport plane during a rescue mission. The service members were attempting to rescue fifty-three American hostages who had been seized during a raid on the US embassy in Tehran in 1979, during the Iranian Revolution. Although this rescue mission was unsuccessful, Iran did eventually release the hostages—but only after they had endured 444 days of captivity.

22 SPACE SHUTTLE *COLUMBIA* MEMORIAL

Section 46

This memorial remembers the seven astronauts killed in 2003, when the *Columbia* burst into flames as it reentered Earth's atmosphere at the end of a sixteen-day scientific mission.

→ **Go back to the pathway and turn right. Look for a large mast, and take the path toward it.**

23 USS *MAINE* MEMORIAL

Section 24

The imposing mast of the USS *Maine*, placed atop a granite base designed to resemble the turret of a battleship, is one of the best-known monuments in the cemetery. The ship was in Havana harbor in Cuba in 1898, during the Spanish-American War, when it was attacked; an explosion tore open the hull, killing more than 260 sailors (230 of whom are buried around this monument). The mast, raised from the harbor floor, was transported back to the United States for this memorial in 1912.

→ **Take Sigsbee Drive (which surrounds the *Maine* memorial) to the end and turn left on Farragut Drive. At the intersection, turn left on McPherson Drive. Jackson Circle will be on your right.**

24 CONFEDERATE SECTION

Section 16

In 1898, a politically misguided and highly disrespectful speech made by President William McKinley in Atlanta advocated the accommodation of Confederate soldiers in Arlington National Cemetery. In the midst of the Spanish-American War, he stated, "Sectional feeling no longer holds back the love we bear each other. Fraternity is the national anthem," adding that "in the spirit of fraternity we should share with you in the care of graves of Confederate soldiers. . . . Every soldier's grave made during the unfortunate Civil War is a tribute to American valor."

By 1902, 262 Confederate remains were moved to this section from burial grounds around the Washington, DC, region. (Other Confederate remains would be moved to this section at later dates; there are now more than

400 here.) Unlike the orderly rows in other parts of the cemetery, they were arranged in rings around a central mound, with distinct headstones of pointed tops different from the federal graves of Union soldiers—or the graves of all subsequent wars. Given the cemetery's strict segregation policy, only white soldiers were included in "the spirit of fraternity."

In 1914, an enormous bronze monument in the middle of the circle was unveiled, funded by the United Daughters of the Confederacy. It was designed by the first Jewish cadet to attend Virginia Military Academy, Moses Jacob Ezekiel (1844–1917), who fought on the Confederate side in the Civil War. The monument—large, elaborate, and offensive in its use of racist tropes—built upon a growing Lost Cause ideology in the South. Topped with a classical female figure wearing a crown of olive leaves who represented the South, it towered over a frieze of life-sized heroic figures of mythic gods alongside soldiers, an enslaved and stereotypical weeping "mammy" figure holding a white infant, and a "master" taking his dutiful enslaved valet with him toward battle. Ezekiel was buried at the base of the monument after his own death.

In 2023, the monument was removed as part of the 2021 National Defense Authorization Act directive to rename or remove all military items that glorified or commemorated the Confederate States of America. (This included ten military bases named for Confederate leaders.) The Sons of Confederate Veterans brought suit against the Defense Department in an attempt to keep the memorial in place, claiming that it "commemorates reconciliation and national unity" rather than glorifying the Confederacy. Although slowed down by the litigation, the army finally removed the offensive monument in December 2023, leaving behind only the granite base as a reminder of the ongoing national reckoning with the repercussions of American slavery.

But that's not the end of the story. Despite the Congressional Naming Commission's decree, which criticized the monument for being "a nostalgic, mythologized version of the Confederacy, including highly sanitized depictions of slavery," the monument is in the process of being reinstated. The Confederate Monument is now held at a storage facility, where it is being refurbished, at a cost of about $10 million. It is expected to return to the grounds of Arlington National Cemetery in 2027.

President Donald Trump issued an executive order in March 2025, "Restoring Truth and Sanity to American History," claiming that "the widespread effort to rewrite history deepens societal divides and fosters a sense of national shame." It orders the restoration of statues that were "removed or changed to perpetuate a false reconstruction of American history, inappropriately minimize the value of certain historical events or figures, or include any other improper partisan ideology."

That last part of the statement, about "partisan ideology," is the most debatable. Statements by Trump and others in his administration have been anything but impartial. US Secretary of Defense Pete Hegseth wrote on social media, "It should never have been taken down by woke lemmings. Unlike the Left, we don't believe in erasing American history—we honor it."

It is unclear at this time if the restored monument will include new signs and if they would be able to provide the sensitive contextualizing needed to educate viewers on its interpretation as a symbol of white supremacy. I am not optimistic.

One other significant part of the cemetery has also been affected by the Defense Authorization Act. As part of this same Naming Commission provision, the Arlington House National Monument, known since 1925 as the Robert E. Lee Memorial (so designated during the ninetieth anniversary of Lee's surrender at Appomattox Court House), has reverted to the name of Arlington

House. Although some military bases that were renamed after the National Defense Authorization Act have gone back to their original names (honoring Confederate military personnel), at this time, I know of no movements to change the name of Arlington House back to the Robert E. Lee Memorial.

→ **Return to McPherson Drive and turn right. The next two memorials will be approximately one hundred feet on your left, past Lawton Drive.**

25 ROUGH RIDERS MEMORIAL

Section 22

The best-known cavalry unit in American history, the Rough Riders were led by future president Theodore Roosevelt during the Spanish-American War. Their fame rests on a decisive battle in Cuba in July 1898, when the unit charged up San Juan Hill. A gray granite pillar displays the First US Volunteer Cavalry's insignia, listing the regiment's battles and the names of those who died. The memorial was dedicated in 1907.

→ **Look to your left for a small plaque close to the ground.**

26 BUFFALO SOLDIERS CENTENNIAL MEMORIAL

Section 22

Just adjacent to the Rough Riders Memorial, look for a low granite marker, dedicated in 1998. Although considerably smaller than the one for the Rough Riders, it complements the larger marker and acknowledges (in its understated way) how white supremacist narratives of valor historically overlook the contributions of soldiers of color.

→ **Continue on McPherson Drive to Lawton Drive (which has looped and intersects with McPherson for a second time). The next site is on your right.**

27 BATTLE OF THE BULGE MEMORIAL

This memorial commemorates the World War II battle that was the last major German counteroffensive on the Western Front. Although the battle ended in victory, it took place under brutal winter conditions and resulted in massive losses: approximately nineteen thousand deaths and seventy-five thousand casualties. The memorial was dedicated in 2006, a gift from the Kingdom of Belgium and the Grand Duchy of Luxembourg.

→ **Just behind the Battle of the Bulge Memorial, you will see a large stone with a Maltese cross.**

28 SPANISH-AMERICAN WAR NURSES MEMORIAL

Section 21

Arlington was not only segregated by race in its early decades; it was also segregated by gender. This "nurses' section" was designated for women who served as contract nurses. The Spanish-American War was the first conflict in which nurses were given a dedicated service unit. Nurses endured fourteen-hour shifts, provided their own uniforms, and worked in challenging (frequently unsanitary and overcrowded) conditions, often with shortages of medical supplies and insufficient staff. This large granite monument with a Maltese cross honors 153 nurses who died during the war—all from disease, as no nurses were killed in combat.

→ **Cross the grass and walk around a copse of trees to find the next memorial.**

29 NURSES MEMORIAL

Section 21

Sculpted by Frances Rich (1910–2007), who served in the US Navy WAVES in World War II, this Art Deco statue in Tennessee white marble is eleven feet tall and surrounded by the graves of 653 nurses. Dedicated in 1938, it marked the professionalism of nurses as military personnel rather than civilian contract workers. Although there have always been male nurses, the memorial depicts nursing service in gendered terms, as an extension of feminine caring roles, and brings a woman's figure into what had previously been a very male cemetery space. The monument looks imposing (and appears even taller) because of its placement atop a slope.

→ **Cut back across the grass to Lawton Drive. Look for a traffic island at the far end of its curve.**

30 SPANISH-AMERICAN WAR MEMORIAL

Arlington National Cemetery includes more Spanish-American War graves and memorials than any other location in the country. As the first war after the Civil War, the Spanish-American War is often credited in publications and tours of Arlington with reuniting the North and South under a single nationalistic effort. But this war turned the United States into a global power and a colonial ruler as it took possession of territories from Spain: Guam, Puerto Rico, and the Philippines. American forces also claimed Cuba as a US protectorate and annexed the independent state of Hawaii. The war inaugurated a new expansionist era in American history. The United States continues to excuse military incursions into other countries, undermining their sovereignty under the banner of spreading democracy.

This large column, topped by an eagle, sits in a prominent location in its own traffic circle; it was donated by the National Society of Colonial Dames.

→ **Go past the row of cannons and cut across the grass, heading down the slope to Memorial Drive. Turn left. The amphitheater will be on your right.**

31 MEMORIAL AMPHITHEATER

The new Memorial Amphitheater was created in 1920, at the end of World War I. Ironically, the first funeral service conducted in the building was for the Confederate veteran Moses Jacob Ezekiel, the sculptor of the controversial and racist Confederate Memorial.

Memorial Amphitheater was configured as a "centerpiece" of Arlington National Cemetery. It can accommodate five thousand people and is the site of large annual services on Easter, Memorial Day, and Veterans Day as well as smaller funeral services. Designed by Thomas Hastings from Vermont marble, the complex includes an open semielliptical outdoor colonnade (inscribed with the names of forty-four battles along the top) as well as an interior chapel and Memorial Display Room for exhibitions in an attached, two-story reception hall building with six columns and a decorative frieze of Greco-Roman sculptures.

The outdoor colonnade is punctuated by arcades; the focal point is an impressive two-story Beaux Arts stage on the eastern side. The names of fourteen army generals and fourteen navy admirals are engraved on the sides of the stage above stylized funerary urns. A ceremonial marble chair adorns the lower stage, surrounded by a deep proscenium arch and the apse above the upper stage. Box seats on either side provide elevated views for honored guests, and marble-topped benches for the public fill the open center.

→ **Go to the rear of the memorial.**

32 TOMB OF THE UNKNOWN SOLDIER

The most distinct feature in the cemetery is the Tomb of the Unknown Soldier, which holds the remains of one soldier from World War I, another from World War II, and a third from the Korean War. Each died in combat, and their remains could not be identified. A soldier from the Vietnam War once occupied a space in the tomb as well but was removed after he was identified through a DNA match. (His remains were returned to his family for burial in St. Louis, Missouri, in 1998.)

The US Army 3rd Infantry Regiment, also known as the Old Guard, guards the tomb day and night. During hours when the cemetery is open to the public, a soldier performs precise choreography in front of the tomb. He or she walks exactly 21 steps across, 21 steps back, then pauses for 21 seconds, makes a quarter turn, pauses for another 21 seconds, and repeats the steps. Changing of the guard occurs on the half hour during summer months and on the hour during the winter, when visitors are fewer.

The original tomb forms the base for a newer monument, added in 1932. The original, smaller monument was often used by visitors to sit atop, and its table-like shape encouraged picnickers. When the American Legion appealed to the US Army to place a sentry to discourage such leisure uses, the cemetery fenced the area, then relented and installed guards from Fort Myer beginning in 1926. In 1948, the US Army reactivated one of its oldest units, the 3rd Infantry Regiment, whose history dated to the colonial era. (Some of its members had previously served at Valley Forge.) In its new iteration, the 3rd Infantry Regiment would be the military's most prominent ceremonial unit, responsible for state funerals, the transfer of repatriated bodies from overseas wars at Dover Air Force Base, and guarding the Tomb of the Unknown Soldier.

The larger memorial kept the original intact, building a solid marble tomb on top designed by architect Lorimer Rich and sculptor Thomas Hudson Jones.

The tomb makes several assumptions. Although meant to represent all Americans, the unknowns are generally assumed to be male (since only combat soldiers were eligible for inclusion), Christian (as the invocation of God on the inscription makes clear), white, and heterosexual.

→ **Up the stairs from the Tomb of the Unknown Soldier you will see double glass doors. These lead to an exhibition hall inside the back of Memorial Amphitheater. On exhibit are gifts from other countries to the cemetery as well as historic photos. A public restroom is also available at this site, located at a side entrance leading underneath the amphitheater.**

Upon leaving the amphitheater museum, take the steps down to the plaza and the pathway to your left. Look for a marble bench to your right.

33 KOREAN WAR CONTEMPLATIVE BENCH

Section 48

Located on the north side of Memorial Amphitheater, find a bench shaded by a mountain ash tree donated by the government of South Korea. Further down the path, a second tree, a Korean white pine, was also donated. This quiet spot was dedicated in 1997. The calm of this little site is in direct contradiction to the war it memorializes, in which approximately three million people—mostly civilians—perished, making it the deadliest conflict of the Cold War era.

→ **Retrace your steps on the path and bear left to skirt the edge of the Tomb of the Unknown Soldier. This path**

will lead you downhill to Roosevelt Drive. Turn left on Roosevelt and follow the signs toward the Kennedy Memorial, crossing the intersections at Farragut Drive and McClellan Drive and continuing. At the corner of Roosevelt and Weeks Drives, look to your left for the next small gravesite, in the second row.

34 RICHARD BYRD GRAVE

Section 2, Grave 4969

Richard Evelyn Byrd (1888–1957) was the first person to fly over both the North and the South Poles—in 1926 and 1929, respectively. For these achievements, he was awarded a Medal of Honor and promoted to rear admiral of the US Navy. He continued exploring Antarctica for the rest of his life; at the time of his last expedition, in 1955, he was sixty-seven. He discovered the largest dormant volcano in Antarctica, Mount Sidley. One of the most highly decorated officers in the US Navy, Byrd was awarded a Navy Cross, Distinguished Flying Cross, and Silver Lifesaving Medal, among other honors. His nonfiction books include *Little America* (1930), *Skyward* (1937), and *Alone* (1938).

→ **Turn left on Weeks Drive and head toward the Kennedy Memorial. Don't enter the Kennedy Memorial yet! Instead, turn left on Sheridan Drive. After passing two paths on your right, look to your left for a large stone (in the third row in) with the name "BONNIN" in capital letters, underneath a small bas-relief of a tepee.**

35 ZITKÁLA-ŠA GRAVE

Section 2, Grave 4703

Gertrude Simmons Bonnin, also known as Zitkála-Ša (1876–1938), was a member of the Yankton Dakota Sioux.

Born on a reservation in South Dakota, she was sent to an Indian boarding school where she was forced to adopt European dress, language, and culture, which shaped her later political activism. (She used both names professionally.) She was secretary of the Society of American Indians and cofounded (with her husband Raymond Bonnin) the National Council of American Indians, which lobbied Congress and the Bureau of Indian Affairs for land claims, improved health care and education, cultural recognition, and voting rights for Native Americans.

Zitkála-Ša continued her education at Earlham College and the New England Conservatory of Music. She is famous as the author of the first autobiography written in English by a Native American that was not filtered through a white editor or translator. She began publishing autobiographical articles in 1900, which were collected as *American Indian Stories* in 1921. She also compiled a collection of Sioux mythology, *Old Indian Legends* (1901), and wrote the first opera by a Native American, *The Sun Dance Opera* (1913). Her nonfiction book, *Oklahoma's Poor Rich Indians* (1924), exposed the theft of Native American lands by the oil industry and led to federal investigations and land reform laws.

Beginning in 1916, the Bonnins lived in the Lyon Park neighborhood of Arlington, Virginia. Although the neighborhood had restrictive covenants at the time, they only specified that African Americans and Jews were banned from buying property, so by this loophole the law did not affect them. Their house at 261 N. Barton Street still stands, and Arlington County named a nearby park in honor of Zitkála-Ša in 2021.

→ **Now take the path on the other side of Sheridan Drive, an alternate entrance to the Kennedy Memorial. You will first pass the graves of Robert and Edward Kennedy along this path, as well as a water feature, on your way to the eternal flame, where John F. Kennedy is buried.**

36 JOHN F. KENNEDY AND THE KENNEDY FAMILY MEMORIALS

On the eastern slope below Arlington House, with an unobstructed view of the National Mall, this memorial to President John F. Kennedy (1917–1963) was dedicated in 1963. Designed by architect John Carl Warnecke, it incorporates an eternal flame similar to the one at the Arc de Triomphe in Paris that marks the French Tomb of the Unknown Soldier. The flame can be clearly seen at night from the National Mall.

Kennedy was the youngest person and the first Catholic to be elected as US president, serving as the thirty-fifth person to hold the office. (President Joseph Biden is the only other Catholic president.) Kennedy served in the US Navy during World War II in the Pacific Theater, where his rescue of sailors from a sinking patrol boat earned him the Navy and Marine Corps Medal, a Purple Heart, and a Victory Medal. He was elected to the House of Representatives and the Senate, representing Massachusetts. Some of his accomplishments in Congress include support for public housing and labor unions. As president, Kennedy focused on the rising tensions of the Cold War and international relations. He formed the Peace Corps and the Presidential Commission on the Status of Women, negotiated a nuclear test ban treaty, reorganized NASA to support further space exploration, and overhauled immigration policy. He is best remembered, however, for his support of civil rights—including policies for affirmative action, equal employment, and the prohibition of racial discrimination in education and public housing that would lead directly to the Civil Rights Act of 1964, enacted by his successor, President Lyndon B. Johnson.

Kennedy was the author of *Why England Slept* (1940), *A Nation of Immigrants* (1958), and, most significantly, *Profiles in Courage* (1956, winner of the Pulitzer Prize in biography). *Profiles* concentrates on eight senators who made decisions of conscience that were initially unpopular. Those senators included John Quincy Adams, Daniel Webster, Thomas Hart Benton, and Sam Houston. A bestseller, the book was later made into a television series of the same name.

Kennedy's funeral was nationally broadcast on television, an event that cemented the popular vision of Arlington as a site for collective mourning. Kennedy is joined at this plot by his wife, Jacqueline Kennedy Onassis; two infants who died shortly after birth; and, slightly further down the path, by his brothers Senator Robert F. Kennedy (who was also assassinated, while campaigning for US president) and Senator Edward Kennedy. Media coverage of the president's funeral led to a massive increase of visitors to the cemetery as well as significantly higher requests for burials.

→ **After passing the eternal flame, continue around the circle. Before you reach the main road on your left, look for the next grave: a large rectangular granite stone on a slight rise.**

37 OLIVER WENDELL HOLMES GRAVE

Section 5, Grave 7004-A

Oliver Wendell Holmes Jr. (1841–1935) was an associate justice of the US Supreme Court from 1902 to 1932. He is particularly known for his progressive opinions on civil liberties and the Constitution and is considered to be among the most influential—and most widely cited—American judges.

Holmes was a brevet colonel in the army during the Civil War, serving in the 20th Massachusetts Volunteer Infantry. He was wounded in battle three times: at Ball's Bluff, Antietam, and Chancellorsville. After the war, he completed a degree in law at Harvard University and then went into private practice for fifteen years while editing the *American Law Review*. Holmes was a professor at Harvard Law School briefly before his appointment to the Massachusetts Supreme Court, where some of his most noted cases included decisions on strengthening antitrust and copyright laws and interpreting the privileges contained in the Bill of Rights. On the US Supreme Court, Holmes advocated interpreting freedom of speech broadly, deferring to decisions of elected legislatures, and upholding regulatory law under the New Deal.

Holmes is the author of the nonfiction works *The Common Law* (1881), *Collected Legal Papers* (1920), and (posthumously) *The Occasional Speeches of Justice Oliver Wendell Holmes* (1962), *The Essential Holmes* (1992), and *The Collected Works of Justice Holmes* (1994). His honors include a memorial garden in his name at the Supreme Court building, his depiction on a US postage stamp, and the designation of his summer home in Beverly, Massachusetts, as a National Historic Landmark.

→ **Continue along the circular path to the end. Make a left on Sheridan Drive and then take an immediate left onto a wood chip pathway.**

38 RUTH BADER GINSBURG GRAVE

Section 5, Grave 7016-1

Justice Ruth Bader Ginsburg (1933–2020) served as an associate justice on the US Supreme Court from 1993 until her death. She is known for her advocacy of gender equality and women's rights; in 1972, she cofounded the Women's Rights Project at the American Civil Liberties Union.

Some of her accomplishments as a justice include supporting abortion rights, striking down the Virginia Military Institute's male-only admissions policy, affirming that mental illness is a protected form of disability, and affirming the right of residents to seek redress from industrial polluters. Although she was in the minority on a case involving pay discrimination based on gender, her eloquent dissent led directly to congressional passage of the Lilly Ledbetter Fair Pay Act in 2008.

Ginsburg cowrote an autobiography, *In My Own Words,* with Mary Hartnett and Wendy W. Williams (2016), and some of her notable decisions were collected in *Decisions and Dissents of Justice Ruth Bader Ginsburg: A Selection* (2020). Among Ginsburg's many honors, she was awarded honorary degrees from thirty colleges and universities, the US Navy named a ship after her, she was featured on a US postage stamp, and a species of praying mantis was named for her. (The insect has a neck plate that resembles a jabot—an ornamental collar that Ginsburg was famous for wearing with her judicial robes.)

→ **The next site is just behind and to the left of the Ginsburg grave.**

39 THURGOOD MARSHALL GRAVE

Section 5, Grave 40-3

US Supreme Court Justice Thurgood Marshall (1908–1993) was one of the nation's most prominent civil rights lawyers. He worked as the NAACP's assistant chief legal counsel, where his most famous case was the 1954 *Brown v. Board of Education* decision, outlawing school segregation. President John F. Kennedy appointed him to the US Court of Appeals for the Second Circuit in 1961, where he wrote over 150 decisions defending the rights of immigrants and people of color. He served as the US Supreme Court's first African American justice for twenty-four years, from 1967 to his retirement in 1991.

His accomplishments as a justice include opposition to the death penalty, support for abortion, a more nuanced interpretation of the Equal Protection Clause of the Constitution, and a broader definition of individual citizens' right to privacy. Among other honors, an airport, courthouse, numerous streets, and schools have been named for him. He was depicted on a US postage stamp and was posthumously awarded the Presidential Medal of Freedom.

→ **Return to Weeks Drive and turn left, heading back toward the visitor center. Turn left on Roosevelt Drive. Take Roosevelt Drive to the end, and cross Eisenhower Drive to enter the pathway back to the visitor center.**

40 BACK TO THE ENTRANCE

Thanks to Montgomery C. Meigs, the District's main contribution to the design of cemeteries is the military cemetery—which was subsequently re-created in every state in the nation. Our ideal of a military cemetery, with rows of identical small white grave markers laid out evenly along a flat landscape, has even influenced designs of military cemeteries internationally.

With its parking lot full of tour buses, its huge gift shop, and its signs reminding visitors to be respectful, Arlington National Cemetery is different from all other cemeteries because it is so hugely popular. Most visitors have some knowledge of the place before they even enter, and some have expectations of their experience that predate their first visit. At the most well-known sites, such as the Kennedy gravesite with its eternal flame and the changing of the guard ceremony at the Tomb of the Unknown Soldier, you become part of a large crowd, especially on a summer weekend. This would be unheard-of at any other cemetery.

Arlington National Cemetery is by the far the best known and best interpreted of all American cemeteries. And yet I found myself constantly at odds with its official narrative. As an institution run by the US Army, Arlington's mission is to create greater meaning out of military history—which often expands into a glorification of warrior culture and timeworn ideas of heroism.

NATIONAL HARMONY MEMORIAL PARK (1962)

7101 Sheriff Road, Hyattsville, MD

National Harmony Memorial Park is a modern, suburban-style cemetery on 142 acres, with rolling grounds and a huge wooden cross at the point of highest elevation. This tour focuses on the eastern side of the property. Despite its modern founding, the cemetery has incorporated the remains of many older burial grounds for people of color.

From the entrance, stay to the left and follow the signs toward the office. Park in the lot in front of the office. Just to the left of the building, enter the grassy area.

Before You Go

https://www.dignitymemorial.com/funeral-homes/maryland/hyattsville/national-harmony-memorial-park/9735
Open 24 hours
Nearest public transportation: Morgan Boulevard Station to bus
Parking and restrooms available

1 NORTHUP-REED SECTION

A modern memorial of etched black granite depicts the faces of two men suspended above an image of the US Capitol, with an enlarged version of the *Freedom* sculpture from the top of the Capitol dome, placed in the center of the image. The memorial, created by an unknown artist, is flanked on either side by plaques honoring two African American heroes.

Solomon Northup (1807 or 1808–ca. 1864) was born

free in New York State, where he farmed, married, and had three children. He supplemented his farming with gigs as a professional violinist. In March 1841, he was recruited by two men who offered Northup high wages to join their touring circus act as a musician. Under this pretense, they took him to Washington, DC. Drugged and kidnapped, he was robbed of his identity papers and imprisoned at the Williams Slave Pen, also known as the Yellow House, once located right off the National Mall at 800 Independence Avenue SW (today the site of the Federal Aviation Administration Building). Northup was placed on a slave ship bound for New Orleans and sold to a series of three different plantation owners in central Louisiana. With the help of a visiting white carpenter from Canada, Northup was finally able to get word to his family after twelve years, and they worked with abolitionists to secure his release.

In 1853 he published a memoir, *Twelve Years a Slave: The Narrative of Solomon Northup*. The memoir made him a national celebrity, and proceeds from the book, as well as speaking tours he made from 1853 to 1857 to support the abolitionist cause, allowed him to purchase property in upstate New York (and his house became a stop on the Underground Railroad). Although his kidnappers were arrested, the case wound through the courts before charges were ultimately dismissed in 1857.

Twelve Years a Slave is a valuable first-person record of human trafficking, the use of slave pens for the internal trade of people from the mid-Atlantic states to the Deep South, and abusive plantation practices in Louisiana. It was a significant tool for the abolitionist cause, and the memoir continues to be praised for its candid and clear writing style. The book has inspired poets, musicians, and filmmakers to create works in response; most recently, the film *12 Years a Slave* won Best Picture at the 2014 Academy Awards. Northup's later life has been poorly documented, and it is unclear where he was buried.

Unknown graves from Columbian Harmony Cemetery (2)

The remains of Philip Reed (ca. 1820–1892), on the other hand, are actually interred at National Harmony. There are no known depictions of Reed (whose name was also spelled "Reid" in many early documents). The image shown on the large monument is misleading: it was taken from a wood engraving of a group of unnamed enslaved people being marched in shackles down Pennsylvania Avenue and should not be taken as a literal depiction. (The image was published in 1815 and has been reprinted many times since.)

Phillip Reed was enslaved to sculptor Clark Mills (see

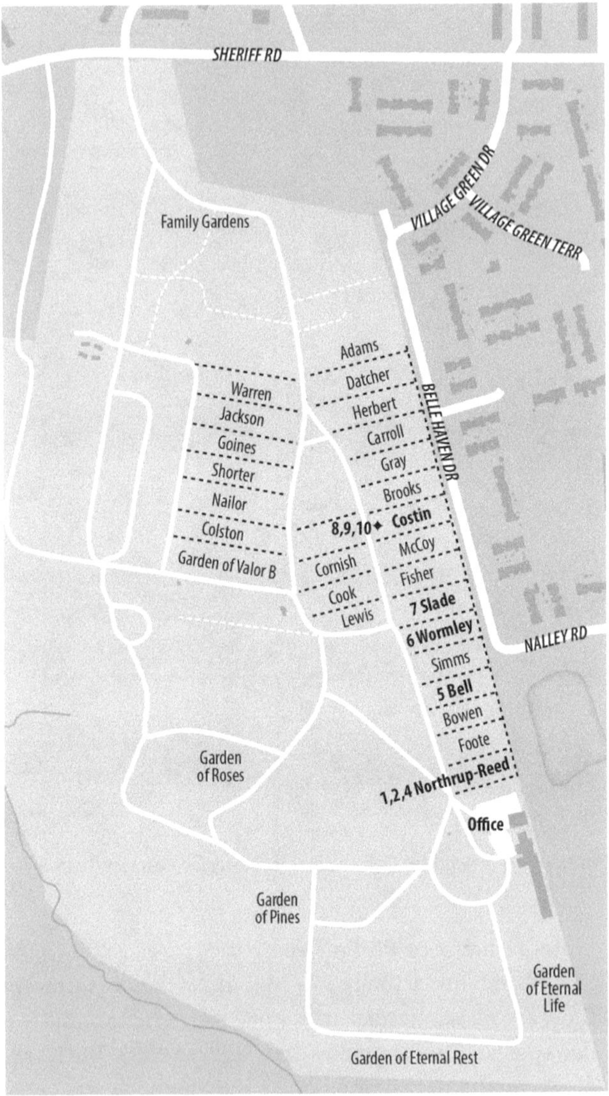

National Harmony Memorial Park

site 18 in the Glenwood Cemetery tour on page 160), and Mills trained him as a master craftsman in bronze casting. Reed was responsible for the final casting and assembly of the Capitol's *Freedom* statue, among other works. (The irony of an enslaved man casting a symbol of national freedom is too acute for words.) Born in South Carolina, Reed was purchased by Mills at about the age of twenty-two and brought to DC. He learned to sculpt in clay and plaster as well as gaining skills in engineering. Reed was put to work in Clark's foundry, once located on Bladensburg Road, for the next two decades. In addition to the *Freedom* statue, Reed is credited with casting two other large bronze public art commissions in Washington: the equestrian statue of Andrew Jackson in Lafayette Square and the equestrian statue of George Washington in Washington Circle.

Reed was emancipated at around age forty-two as part of the District of Columbia Compensated Emancipation Act (1862), when slavery was outlawed in DC nine months prior to the enactment of the national Emancipation Proclamation. Clark's petition for Reed's freedom described him as mixed race, "short in stature, in good health, not prepossessing in appearance but smart in mind." Clark received $350.40 in compensation for the mandatory release of Reed. (Clark also received compensation for ten others he had held in bondage.) Once freed, Reed stayed in DC (at an address near the National Mall at Third and C Streets SW), worked as a plasterer, and married twice. His remains were moved twice after he died. He was first buried in Graceland Cemetery, and when that burial ground was closed in 1894, his remains were moved to Columbian Harmony Cemetery. In 1960, he was moved to National Harmony as part of a mass reburial, and the exact location of his remains is no longer known.

In addition to the tribute here, Reed is remembered with an exhibit and full-sized plaster cast of *Freedom* at the US Capitol Visitor Center. Among the many named and unknown enslaved people who helped build the Capitol, his life remains the best documented.

→ **Look for the row of markers flush with the ground to the left of the monument.**

2 COLUMBIAN HARMONY CEMETERY UNKNOWNS

In 1825, the Columbian Harmony Society was founded, a mutual-aid group open to free African American males aged twenty-one or older. Members paid an initiation fee of $15 and monthly dues of 25 cents. They pledged to assist one another in times of sickness, infirmity, or accident and to attend the funerals of all members once deceased. Monthly dues covered the cost of medical expenses and funerals (up to $25 for a member, $15 for a member's wife, and $7.50 per member's child). The Society followed the common model of other relief organizations of the period, with a constitution and bylaws.

In 1828, the Society was able to open its own dedicated burial ground, and Harmoneon Cemetery became the first African American cemetery established in DC. It was located south of Florida Avenue, bounded by Fourth, Sixth, and S Avenues NW and Rhode Island Avenue, on 1.3 acres that quickly filled to capacity. The society paid $100 for the grounds. (That land, in the Shaw neighborhood, is now almost completely residential, with a combination of apartments and single-family houses.)

In 1852, the District passed an ordinance that forbade the founding of new burial grounds within the old city limits (that is, the downtown areas) as well as the expansion of existing cemetery grounds. The DC government followed that law up in 1856 with another ordinance, mandating that all cemeteries located south of Florida Avenue relocate further out, in what was then Washington County. In 1857, the Society was able to move to a larger plot of 17 acres at the intersection of Rhode Island

Avenue and Brentwood Road. (The location was then considered part of Washington County, not Washington City. The cemetery at this location would later expand to 34 acres in 1886.) The Society paid $4,046 for the new property, now named Harmony Cemetery, a purchase made possible in part by the sale of the original Harmoneon property once human remains had been moved. Members made improvements to the site, including roads, drains, and landscaping. In 1899 they built a chapel, and in 1912, a lodge for a sexton.

By the 1920s, the area surrounding Harmony Cemetery was developed into housing reserved for white buyers through the use of racially restricted covenants. As Society membership declined and the number of lots remaining for sale dwindled, the cemetery's increasing financial troubles brought complaints of lack of maintenance. In response, the cemetery sold off portions of the property to developers in 1903, 1923, and 1928 to stay solvent. By 1950, the cemetery had run out of space for new burials, and in 1952, the owners were charged with neglect and violating public health rules.

In 1958, new property for National Harmony was purchased. Real estate investor Louis H. Bell committed to fund the relocation of all interments in exchange for rights to develop the land. About 37,000 graves needed to be moved, the largest cemetery relocation in DC history. The DC Department of Health streamlined the process in 1960 by issuing a single mass removal permit rather than a permit for each individual (as had been the standard practice previously). From the start, there were problems identifying disinterred bodies, as remains were found that did not correspond to existing records, and some grave markers had shifted or fallen. The company subcontracted to handle the removal of bodies did not move corresponding grave markers, further complicating the process of ensuring the respectful and dignified disposition of those reburied. The removal process took place over the course of two years.

On July 1, 1962, a dedication ceremony took place at National Harmony Memorial Park. Over the next several years, improvements to the new property were made, including clearing of trees, laying sod, and placing asphalt roads. The cemetery set up a perpetual care fund to prevent the kind of problems of neglect experienced at Harmony Cemetery.

In this section, you can see a row of modern plaques marking some of the places where unknown remains were reburied. Other plaques like these can be found scattered throughout the cemetery grounds.

3 UNKNOWNS UNMENTIONED

National Harmony is notable for reinterments of a large number of earlier cemeteries. In addition to the largest number from Columbian Harmony Cemetery, remains were also brought to this spot from Harmoneon Cemetery, Graceland Cemetery, Payne's Cemetery, Hillsdale Cemetery, the Colored Union Benevolent Association grounds (now part of Walter Pierce Park in Adams Morgan), and Rosemont Cemetery, as those properties were closed. National Harmony Memorial Park has thus become, by default, the primary place where African Americans from the greater DC region have historically been laid to rest.

In 1965, the cemetery accepted remains from Rosemont (now the site of the Stanton Glenn Apartments on Stanton Terrace SE), and in 1969 a smaller number from Payne's (now the site of Fletcher-Johnson Middle School on Benning Road SE). These later reinterments were the result of new construction on former cemetery plots. The most recent additions, and the most numerous, were remains left behind from the Columbian Harmony plot. These remains were originally thought moved, but they later came to light as new development was constructed around the Rhode Island Avenue–Brentwood Metro station.

→ **Look for the next site in the next row down.**

4 PAUL EDWARD SLUBY GRAVE

Northup-Reed, Lot 87-B

Paul E. Sluby Sr. (1934–2019) is best known as the region's premier researcher and historian of cemeteries. It is only fitting that he be given a place of honor here.

Sluby was born in Pennsylvania. From 1954 to 1957, he worked for the US Army in Stuttgart, Germany. He moved in DC in 1961 to work as a helicopter pilot for the DC police and retired in 1980, after nearly twenty years. In 1973, he became the first African American board-certified genealogist in the nation, and in 1977, he cofounded the Afro-American Historical and Genealogical Society (AAHGS). He served as director of the National Genealogical Society from 1978 to 1980.

Sluby's great passion, however, was uncovering the history of DC-area burial grounds, especially those that were no longer active or had been moved. He painstakingly researched, transcribed, and published records of burials at Holmead's Cemetery, Presbyterian Cemetery, Payne's Cemetery, Eastern Methodist Cemetery, Rock Creek Cemetery, the Joseph F. Birch Funeral Home, and Columbian Harmony Society. His most significant publication, the capstone to all his research, was the pioneering *Bury Me Deep: Burial Places Past and Present in and Nearby Washington, D.C.; A Historical Review and Reference Manual* (2009). Like many others, I am indebted to him for his meticulous contributions to DC history.

→ **Walk along the fence line back toward the entrance. Granite markers give the name of each section,**

honoring the Columbian Harmony Society founders, all of whom were buried in this cemetery's earlier burial grounds. The third named section is our next stop.

5 BELL SECTION

This section of the cemetery is named for George Bell (1761–1843), cofounder of the first school for African Americans in DC (1807). Bell was born enslaved and never learned to read or write, but he believed passionately in the importance of education. After his wife purchased his freedom, he worked as a carpenter and caulker at the Washington Navy Yard. Bell cofounded the Resolute Beneficial Society (a forerunner to the Columbian Harmony Society), which not only provided care for sick members and funerals for those who had died but was also a force in the abolitionist movement in the city, protesting slave holding pens and the slave trade and operating Underground Railroad stations in local homes and businesses. With Nicholas Franklin and Moses Liverpool, two other free African American men who had been born enslaved, he built a one-story schoolhouse in the Capitol Hill neighborhood named Bell School. The men considered their educational activities an extension of their abolitionism.

Note that most gravestones in this area are placed flush with the ground. This modern suburban cemetery design is easier to mow and maintain and emphasizes expansive views of extended lawn. While I sometimes feel that such landscapes lack character, the openness is the point: it becomes the central feature, an expansive green space that symbolizes democratic ideals of freedom, fairness, and impartiality. The design provides users common ground and scenic vistas without barriers or an implied hierarchy of monuments based on wealth. This design was a reaction against the visual clutter of earlier Victorian burial grounds. It seemed cleaner, healthier, and more modern, and it expressed a belief in the equality of all after death.

→ **Continue to walk, crossing into two more named sections.**

6 WORMLEY SECTION

This section is named for James Wormley (1819–1884), a free African American man born in Washington who operated boardinghouses in the city beginning in 1855. He opened Wormley's Hotel, renowned for its fine food and extensive wine cellar, in 1871. Located at 1500 H Street NW, the property remained in his family until 1897; it is now the site of the Union Trust Company building.

Wormley was instrumental in the founding of two public schools, advocating successfully for the education of children of African descent whose parents paid taxes but whose children were denied entry until 1871, when segregated schools were established. The US Congress agreed to fund the first segregated public elementary school for African American scholars, the Sumner School, located at 1201 T Street NW. Wormley also cofounded a second school in Georgetown, which was named for him, and he chaired the committee that oversaw its construction. The Wormley School opened in 1885 and operated until 1952. (That building has since been converted to condominiums).

Wormley's Hotel, located near Lafayette Square, was favored by wealthy white patrons who were politically prominent. James Wormley developed a network of relationships with powerful elected officials, diplomats, and business leaders. His hotel became a social hub, hosting large diplomatic parties such as the 1878 Spanish Ball. It was most famously the site, in 1877, of secret meetings between Rutherford B. Hayes and Samuel J. Tilden over the contested presidential election of 1876. These closed-door deliberations resulted in the presidency of Hayes and the Compromise of 1877, which ended Reconstruction with the removal of federal troops from Southern states.

→ **Walk into the next named section.**

7 SLADE SECTION

This section is named for William Slade (1815–1868), who worked as an usher and valet in the White House during the Lincoln administration and as White House steward for President Andrew Johnson.

Slade was born free and moved to DC at some point prior to 1843 with his wife, Josephine. They had seven children, all but the eldest born in Washington, and lived in a house once located on Massachusetts Avenue between Fourth and Sixth Streets NW. His earliest jobs in the city were operating a boardinghouse, working as a messenger for the US State Department, and serving as a porter at the Metropolitan Hotel. Slade was an elder in the Fifteenth Street Presbyterian Church, an active member of the Contraband Relief Society, and president of the Social Civil and Statistical Association. He was also an original cofounder of the Columbian Harmony Society.

Slade is most famous for his close relationship with Abraham Lincoln, who was said to have tested out parts of public speeches on his valet and trusted him with intimate details about his household. Slade used his access to advocate directly to Lincoln for the right of Civil War troops of color to elect their own officers and to champion emancipation.

→ **Walk down three more named sections to the Costin section, marked by a large fir tree. Look for the next grave in the fourth row down from the tree.**

8 ELIZABETH KECKLEY GRAVE

Lot 113, Grave 7

Elizabeth Hobbs Keckley (1818–1907), a talented and well-known seamstress to upper-class white women in DC, purchased her freedom and that of her son. She became known as the personal attendant and confidante of Mary Todd Lincoln. She lived in DC from 1860 through 1892 and again in the late 1890s until her death, and she founded the Contraband Relief Association in 1862 to provide aid to formerly enslaved individuals. Her memoir, *Behind the Scenes: Or, Thirty Years a Slave and Four Years in the White House,* was published in 1868. Keckley's remains were moved here from Columbian Harmony Cemetery, and the memorial plaque, which reproduces her likeness and her signature, was added to these grounds in 2010.

→ **Look three graves to your left for the next site.**

9 OSBORNE PERRY ANDERSON GRAVE

Lot 114, Grave 5

Osborne Perry Anderson (1830–1872) was born free in West Fallowfield, Pennsylvania, and educated at Oberlin College. He was a printer by trade. In 1858, he volunteered to work with abolitionist John Brown, and he was the only African American who took part in the raid on Harpers Ferry to survive. From Canada, where he moved afterward, he wrote a first-person account, *A Voice from Harper's Ferry* (1861). Anderson enlisted in the Union Army at the start of the Civil War, serving as a noncommissioned officer. He died of tuberculosis at age forty-two while traveling through DC.

→ **Look one grave over and one row back for the next two sites.**

10 TWO CIVIL WAR SOLDIERS

Costin (Lot 121, Grave 1) and Brooks (Lot 128, Grave 4)

Side-by-side graves honor two Civil War Medal of Honor recipients, Thomas R. Hawkins and Christian A. Fleetwood. The two were among a group of thirteen men who were the first African Americans to be awarded medals by the US Congress. Both were originally buried at Columbian Harmony Cemetery and later reburied here.

Thomas R. Hawkins (ca. 1840–1870) was awarded the Medal of Honor, the country's highest military decoration, for his actions to "rescue the regimental colors" during the Battle of Chaffin's Farm. Hawkins joined the US Army's 6th US Colored Infantry in Philadelphia and rose to the rank of sergeant major, the highest rank allowed for soldiers of color at that time. Hawkins survived the Civil War but died in 1870, at age twenty-nine or thirty, of cancer.

Christian A. Fleetwood (1840–1914) was born free in Baltimore, graduated from Ashmun Institute (a forerunner to Lincoln University), and worked, prior to the Civil War, as publisher of a newspaper, the *Lyceum Observer.* He enlisted in the 4th Regiment of the US Colored Infantry in 1863 and also rose through the ranks to become a sergeant major, seeing action in North Carolina and Virginia. Like Hawkins, he was also awarded the Medal of Honor for actions in the Battle of Chaffin's Farm; his medal was later donated by his daughter to the collections of the Smithsonian National Museum of American History. He served for three and a half years and wrote a nonfiction book, based in part on his experiences, titled *The Negro as Soldier* (1895).

After the war, Fleetwood worked as a clerk at Freedman's Savings and Trust Company, then for three decades at the War Department. He also instructed the Colored Washington High School Cadet Corps and helped organize DC's first African American National Guard unit. Although deaf in one ear, Fleetwood was a fine musician and choirmaster, and he organized the American Orchestra Club to perform concerts at DC churches. He and his wife, Sara (who was an impressive community leader herself and worked as superintendent of nurses at Freedmen's Hospital), were active in numerous charitable works. During the Depression of 1893, the Fleetwoods helped organize other well-to-do African American families to donate funds to purchase and dispense coal, food, clothing, and other supplies, using their private home in the LeDroit Park neighborhood as a hub for the storage and dispersal of donated goods.

→ **Walk back toward the office either on the grass, as you came, or along the roadway.**

11 CEMETERY NOTABLES

Some of the most significant early leaders of DC's African American community are buried in this cemetery, but their graves are unmarked, due to the confusion of mass reinterments from other cemeteries. We honor their memories.

Anthony Bowen (1809–1871) was born enslaved in Prince George's County, Maryland; he moved to DC in 1826 and purchased his freedom in 1830. Bowen was a cofounder of St. Paul AME Church in 1856 and ran the church's Sunday Evening School, where adults as well as children could learn basic literacy and math skills as well as Bible study. The church and school initially met in his home in the 900 block of E Street NW (now the site of the Southeast-Southwest Freeway). His home was also an Underground Railroad stop, and Bowen is credited with helping dozens of enslaved people escape to freedom. He was the first African American clerk hired to work for the US Patent Office, starting as a laborer and working his way up to a coveted clerkship. Bowen was the cofounder, in 1853, of the first YMCA for African Americans in the nation; it was later named for him. A DC public elementary school was also named in his honor.

Solomon G. Brown (1829–1906) was a poet and the first African American employee hired by the Smithsonian Institution. He was also a popular lecturer and an avid amateur naturalist. Brown helped found the Hillsdale neighborhood of Anacostia and served three consecutive terms as a delegate to the Territorial Government of the District of Columbia. His poems were widely published in African American newspapers across the United States. Brown's house on Elvans Road in Anacostia no longer stands. He was originally buried in the Hillsdale Cemetery, near today's Suitland Parkway, and his remains were moved twice before finally finding rest at National Harmony.

Rev. John F. Cook (1810–1855) was born enslaved and trained as a shoemaker, but he was freed by his aunt Alethia Tanner, who purchased an astounding total of twenty-two family members and friends, releasing them from bondage. He was educated at John W. Prout's Columbian Institute, a private, segregated school in DC, and worked in government positions as a messenger and clerk. Cook was a builder of several significant institutions serving people of color in DC: he founded the Philomathean Talking Society, a membership organization where African American men could debate issues of slavery, temperance, and politics. In 1834, he took over Prout's school, renaming it the Union Seminary, and raised the prominence of that institution. He studied for the ministry while teaching and founded the Fifteenth Street Presbyterian Church in 1841. The first church building was located at Fifteenth between I and K Streets NW. It moved to its current location, at 1705 Fifteenth Street, in 1918; the church, still standing on that spot, was rebuilt in 1979. Cook was renowned for the dignity and force of his public speaking.

Cook's daughter-in-law, Helen Appo Cook (1837–1913), was a leader in the women's club movement. She was a cofounder and leader of the Colored Women's League, organized in DC in 1892, which later merged with another organization to become the National Association of Colored Women. She was a member of the Niagara Movement, the predecessor to the NAACP, which was formed to advocate nationally for civil rights, and she attended (and spoke at) suffrage association meetings. She also hosted the elite Booklovers literary salon in her home. Cook held leadership positions in the National Association for the Relief of Destitute Colored Women and Children for nearly thirty-five years. She gave a number of well-regarded public speeches at such events as the National Conference of Mothers, the Atlanta Conference of Negro Problems, and the National Conference of Colored Women of America. Cook was married to John Francis Cook Jr. (who served as a DC tax collector and a trustee of Howard University) and had five children. At the time of her death, she and her husband were the wealthiest African American family in the District.

Paul Jennings (1799–1874) is the author of *A Colored Man's Reminiscences of James Madison* (1865), the first memoir of a servant's life in the White House. Born into slavery, Jennings was owned by the Madisons and, as a young boy, traveled with them to Washington to serve in the White House when James Madison was elected to be the fourth US president. His mother was another Madison slave, and his father was reported to have been a white man named Benjamin Jennings, an English trader living in Chesterfield, Virginia. While living in the White House, Paul Jennings witnessed the British occupation of DC in 1814 (during the protracted War of 1812). He returned to Virginia with his "masters" and was present at James Madison's death in 1836. He moved back to DC with Dolley Madison, residing with her in Lafayette Square. When Dolley Madison became impoverished, she sold off her remaining slaves, including Jennings, who was sold first to the insurance agent Pollard Webb in September 1846 and then, ten months later, to Senator Daniel Webster. The senator freed Jennings but made him continue to work for him to pay off his freedom at the rate of eight dollars a month. In 1848, Jennings helped plan a major (and ultimately unsuccessful) escape of seventy-seven slaves on the schooner *Pearl.* He later worked for about fifteen years as a laborer at the Pension Office of the Department of the Interior. He married three times, and three of his sons fought for the Union in the Civil War. He died in the home he owned at 1804 L Street NW (now razed, in the Farragut Square neighborhood) at age seventy-five.

Mary Ann Shadd Cary (1823–1893) was an educator, journalist, and orator who became the second African American female lawyer in the United States when she graduated from Howard Law School in 1870. She organized the Colored Women's Progressive Franchise in 1880 to fight for women's rights. She is the author of *A Plea for Emigration, or, Notes of Canada West*. Her house at 1421 W Street NW, where she lived from 1881 to 1885, is a National Historic Landmark and marked with a plaque.

12 BACK AT THE OFFICE

Over a two-mile-long stretch of the Potomac River in King George County, Virginia, fifty-five headstones were recovered along the shoreline and underwater. They have now been brought to National Harmony and are being stored in the workshop behind the office, awaiting restoration. Broken pieces of the cemetery's original mausoleum and chapel from Columbian Harmony Cemetery were also recovered. None are currently on public display.

The headstones were discovered by Virginia State Senator Richard Stuart and his wife, Lisa Stuart, when they purchased a farm in King George County in 2016. Louis Bell, who purchased the land that was Columbian Harmony Cemetery, was required to move the remains of bodies but not the headstones. When the headstones were dug up, he sold them as scrap, and several truckloads were purchased by the farm's former owner as erosion control riprap.

The Sons and Daughters of Harmony Cemetery, a nonprofit group founded in 2020, oversaw the headstone recovery process and the return of the stones to National Harmony. Plans are underway for a new memorial garden at the cemetery, where the stones can be displayed and their story told. As you drive out of the cemetery, look to your right after you pass Section E and just before you turn onto Sheriff Road. Current plans are to build the garden on the wooded eastern slope by the entrance, although unfortunately, at the time of this writing, a designer has not yet been selected and the timeline for completion remains unclear. Funding for the memorial, originally hoped to come through the governor's office, was never approved, which has delayed plans.

→ **To reach the final stop, you will need to leave the cemetery grounds and drive approximately eight miles back into DC along Route 50 and Rhode Island Avenue NE. Turn left into the Rhode Island Row shopping center and look for parking.**

13 RHODE ISLAND AVENUE–BRENTWOOD METRO STATION

919 Rhode Island Avenue NE

A commemorative plaque, installed in 1981, is set in a concrete wall facing the Metro station exit. The plaque reads, "Former Site Columbian Harmony Cemetery 1857–1959. Many distinguished black citizens including civil war veterans were buried in this cemetery. These bodies now rest in the new National Harmony Memorial Park Cemetery in Maryland."

This was not considered sufficient: a second plaque was added, along with a flagpole, in the 2010s. It can be found on a rather isolated traffic island at the outer edge of the bus loop. That plaque reads,

> This area, including that of the adjacent shopping center, was once the site of Columbian Harmony Cemetery. The cemetery, established in 1828 "for free persons of color," was originally located near 6th and S Streets, NW, Washington, D.C. Relocation of Harmony Cemetery to this area began in 1857 and the cemetery was active here about one hundred years. During that time about 37,000 interments of eminent citizens were made in these once hallowed grounds. This included 531 Civil War Union soldiers, whose remains were later removed to Arlington National Cemetery, in Virginia. In 1959, all human remains in Harmony Cemetery were disinterred and removed to National Harmony Memorial Park, in Largo, Maryland. This memorial serves to help preserve the memory of the historically important Harmony Cemetery site and to honor the loved ones once interred here.

Unfortunately, this plaque is misleading in one major respect: all the human remains were not disinterred. Louis Bell, who purchased the cemetery, made a fortune on land sales to the DC government when he took over the original Harmony Cemetery. The city initially planned to build a highway over the land. When those plans were scrapped, they sold the land to the Washington Metro. Although Bell made a legal and binding commitment to unearth all the buried remains in exchange for developing the land, he left many bodies behind. The exact number is unclear.

When the Metro station and a parking lot for impounded vehicles were built from 1976 to 1979, coffins, cloth fragments, and human remains were discovered, proving that Bell only partially disinterred the cemetery despite court records with his affidavits stating that all this work was complete. More remains were uncovered in 2012, when a new residential and retail complex called Rhode Island Row was constructed, and in 2016, when the Visionary Square Senior Residences were built (along with the installation of new storm drainpipes). Those remains were eventually moved to National Harmony Memorial Park.

The DC Department of Transportation, working with Metro, announced plans to create a memorial plaza on a grassy knoll adjacent to the station, at the corner of Sixth Street and Rhode Island Avenue NE, as early as 1982. In the intervening years, that land was developed. It appears now that the city's plans for the memorial plaza have been dropped. What is left are the two plaques. It seems that all the best intentions for proper commemoration of our beloved ancestors have—once again—come up short.

OTHER SITES OF INTEREST

Two dozen additional recommended mortuary sites are listed here in the order in which they were founded.

1 MOUNT VERNON, CA. 1760–1863

3200 Mount Vernon Memorial Highway, Mount Vernon, VA

The family cemetery on the grounds includes the George Washington family tomb and a slave cemetery, with the remains of seventy individuals, marked by a modern memorial. Washington inherited just over two thousand acres when he inherited Mount Vernon in his twenties. He would expand it gradually, over the next twenty-five years, to almost eight thousand acres. What remains today is the mansion and over a dozen historic outbuildings, four gardens, and three burial areas.

George Washington (1732–1799) and Martha Washington (1731–1802) were interred in the deteriorating family vault (still standing, although emptied of Washington relatives and today little visited). After the vault was robbed, they were transferred to the new tomb in 1831. The details of the robbery are almost comical: a former gardener at the estate, angry at being fired, slipped onto the grounds and stole what he believed to be the president's skull. In actuality, the grave he robbed belonged to the in-laws of a nephew—but the tomb was in such disarray from seasonal flooding that about twenty family coffins were stacked up atop sawhorses—so his mistake was perhaps understandable. The culprit was caught the next day and the skull returned. This desecration forced the issue: the old family tomb was finally closed up for good and a new one built on higher ground.

Clockwise from upper left: Mount Vernon (1), new tomb; Smithson tomb at the Smithsonian Institution Castle (18); grave markers at National Capital Hebrew Cemetery (19); marker at Hillwood Estate Pet Cemetery (22)

A daily wreath-laying ceremony takes place at the new brick tomb, where two marble sarcophagi (erected in 1837) are inscribed "Washington" and "Martha, Consort of Washington." In front of the tomb, two obelisks were erected in memory of later owners of Mount Vernon: Bushrod Washington (1762–1829), a Supreme Court justice, who is buried in the inner vault along with his wife, Anna Blackburn Washington (1768–1829), and John Augustine Washington (1736–1787), who is buried in West Virginia. Two additional obelisks to the right of the tomb were erected to the memory of two women, Eleanor Park Custis Lewis, Washington's granddaughter (1779–1852), and Mary Eliza Angela Lewis Conrad, Washington's grand-niece (1813–1839).

Daily wreath-laying also takes place at the Slave Memorial located about fifty yards southwest of the tomb. Designed by architectural students from Howard University, this memorial on the site of a cemetery of enslaved persons opened to the public in September 1983. A truncated granite column represents "life unfinished" in the center of three concentric circles. An older marker, dating to 1929, remains in place. It reads, "In honor of the many faithful colored servants of the Washington family." From 2014 to 2017, archeologists began mapping the slave cemetery to better interpret the site and have found approximately fifty graves, none with their original markers.

Over his lifetime, between the ages of eleven and sixty-six, Washington owned or managed about 670 enslaved human beings. He held 317 people in bondage at the time of his death and stipulated in his will that 123 people should be set free upon Martha's death—which did not include the enslaved people owned by his wife's estate, who were not legally eligible for the same terms of freedom. He also made provisions for the lifetime support of freed elderly or ill people he had once enslaved. He is the only US president to have emancipated the people he owned.

2 OLD PRESBYTERIAN MEETING HOUSE BURIAL GROUND, 1774–1831; 1809

323 South Fairfax Street, Alexandria, VA, and 600 Hamilton Lane, Wilkes Street Cemetery Complex

Some three hundred persons are buried in grounds surrounding the church, including George Washington's personal physician, Dr. James Craik (1727–1814); John Carlyle, a founding trustee of Alexandria (1720–1780); and a number of patriots of the Revolutionary War. The Tomb of an Unknown Soldier of the American Revolution lies on the northern side of this graveyard.

The church operates a second cemetery, the Presbyterian Cemetery on Hamilton Lane, which is part of the Wilkes Street Cemetery Complex. This second cemetery opened in 1809 and includes soldiers who served in the Revolutionary War, the War of 1812, and the Civil War. Also interred at this location are former mayors, merchants, ship captains, and prominent business owners from Alexandria.

3 QUAKER CEMETERY, 1807–1890, AND THE COLORED UNION BENEVOLENT ASSOCIATION, 1870–1890

Walter Pierce Park, Adams Mill Road and Calvert Street NW, DC

No grave markers can be seen at this site (now a public park), but it has been the subject of ongoing archeological studies, much of the work conducted by Howard University students under the direction of Professor Mark E. Mack. The Colored Union Benevolent Association was also referred to as the Free Young Men's Burial Ground and Mt. Pleasant Plains Cemetery. The earlier Quaker cemetery was open to all, including paupers, and graves were intentionally left unmarked to emphasize equality in death.

Notable burials here include Amelia Edmonson (ca. 1789–1874) and her sons Ephraim (ca. 1818–ca. 1890) and Richard (ca. 1821–1879), who took part in the largest escape attempt of enslaved persons in the country aboard the *Pearl*. The schooner sailed from Washington Harbor down the Potomac River to the convergence with the Chesapeake Bay, but it was intercepted and all the people aboard recaptured. Also interred here is abolitionist Luke Carter (?–1857), who sheltered enslaved people in his home before they boarded the ship. At least 45 soldiers, sailors, scouts, and spies who served in the Civil War and Indian Wars are interred here, including Lucy Ann Walker (ca. 1814–1880), an African American laundress who worked in Confederate camps and relayed messages to Union troops; Eli Gales (?–1889), who served on ships in the Potomac Flotilla, routing Confederate forces in the waterways around Washington; and John Shorter (ca. 1814–1885), cofounder of the Quaker Cemetery, who lobbied Congress to provide equal pay to African American military personnel. The exact number of remaining graves is unclear, since some disinterments took place in 1890, when the National Zoo expanded, and more graves were removed when Adams Mill Road was widened. Remains were disinterred again in 1940, when a developer purchased some of the land. Other gravesites may have been lost due to erosion.

Today the park holds basketball courts, a dog area, and a children's playground. A series of informational markers about the cemeteries can be seen at the west end of Walter Pierce Park. In 2024, DC Parks and Recreation added an Ancestors Pavilion to the east end with nine signs describing the site's history, how research was conducted, and an alphabetical list featuring the names, ages, and death dates of 8,428 people known to be buried at this site.

4 ST. MARY'S CATHOLIC CHURCH CEMETERY, 1819

1350 Baltimore Road, Rockville, MD

This cemetery, surrounded by major roads on all sides, is famous as the final resting place of F. Scott Fitzgerald (1896–1940) and Zelda Fitzgerald (1900–1948). Their grave includes a quotation from *The Great Gatsby:* "So we beat on, boats against the current, borne back ceaselessly into the past."

5 GEORGETOWN VISITATION CEMETERIES, 1821

1500 Thirty-Fifth Street NW, DC

These sites are located on the private campus of Georgetown Visitation Preparatory School, one of the oldest Catholic girls' schools in the United States; there is no public access. Three separate areas were set aside for the burial of Jesuits, only one of which is still in use. A brick-lined burial crypt under the Chapel of the Sacred Heart holds the remains of three priests who were leaders of Georgetown College (as it was then known): Father Leonard Neale (1746–1817), Father Joseph-Pierre Picot de Clorivière (1768–1826), and Father Robert Plunkett (1752–1815). Thirty-three nuns are also buried there. Two other cemeteries also make up this group: the Garden Cemetery, used from 1841 to 1887, and the New Cemetery, opened in 1887 and still in use by the Order of the Visitation of Mary. The New Cemetery is in a small square of land west of the Visitation parking lots. In keeping with the order's mandate to live simply, each gravestone is identical, inscribed with a name, date of death, and the number of years each person remained a faithful member of the convent.

6 HOLY ROOD CEMETERY, 1832

2126 Wisconsin Avenue NW, DC

The oldest Catholic burying ground in Washington is located at one of the city's highest elevations. Approximately seven thousand burials (with as many as one thousand believed to be free and enslaved African Americans) are on this 6.5-acre site owned by Georgetown University. The cemetery is notable for the large number of graves of Irish immigrants who came to the region to build the C&O Canal. The original grounds were enlarged and improved as a result of the charitable donations of W. W. Corcoran (who also endowed Oak Hill Cemetery). By the 1980s, the land was so poorly maintained that the university began exploring options to remove bodies and use the land for other purposes, but after a legal challenge, they recommitted to the cemetery and began restoration in 2018. Since that time, new landscaping, paths, and a columbarium have been built.

7 ST. ELIZABETHS HOSPITAL CEMETERY, 1856–1983

Martin Luther King, Jr. Avenue SE, DC

Two cemeteries, on the east and west campuses, contain the graves of military veterans from the Civil War, Spanish-American War, and World War I as well as of civilians who were patients at the hospital. In 2021, parts of the West Cemetery, containing Civil War–era graves, collapsed down a hillside and were temporarily shored up with gravel and concrete—a stabilizing process that allows for a more permanent solution in the future. Poor recordkeeping makes an exact estimate of the numbers interred difficult, but the St. Elizabeths cemeteries are thought to be some of the earliest cemeteries in the nation that did not segregate the bodies of African Americans. The grounds historically included the Government Hospital for the Insane, the Union General Hospital, the Navy General and Quarantine Hospital, and an Artificial Limb Manufacturing shop. There is limited public access.

8 IVY HILL CEMETERY, 1856

2823 King Street, Alexandria, VA

Located on twenty-two hilly acres that span the Timber Branch creek, Ivy Hill started as a family cemetery in 1811 and later became a community cemetery. The site has a range of large mature trees and a memorial to Alexandria firefighters near the entrance. Perhaps the most famous person buried at Ivy Hill is aerospace engineer Wernher von Braun (1912–1977), who escaped justice for his Nazi war crimes when he moved to the United States following World War II. Von Braun did pioneering work for the US Army and NASA on rockets and the launch vehicle for the Apollo spacecraft. Benjamin Franklin Stringfellow (ca. 1840–1913), famous as a Confederate officer and spy for Robert E. Lee and J. E. B. Stuart, is also buried here, as is modernist architect Charles M. Goodman (1906–1992), who designed Washington National Airport, the distinctive barrel-roof townhouses in the Southwest Waterfront district of DC, and the Hollin Hills neighborhood of Alexandria.

9 PROSPECT HILL CEMETERY, 1858

2201 N. Capitol Street NE, DC

A German American cemetery, Prospect Hill holds the remains of a number of beer brewers, almost two hundred Civil War Union veterans, and three people associated with the murder of President Abraham Lincoln: George A. Pankhurst (1841–1890), an actor who was on stage at Ford's Theater when the president was shot and witnessed John Wilkes Booth's escape; William Petersen (1810–1871), a tailor who owned the house across the street from Ford's Theater, where Lincoln was taken after being shot and where he ultimately died; and Petersen's wife, Anna Klomann Petersen (1819–1871), who ran the boardinghouse. August Gottlieb Schoenborn (1827–1902), the architect who designed the iron dome for the US Capitol, is also interred here. A large section of the original cemetery was taken by eminent domain for the widening of North Capitol Street, reducing the size of the graveyard to nine acres. The resulting cemetery is a simple circular carriage drive, with two walking paths forming a cross in the middle of the circle.

10 CONTRABANDS AND FREEDMEN CEMETERY, 1864–1869

1001 S. Washington Street, Alexandria, VA

A park preserves the site of a Civil War–era burying ground for African Americans, including Union soldiers and formerly enslaved people who escaped bondage as "contrabands." Under the auspices of the US military governor of Alexandria, a plot of 1.5 "abandoned" acres was seized and the local pastor Rev. Albert Gladwin, who served as superintendent of contrabands, kept burial records for the cemetery's first two years. Survey maps show that the land was recognized as a cemetery through at least 1939, but it was then used for commercial purposes until the city began archeological explorations beginning in 1996. A rededication ceremony was held in 2007; the park now contains a large memorial sculpture by C. J. Howard. Although no aboveground remnants of graves can be seen, ground-penetrating radar was used to locate approximately 1,800 remains. The National Park Service included the cemetery on the African American Civil Rights Network beginning in 2021. (See page 203 in the Alexandria National Cemetery tour for additional information.)

11 JEWISH CONGREGATIONS COMBINED CEMETERIES, 1869

1380–1400 Alabama Avenue SE, DC

This group of cemeteries on seven acres, still in active use, includes Elesavetgrad Cemetery (named for a town in Russia) and the burial grounds for six synagogues:

Ohev Sholom Cemetery, Adas Israel Congregation Cemetery, Bet Mishpachah Cemetery, Chesed Shel Emes Cemetery, Kesher Israel Cemetery, and Washington Hebrew Memorial Park. Some of the cemeteries are separated by a chain-link fence, but others simply flow into one another. The site is tucked into a mostly flat, wooded area between public housing and some newer developments. A caretaker's house on the site includes some lovely exterior mosaics. Most headstones are bilingual, in English and Hebrew, and many are decorated with Stars of David, open books, or menorahs.

12 BLACK BAPTIST CEMETERY, 1885–1899(?)

500 Holland Lane, Alexandria, VA

Now preserved as part of Alexandria African American Heritage Park, this is the oldest-known intact African American cemetery in Alexandria. Founded by the Silver Leaf (Colored) Society of Alexandria, the property displays five complete headstones and one partial headstone. The remaining twenty-three known interments at this site are unmarked. The park, located along Hooff's Run, also contains walking paths, interpretive signs, and modern commemorative sculptures by Jerome Meadows.

13 MOUNT SALVATION BAPTIST CEMETERY, 1888–1974

1961 N. Culpeper Street, Arlington, VA

This African American cemetery behind a Baptist church has been designated a local historic district, marked by a plaque as of 2022. Only the cemetery has the historic designation; the church is the fourth built at this location and is not part of the designation. The remains of eighty-nine people have been verified, but there are likely more people buried here, as records were only kept from 1916 to 1974. Many are descendants of the original settlers, a group of formerly enslaved people who were forced out of Freedman's Village (now the site of Arlington National Cemetery) and developed one of three lively communities of color in Arlington County beginning in the 1880s. Note the use of yucca plantings at this site. The yucca is a traditional plant used by African Americans to represent eternal memory—and sometimes signaling a wish to keep restless spirits in their graves. Where gravestones were not possible, especially in the case of the unmarked graves of enslaved people or in communities where the cost of a stone marker was too prohibitive, a yucca could be used to mark the burial site, as the plant continues to grow for an extremely long period of time. This tradition continues in African American burial grounds, even where graves are now well marked.

14 SCOTTISH RITE TEMPLE, 1891, 1954

1733 Sixteenth Street NW, DC

The House of the Temple was designed by architect John Russell Pope based on one of the Seven Wonders of the Ancient World—the Tomb of Mausolus in Halicarnassus, Turkey. The Temple contains the remains of two former Masonic sovereign grand commanders, General Albert Pike (1809–1891) and General John Henry Cowles (1863–1954).

15 LOMAX AFRICAN METHODIST ZION CHURCH CEMETERY, 1894–1982

2704 S. Twenty-Fourth Road, Arlington, VA

Arlington County's oldest historically African American church was founded in Freedman's Village in 1866, under the name Little Zion Church, and moved to this location in 1874, when it was forced out by the expansion of Arlington National Cemetery. The present church, built in the Gothic Revival style, is the second built on this location. The cemetery holds the remains of approximately 107 people buried after 1894; earlier interments that are unmarked may date to earlier years. The cemetery is part of a designated local historic district and is listed on the National Register of Historic Places.

16 HISTORIC WOODLAWN CEMETERY, 1895–1969

4611 Benning Road SE, DC

The final resting place of some of the most prominent African American residents of the region, Woodlawn is listed by the DC Preservation League as one of the District's most endangered historic places. It comprises nearly twenty-three acres and includes the remains of over thirty-six thousand individuals, including celebrated legislators, ministers, teachers, writers, lawyers, and activists. Woodlawn also received the reinterred remains of bodies from earlier historic Black burial grounds within DC after they closed, particularly Graceland Cemetery. The property was added to the National Register of Historic Places in 1996; since 1972, the cemetery has been administered by the nonprofit Woodlawn Cemetery Perpetual Care Association. Only one internal road from the original rural design of winding carriage paths remains. The hilly site is filled with overgrowth and debris, and the remaining grave markers not toppled or broken bear little relation to what lies below. Despite plans for restoration, the Association is plagued by a lack of funding needed to preserve this formerly celebrated site of remembrance. The cemetery is open to the public on only five holidays each year.

17 FRANCISCAN MONASTERY OF THE HOLY LAND IN AMERICA, 1898

1400 Quincy Street NE, DC

The Franciscan Monastery is famous for its gardens, which include full-size replicas of sacred shrines, including Mount Calvary, the Holy Sepulcher in Jerusalem, and the Lourdes Grotto. Guided tours, led by friars, include visits to the neo-Byzantine interior of the Memorial Church of the Holy Sepulcher and the replica Roman catacombs—two of which contain real relics. The bones of St. Benignus (minus his skull, which is preserved in a church in Italy) are arranged in a triangular wooden and glass box above a marble statue of the saint. You can clearly make out rib bones on display. In addition, the skeleton of a young child, St. Innocent, thought to be a martyr from the second century, was imported from the catacomb of St. Callixtus in Rome sometime during the 1920s. He is dressed in fancy robes, holding a palm frond, with a doll's face made from wax: his skeleton is visible only at his hands and feet.

18 SMITHSONIAN INSTITUTION CASTLE, 1904

100 Jefferson Drive SW, The National Mall, DC

The remains of donor James Smithson (1765–1829) were reinterred in the Smithsonian Institution's oldest building, now a visitor's center, in 1904. At the prompting of Alexander Graham Bell, the reinterment ceremony took place seventy-six years after Smithson's death in Genoa, Italy, when the cemetery in San Benigno (where he was originally laid to rest) was demolished. His remains now rest inside an ornate marble sarcophagus carved with images of snakes, birds, flowers, and moths, balanced on lion's paws, and topped with a seedpod finial. In 1973, the tomb was briefly reopened so modern researchers could examine his skeleton. An exhibit on Smithson's life accompanies the tomb. It includes some of his former books and belongings and a display of the zinc carbonate mineral named in his honor: smithsonite.

19 NATIONAL CAPITAL HEBREW CEMETERY, 1910

4708 Fable Street (near Southern Avenue), Capitol Heights, MD

Straddling the line between Southeast Washington, DC, and Maryland, this cemetery creates a bend in Southern Avenue's straight boundary line to accommodate a plot of 2,750 graves. The cemetery serves three operating synagogues—Beth Sholom and Talmud Torah (Potomac, Maryland), Ohev Sholom Talmud Torah / The National Synagogue (DC), and Young Israel Shomrai Emunah (Silver Spring, Maryland). It also served various smaller Jewish congregations and communities that no longer exist: Ezras Israel, the Yom Tov Society, the Workman's Circle, and the fraternal organizations National Capitol Lodge, George Washington Lodge, and Friendship Lodge. The grounds include a caretaker's house (built in 1961). This graveyard is notable for the large number of grave markers made to resemble stylized tree stumps. This iconography of stumps and cut logs—either single ones or in triangular piles—symbolizes a life cut short. Some of the markers also include twining vines, knotholes, and other lovely naturalistic details. Many feature two carved hands, the Hands of the Kohanim, meant to show that the bearers derived from an ancient priestly family and to give viewers of their graves their special blessing. Modern fans of *Star Trek* will recognize the symbol, with the space between the middle fingers, which actor Leonard Nimoy adopted for his character Spock. There are also three separate areas at the edges of the cemetery set aside for infant burials.

20 WASHINGTON NATIONAL CATHEDRAL, 1917

3101 Wisconsin Avenue NW, DC

The second-largest cathedral in the nation contains the burial crypts of 206 individuals, of which 37 are full-body remains and the remaining are cremated remains. Burials include President Woodrow Wilson (1856–1924), the only US president buried in DC, and First Lady Edith Bolling Wilson (1872–1961); author and activist Helen Keller (1880–1968) and her teacher and lifelong companion Anne Sullivan (1866–1936); philanthropist and author Isabel Anderson (1876–1948); Admiral George Dewey (1837–1917); and Matthew Shepard, tortured and murdered at age twenty-one, whose death was a catalyst for LGBTQ+ rights (1976–1998).

21–23 PET CEMETERIES

Dumbarton Oaks Park Pet Cemetery (1920s–1940), 3100 R Street NW and Lovers' Lane, DC

Hillwood Estate Pet Cemetery (1950s–1980s), 4155 Linnean Avenue NW, DC

Aspin Hill Memorial Park (1920–2018), 13630 Georgia Avenue, Silver Spring, MD; entrance on Aspen Hill Road

Within the woodland garden landscape of Dumbarton Oaks Conservatory, philanthropists Mildred Bliss (1879–1969) and Robert Bliss (1875–1962) set aside a small burial ground for family pets: six dogs and two horses, whose graves are marked with natural stones engraved with each pet's name. To reach them, you must hike down Lovers' Lane to the Conservatory trail, then cross to the opposite side of Dumbarton Run, where you'll find the gravestones at the high point of one of the "meadow rooms" surrounded by woodlands. The small, naturalistic cemetery is beautifully incorporated into the landscape.

At Hillwood, the pet cemetery is more formal, with headstones for the pets of businesswoman and philanthropist Marjorie Merriweather Post (1887–1973) surrounding a brick pathway amid plantings of forget-me-nots and vinca. Cast cement statues of dogs, some holding fruit baskets in their mouths, frame the entrance to the small diamond-shaped plot. In this shady setting, you'll find the graves of two international show champions as well as family favorites Scampi, Lady Margaret, Coco, and Petit Chou. For those combining a walk through the grounds with a tour of the historic mansion, make sure you stop in the first-floor library to find a miniature canopied French bed in pink silk from the 1700s and the nearby photo documenting that Scampi, a schnauzer, used the antique as his dog bed.

Aspin Hill—named after an English dog kennel—was founded by two dog breeders, Richard and Bertha Birney (both ?–1944). Its twenty acres hold the remains of over fifty thousand pets—mostly dogs and cats but also monkeys, birds, goats, hamsters, frogs, fish, turtles, and snakes. There are also graves of thirteen human beings who chose to be buried close to their pets. Since 2007, the cemetery has been operated by the Montgomery County Humane Society, and the property is now considered full, with no additional plots for sale. Among the notable pets buried here are seven dogs belonging to FBI director J. Edgar Hoover; Jiggs, the dog from the *Our Gang* movie series; and Rags, the mascot of the First Division in World War I. Also on site are a gable-roof kennel and a 1930s brick bungalow where the founders once lived. Some favorite graves to look for include those for Bunny (a bulldog) and Robin Goodfellow (a greyhound) as well as a mausoleum for another dog, Mickey.

24 FOLGER SHAKESPEARE LIBRARY, 1936

201 E. Capital Street SE, DC

A white marble library designed by architect Paul Philippe Cret (1876–1945) houses the cremated remains of donors Henry Clay Folger (1857–1930) and Emily Jordan Folger (1858–1936), who are inurned in the Reading Room wall of the institution, near their portraits and a bust of William Shakespeare.

ACKNOWLEDGMENTS

I am indebted to the managers and staff of individual cemetery sites who took the time to speak with me and answer my many questions. My gratitude as well to Mark Mones and Eric Brandt at the University of Virginia Press for their crucial encouragement and support. Many thanks to Laura Reed-Morrisson of Bluestar Editorial for her keen eye for detail. And I would be completely remiss if I did not also thank my beloved Tracey Meikle, who walked every single one of these tours along with me, often multiple times, as I wrote this book.

SOURCES

I am indebted to several researchers who came before me and whose work I relied upon to create this book. In 2009, Paul E. Sluby self-published his magisterial text, *Bury Me Deep: Burial Places Past and Present In and Nearby Washington, D.C.; A Historical Review and Reference Manual*. Based on decades of study, this book remains the most important resource for understanding how the city's burial grounds have changed over time. I also made use of some other general reference books and pamphlets, including James M. Goode's *The Outdoor Sculpture of Washington, D.C.: A Comprehensive Historical Guide* (Smithsonian Institution Press, 1974), Anne O. Brockett's *Gone But Not Forgotten: Cemeteries in the Nation's Capital* (DC Historic Preservation Office, 2012), and the second edition of Dean W. Holt's *American Military Cemeteries* (McFarland, 2010).

I found the individual websites of several cemeteries extremely helpful and made extensive use of the Find a Grave website. I repeatedly accessed the archives of the *Washington Post*, *Washingtonian Magazine*, *DCist*, the *Georgetowner*, the *New York Times*, the *Washington Evening Star*, CBS News, and the *Records of the Columbia Historical Society of Washington, D.C.*, to illuminate issues each cemetery bought to light. The District of Columbia Register and the nomination records of the National Register of Historic Places, managed so ably by the National Park Service, were often invaluable. I referred to the Maryland Historical Trust's Inventory of Historic Properties as well as the Library of Congress Historic American Landscapes Survey and the National Cemetery Administration records of the US Department of Veterans Affairs.

For individual cemeteries, I would recommend the following sources.

Andrews, Owen, and Cameron Davidson. *A Moment of Silence: Arlington National Cemetery.* Washington, DC: Elliott & Clark Publishing, 1994.

Bates, Barbara. *African American Men on the District of Columbia War Memorial and the 16th Street War Memorial Trees and Markers.* The Association of Oldest Inhabitants of DC, November 2020.

Calamito, Katlyn, Amanda Gallagher, Rebecca Kaliff, and Alexis Zilen. "What Lies Beneath: Documenting the History of the Columbian Harmony Cemetery." Humanities Truck exhibit, 2021. https://humanitiestruck.com/what-lies-beneath/.

Carroll, Thomas D. *Up on the Hill: An Oral History of the Halls Hill Neighborhood in Arlington County, Virginia.* Arlington, VA: Cultural Affairs Division of the Arlington County Department of Parks, Recreation and Community Resources, 2002.

Craughwell, Thomas J. *Stealing Lincoln's Body.* Boston: Belknap Press, 2007.

Eggener, Keith. *Cemeteries.* New York: W. W. Norton; Washington, DC: Library of Congress, 2010.

Exton, Peter, and Dorsey Kleitz. *Milestones into Headstones: Mini Biographies of Fifty Fascinating Americans Buried in Washington, D.C.* McLean, VA: EPM Publications, 1985.

Faust, Drew Gilpin. *This Republic of Suffering: Death and the American Civil War.* New York: Vintage Books, 2008.

Ferguson, Ernest B. *Freedom Rising: Washington in the Civil War.* New York: Vintage Books, 2004.

Forman, Stephen M. *A Guide to Civil War Washington.* Washington, DC: Elliott & Clark Publishing, 1995.

Greenly, Mark D. "Those Upon Whom the Curtain Has Fallen: Past and Present Cemeteries of Old Town, Alexandria, with Walking Tours of Old Town." Alexandria Archeology Publications 88. Alexandria, VA: Office of Historic Alexandria, 1996.

Harrold, Stanley. *Subversives: Antislavery Community in*

Washington, D.C., 1828–1865. Baton Rouge: Louisiana State University Press, 2003.

Higgins, Peter T. *Buried in Georgetown: A Brief Look at Cemeteries and Burial Grounds in Georgetown, Washington, D.C.* Washington, DC: Tender Fire Books, 2022.

Jacob, Kathryn Allamong. *Capital Elites: High Society in Washington, D.C. After the Civil War.* Washington, DC: Smithsonian Institution Press, 1995.

Johnson, Abby Arthur, and Ronald Maberry Johnson. *In the Shadow of the United States Capitol: Congressional Cemetery and the Memory of the Nation.* Washington, DC: New Academia Publishing, 2012.

Kirchick, James. *The Secret City: The Hidden History of Gay Washington.* New York: Henry Holt, 2022.

Kuehn, Henry H. *Architects' Gravesites: A Serendipitous Guide.* Cambridge, MA: MIT Press, 2017.

Laqueur, Thomas W. *The Work of the Dead: A Cultural History of Mortal Remains.* Princeton, NJ: Princeton University Press, 2015.

Lesko, Kathleen M., Valerie Babb, and Caroll R. Gibbs. *Black Georgetown Remembered.* Washington, DC: Georgetown University Press, 1991.

McElya, Micki. *The Politics of Mourning: Death and Honor in Arlington National Cemetery.* Cambridge, MA: Harvard University Press, 2016.

Mills, Cynthia. *Beyond Grief: Sculpture and Wonder in the Gilded Age Cemetery.* Washington, DC: Smithsonian Institution Scholarly Press, 2014.

Nunley, Tamika Y. *At the Threshold of Liberty: Women, Slavery, and Shifting Identities in Washington, D.C.* Chapel Hill: University of North Carolina Press, 2021.

Pinsker, Matthew. *Lincoln's Sanctuary: Abraham Lincoln and the Soldiers' Home.* New York: Oxford University Press, 2003.

Rainville, Lynn. *Hidden History: African American Cemeteries in Central Virginia.* Charlottesville: University of Virginia Press, 2014.

Ricks, Mary Kay. *Escape on the Pearl.* New York: William Morrow, 2007.

Sloane, David Charles. *Is the Cemetery Dead?* Chicago: University of Chicago Press, 2018.

Williams, Talmadge T. *A Guide to the Historic Sites of a Long and Proud Heritage: African American History in Arlington, Virginia*. Arlington, VA: Arlington Economic Development, undated.

Worpole, Ken. *Last Landscapes: The Architecture of the Cemetery in the West*. London: Reaktion Books, 2003.

INDEX

Italicized page numbers refer to illustrations.